IMAGES
of America

SALISBURY

ON THE COVER: The Coca-Cola plant was located on East Council Street, adjacent to the Southern Railway tracks. T.A. Snyder was an early manager of the plant. A new facility was constructed on South Main Street in the 1930s. This building still stands today and can be seen from the platform of the Salisbury depot. (Courtesy Edith M. Clark History Room of the Rowan Public Library.)

IMAGES
of America

SALISBURY

Larry Neal and
the Rowan Museum

ARCADIA
PUBLISHING

ISBN 978-0-7385-9842-0

Published by Arcadia Publishing
Charleston, South Carolina

Printed in the United States of America

Library of Congress Control Number: 2012949479

For all general information, please contact Arcadia Publishing:
Telephone 843-853-2070
Fax 843-853-0044
E-mail sales@arcadiapublishing.com
For customer service and orders:
Toll-Free 1-888-313-2665

Visit us on the Internet at www.arcadiapublishing.com

This book is dedicated to the memory of my father, Larry K. Neal Sr., and to those who have preserved the history of Salisbury and Rowan County for the benefit of future generations.

Contents

ACKNOWLEDGMENTS

I would like to thank Kaye Brown Hirst and the Rowan Museum for their interest in a book on the history of Salisbury. I would also like to thank Arcadia Publishing for having the confidence in my writing this book. Salisbury has over 250 years of history and a story that deserves to be told. At the Rowan Museum, I would like to thank Tricia Creel, who graciously allowed me to take over her desk in the afternoons to scan images. Mary Jane Fowler, the museum curator, helped me understand the museum's collections and provided information for image captions.

Further assistance was given by Gretchen Witt, who oversees the Edith M. Clark History Room of the Rowan Public Library. Not only is this part of the library helpful to genealogists, it also holds books on Salisbury and Rowan County as well as a large image collection. Their resources, including a well-designed and informative website, aided in composing this book. Susan Sides, president of the Board of Trustees of the Historic Salisbury Foundation, had previously written books on historic postcards of Salisbury and Rowan County, which also aided in the preparation of this book.

I would also like to thank Katie McAlpin of Arcadia Publishing, who graciously worked with me through the ups and downs of the editing process. I also want to give credit to my late uncle, William "Billy Don" Booth, who helped spur my interest in books and writing through his own books, written several years ago. I would be remiss if I did not thank my wife, Traci, and daughter, Kerstin, for their understanding while I worked evenings and weekends on the computer. Kerstin really missed her playtime with daddy! I continue to hope she will gain an appreciation of history as she grows older.

INTRODUCTION

Rowan County was formed in 1753 from Anson County. Named after Matthew Rowan, the county originally incorporated the land comprising adjacent current counties touching the borders of Virginia and Tennessee. The city of Salisbury developed along early trading routes first used by Native Americans living near the Yadkin River. Salisbury's importance also grew due to the presence of the county courthouse, which brought continued development to the city.

At the time of the American Civil War, Salisbury was the location of a relatively new courthouse, built in 1855, and a Confederate prison that held captured Union soldiers. By 1865 and the end of the war, the prison had been destroyed, but the city remained intact and looked toward the future.

By the 1880s, Salisbury had developed a flourishing downtown centered on the fountain in the square, at the intersection of Main and Innes Streets. Stores, stretching for several blocks on North and South Main, carried everything from general merchandise, clothes, and shoes, to dry goods and groceries. It was during this time that one of Salisbury's greatest photographers began his long and interesting career.

Theodore Buerbaum, an immigrant from Germany, married his wife in 1885 and, around the same time, opened a bookstore/general store at 106 South Main Street. He needed something to attract people to his store, which led to his hobby of photography. He began taking photographs of Salisbury—businesses, homes, attractions, and more—and sent them back to Germany to be printed into postcards. These postcards became popular for tourists and local citizens alike. The images helped record a time of great prosperity for Salisbury, with the development of the Fulton Heights neighborhood, construction of the streetcar line to Spencer, and the completion of the Grubb Building, known today as The Plaza. The changes from the late 19th to the early 20th centuries are well documented thanks to his efforts. Today, the Rowan Museum's collection includes Buerbaum's original photograph book, which contains many images from this period. One of the purposes of this book is to showcase these original photographs, many of which have not been seen by the general public.

In the beginning of the 20th century, two products were developed that put Salisbury not only on the map but in the minds and stomachs of Rowan County residents. The first was Stanback Headache Powder, invented by Dr. Tom Stanback in a Thomasville drugstore. In 1911, he moved his headquarters to Spencer, so he could try out the powder on railroad workers. He moved the company to Salisbury a few years later. A full production facility was later built on South Main Street, and it remained in operation until 1998, when the company was sold.

Cheerwine, a cherry-flavored soft drink, was invented by L.D. Peeler in 1917. He was looking for a different flavor to create a new drink and came across some cherry varieties from a traveling salesman. Cheerwine became an instant success but was only available in Rowan County. The distinctive bottle design had angled straight sides and embossed cherries when production started but soon incorporated an intertwined "CW" logo. Today, Cheerwine is sold in 11 southern states and can be ordered and shipped anywhere in the world.

Rowan County's 200th anniversary celebration in 1953 included a large parade down Main Street in Salisbury. This parade was reminiscent of grand parades held in the early 1900s with plenty of floats, homemade decorations, and dignitaries. One interesting part of the celebration was the "Brothers of the Brush," in which the men of Salisbury and Rowan County agreed to grow beards and mustaches to duplicate that "old-time look." Pres. Dwight Eisenhower made a speech at Catawba College during the celebration. The Rowan Museum was formally started in 1953 under the direction of Alice Slater Cannon Guille, lifelong resident of Salisbury and Rowan County.

Several local citizens have become household names through the years. Andrew Jackson was an early celebrity, studying law in Salisbury. Sidney Blackmer, who grew up in Salisbury, eventually became a famous film and television actor with a career spanning more than 50 years, from 1914 to 1968. His last movie was Roman Polanski's *Rosemary's Baby*. His home has been saved and awaits restoration. Without a doubt, the person most associated with Salisbury is Sen. Elizabeth Hanford Dole. Born in 1936, she graduated from Duke University in 1958, eventually earning a Harvard law degree in 1965. She served as the secretary of the Department of Transportation from 1983 to 1987 under Pres. Ronald Reagan, working closely with the National Highway Transportation Safety Administration. She served as secretary of labor under Pres. George H.W. Bush from 1989 to 1990. Dole may be best remembered as a US senator from North Carolina, serving from 2001 to 2007.

Life in Salisbury continued basically unchanged through the 1970s, but developments began to occur during the final decades of the 20th century. Most of the large textile mills closed as companies moved production out of North Carolina. The Southern Railway closed Spencer Shops completely in 1979, causing many railroad workers living in Salisbury to relocate out of state. The old passenger depot was seeing only one train a day, the "Southern Crescent." This was a far cry from the multiple trains passing through during the 1930s and 1940s. The downtown area also suffered, first from a disastrous fire that damaged several stores, then from the construction of the Salisbury Mall in the 1970s. The 1990s, though, brought a renewed interest in historic preservation, thanks in part to the Historic Salisbury Foundation. Historic properties, including houses and businesses, were restored. In 1996, the restoration of the train depot was completed. Today, the Historic Salisbury Foundation purchases property deemed too historically important to lose and seeks new owners willing to rejuvenate and maintain the properties. The downtown shopping areas were also revitalized, based around venues including the Meroney Theater, The Plaza building, and longtime local merchants.

Rowan County's 250th anniversary celebration in 2003 was orchestrated by the Rowan Museum and chaired by Kaye Brown Hirst. A big parade, sponsored by Cheerwine, stretched down Salisbury's Main Street. Salisbury continues to take pride in its history and is looking toward the 300th anniversary celebration! Today, Salisbury is a growing city with a vibrant downtown, improved interstate access, and a growing population and economic base. One of the city's latest adventures is Fibrant, a fiber-optic network for telephone and internet service. The city of Salisbury is embracing the 21st century while never forgetting the past.

One

Early Salisbury

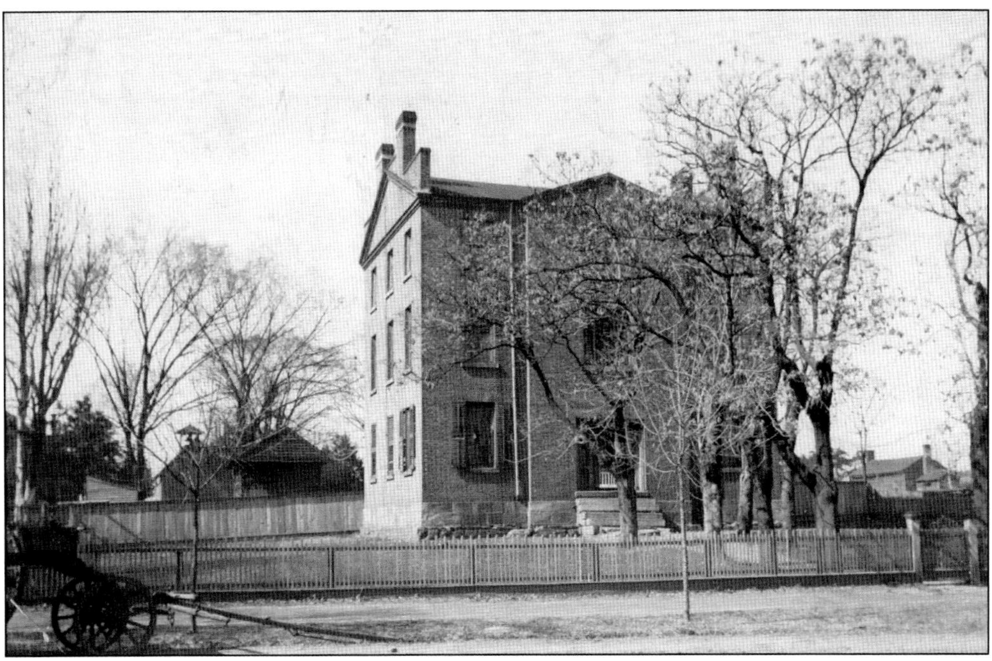

The Rowan County Jail is seen here in the 1890s. The building was on Main Street, adjacent to the courthouse. St. Luke's Episcopal Church is visible in the background. (Courtesy Rowan Museum Collection.)

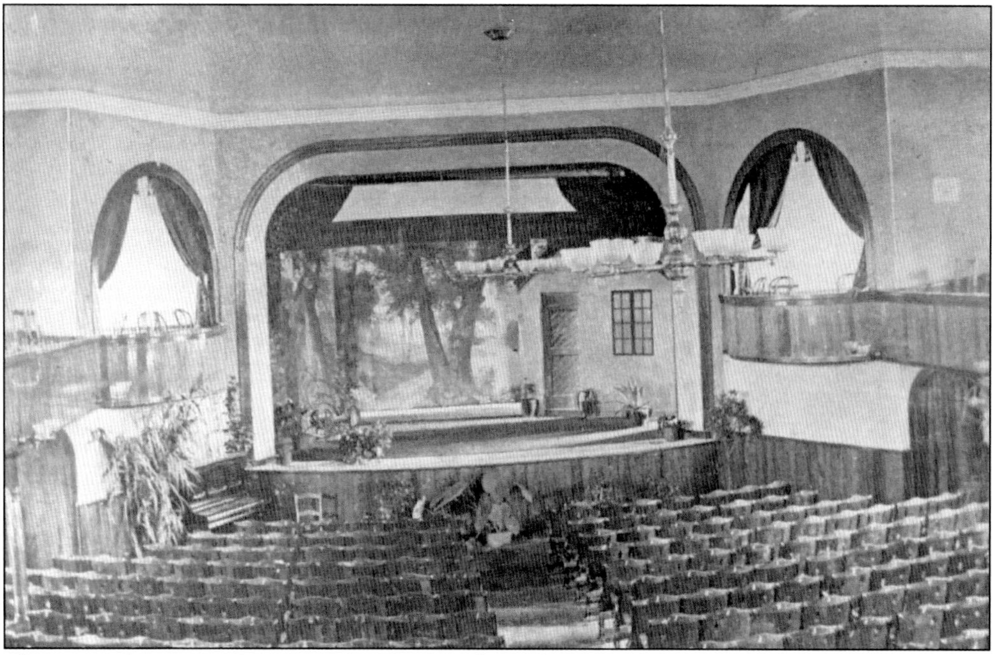

The original Meroney Opera House is seen in these photographs around 1894. A second Meroney Opera House, constructed in 1905, remains today as the Meroney Theater, operated by the Piedmont Players. (Both, courtesy Rowan Museum Collection.)

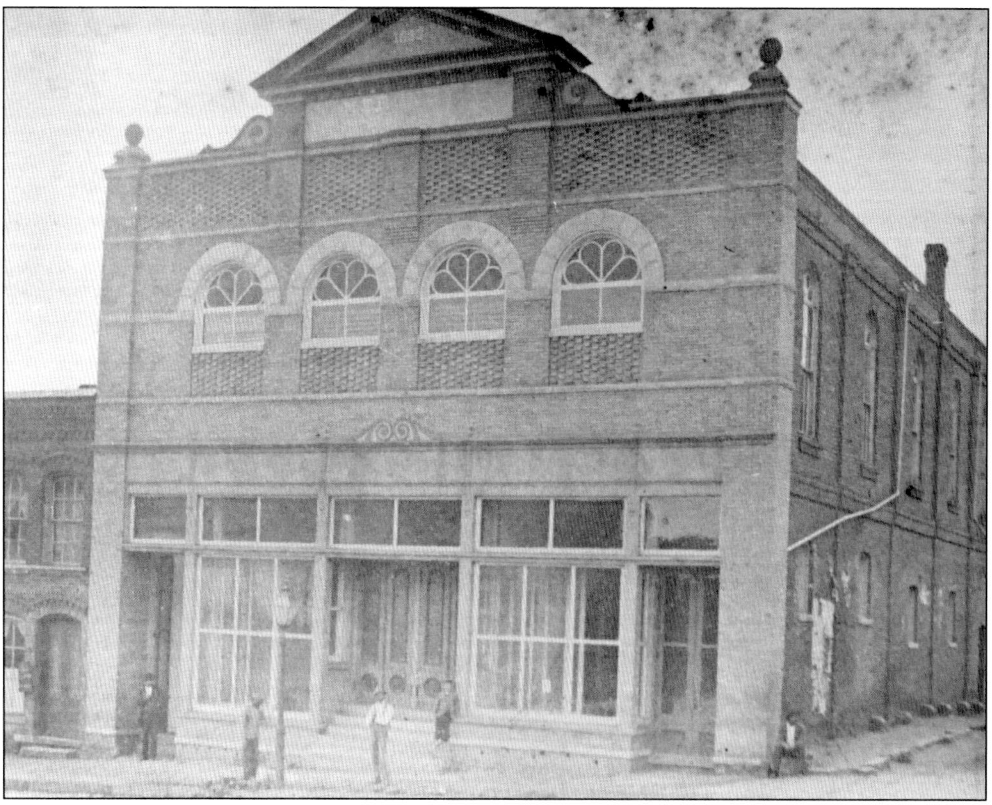

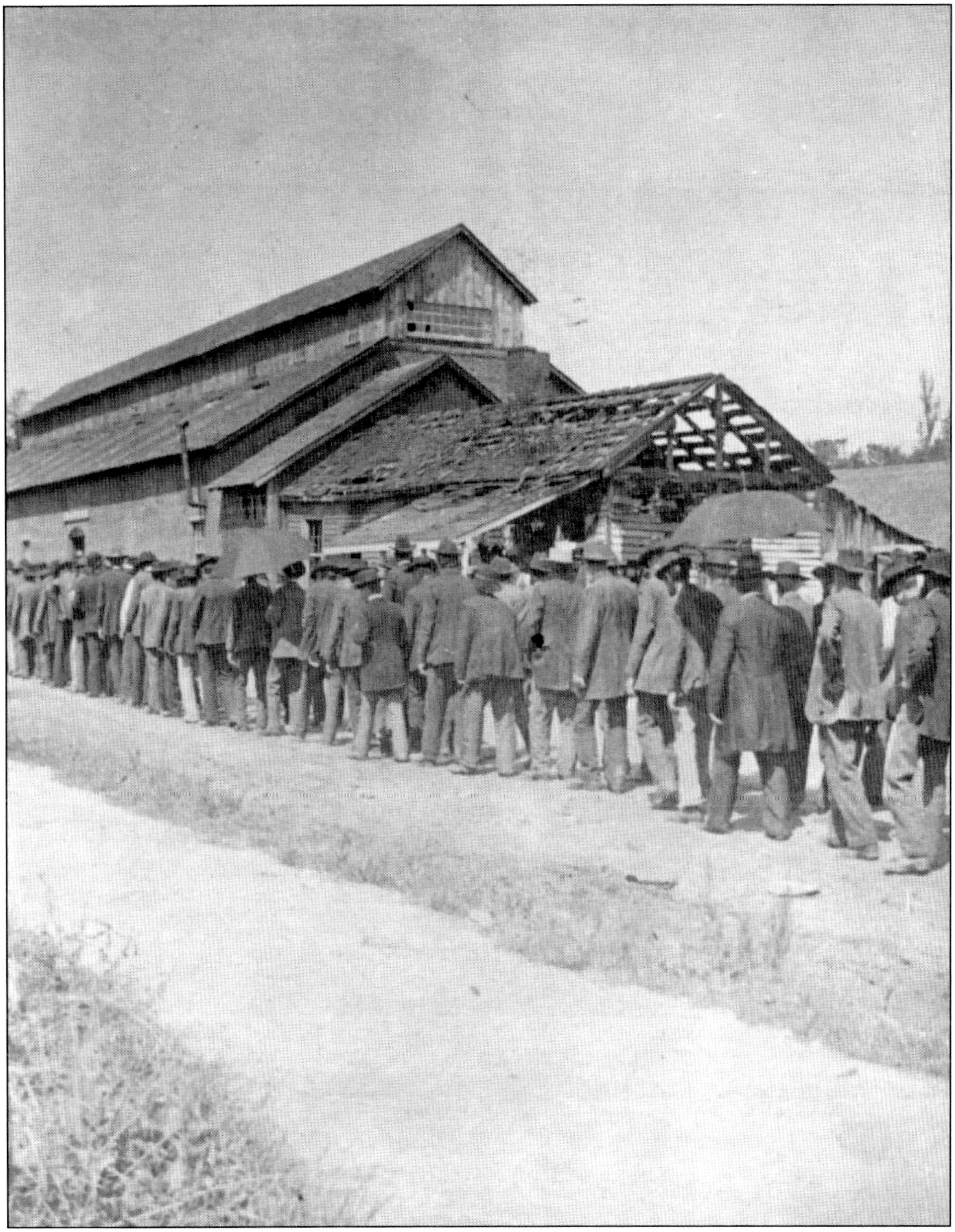

In 1894, the Confederate veterans held their annual dinner at a warehouse on the corner of Fisher and Church Streets. North Carolina, like many Southern states, continued to pay a pension to Civil War veterans until their death. Annual meetings like this one in Salisbury allowed these men to recollect the past and catch up with friends. (Courtesy Rowan Museum Collection.)

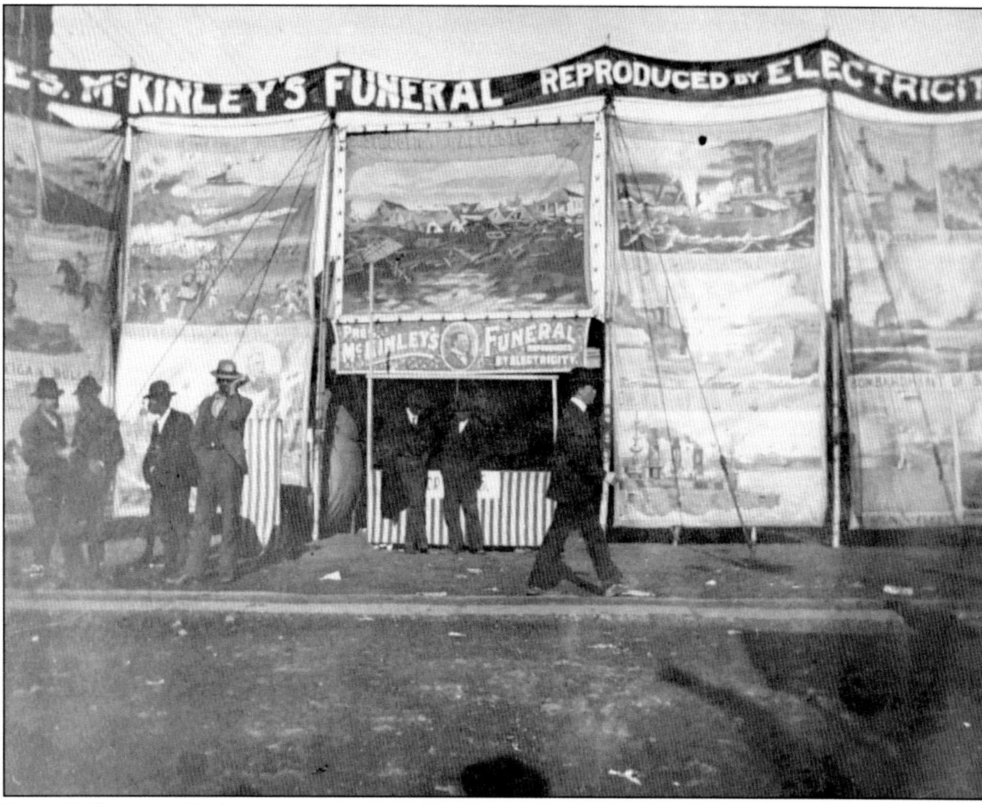

Pres. William McKinley was assassinated in September 1901 in Buffalo, New York. The nation experienced widespread grief, and his funeral was preceded by a train carrying his body to Canton, Ohio. His funeral was filmed by Edison Studios, and copies were shown at carnivals across the United States. His death was still on many minds as this carnival visited Salisbury in November 1901. (Courtesy Rowan Museum Collection.)

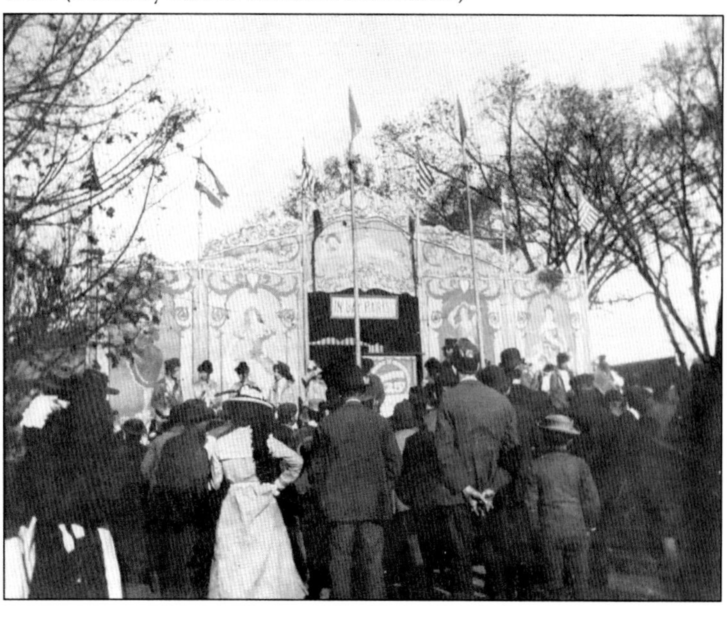

The 1901 carnival brought many interesting displays, including this exhibit, entitled In Gay Paris. For many, traveling to Europe was impossible. For the cost of a quarter, though, they could experience another part of the world. (Courtesy Rowan Museum Collection.)

Sideshows have always been a mainstay of carnivals, and this was no exception. Here, Ki-Lo, from Egypt, would eat live poisonous rattlesnakes. The sign on the post alludes to another exhibit, in which a statue apparently came to life. (Courtesy Rowan Museum Collection.)

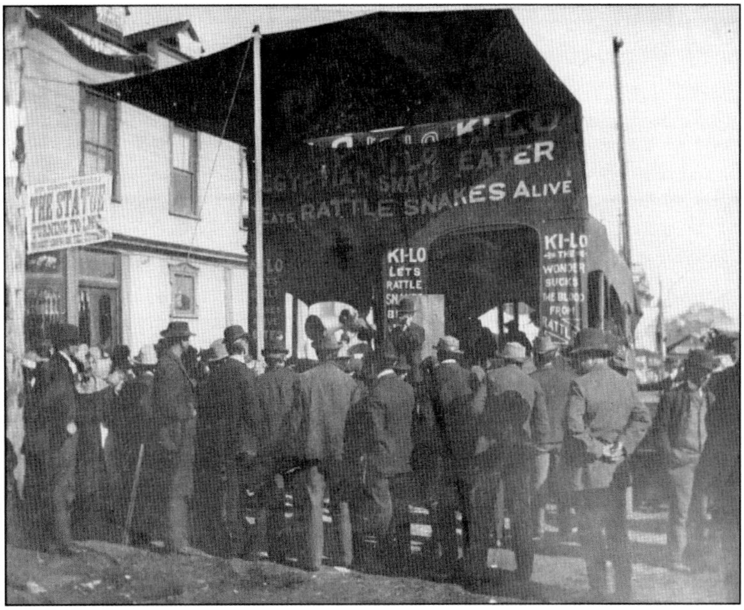

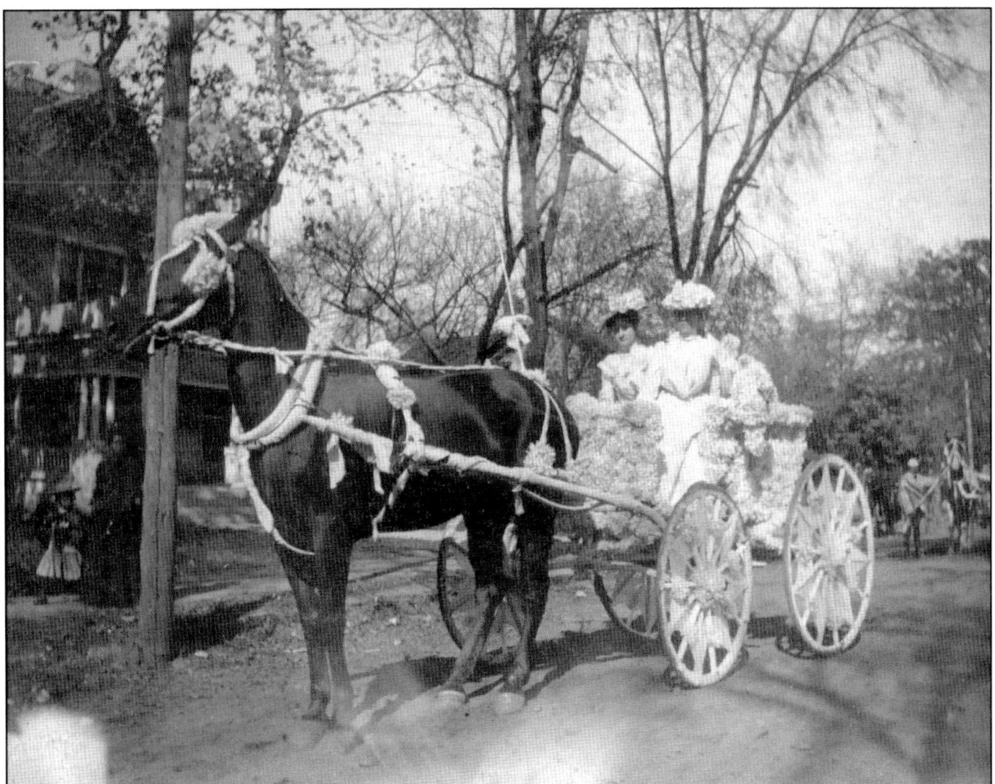
The locals of Salisbury also participated in the 1901 carnival. Here, Annie Wetmore and a Miss Mallett are ready to ride a decorated buggy, possibly as part of a parade. Other buggies were decorated in a similar fashion. (Courtesy Rowan Museum Collection.)

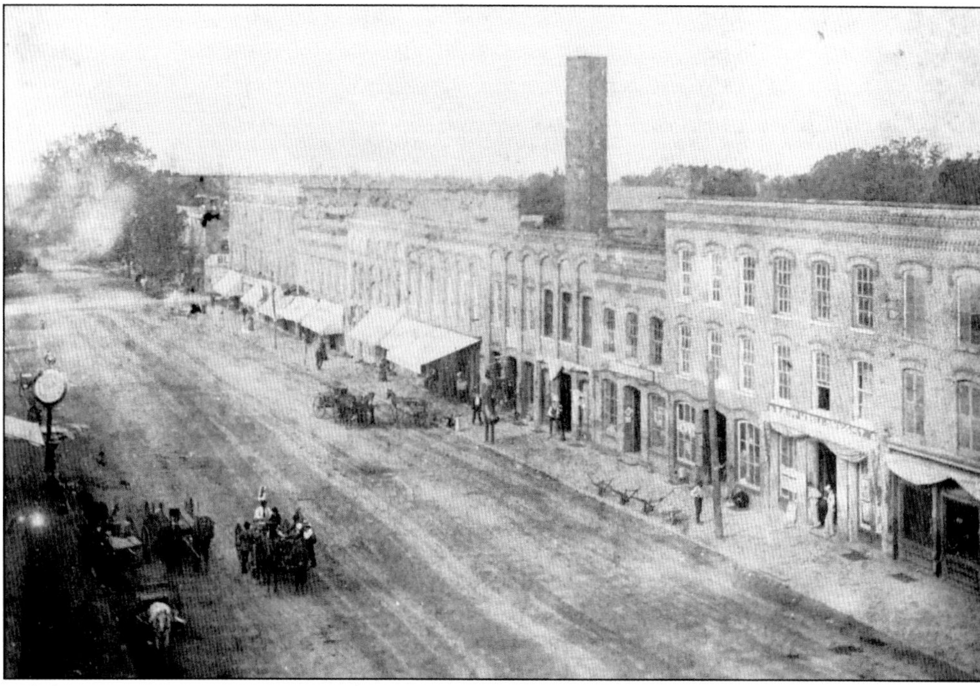

Salisbury's Main Street is seen in these two images from the turn of the 20th century. The above photograph was taken before 1905, as streetcar tracks have not yet been laid. The photograph below was taken from the standpipe, which served as an early water tower for the city. (Both, courtesy Rowan Museum Collection.)

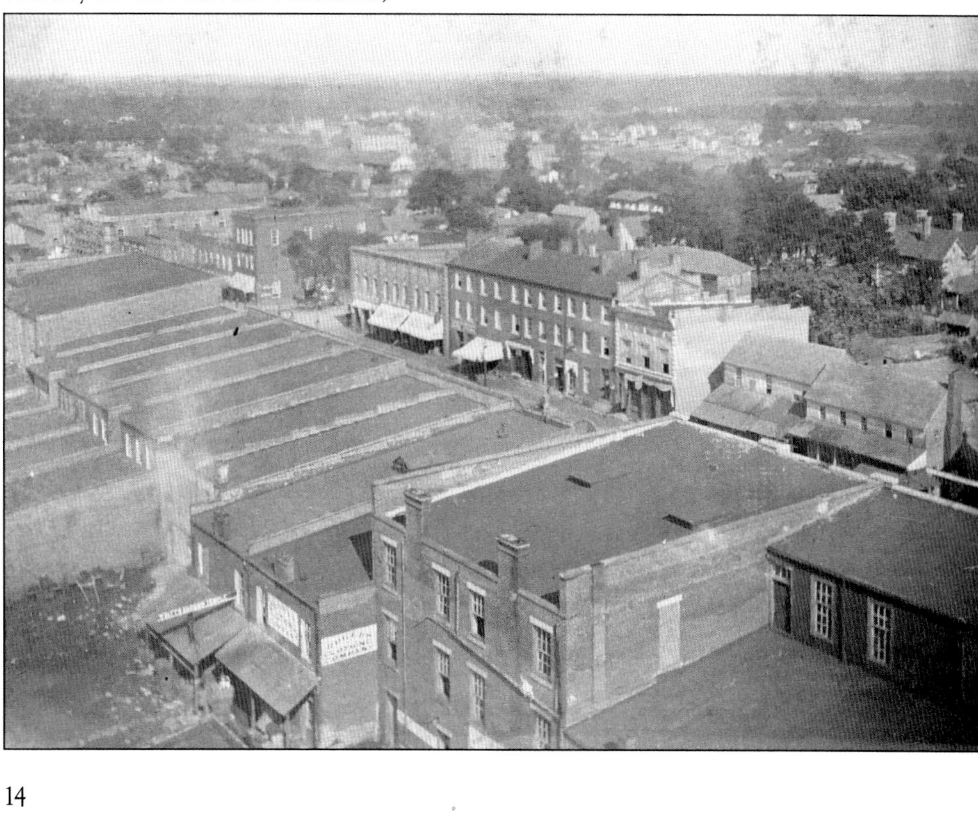

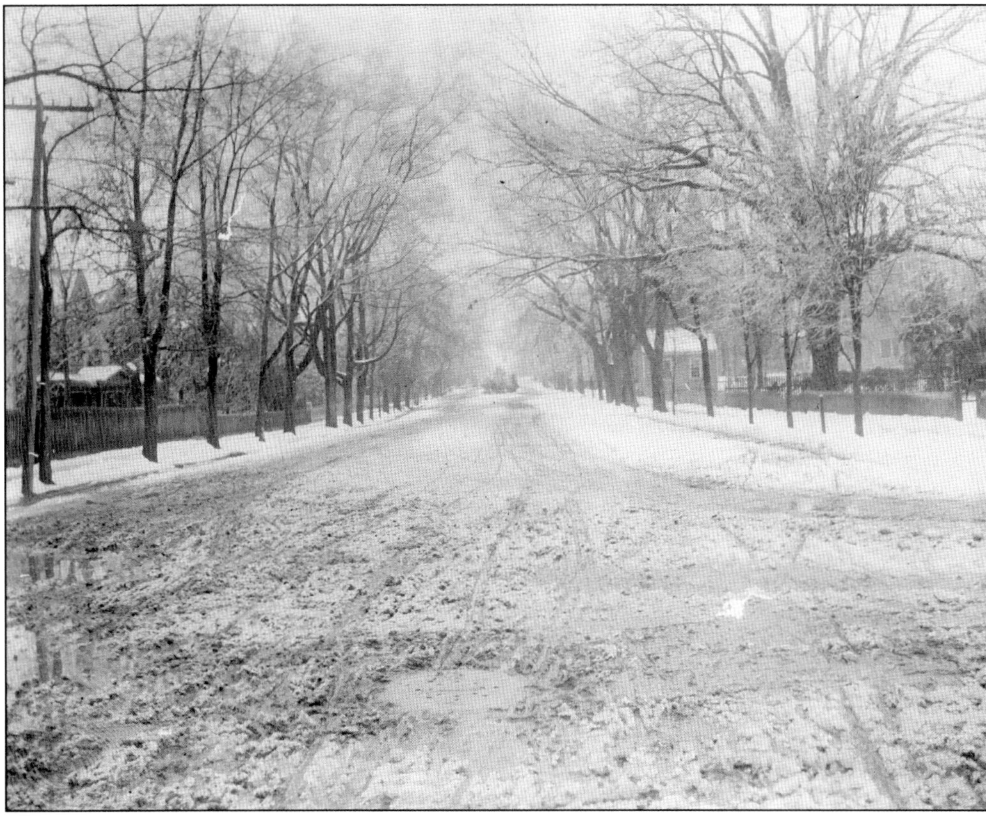

The winter scene of old Salisbury shown above is from the intersection of Fulton and Innes Streets, near Dr. Rumple's office, looking toward the square. The photograph below shows the intersection of South Fulton and West Fisher Streets. (Both, courtesy Rowan Museum Collection.)

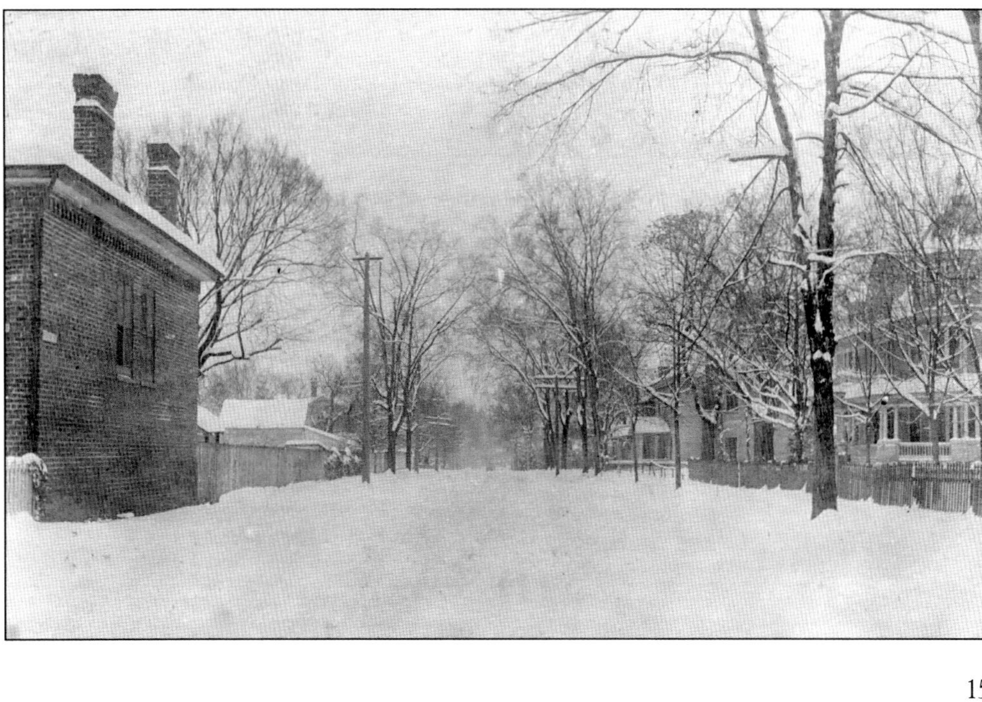

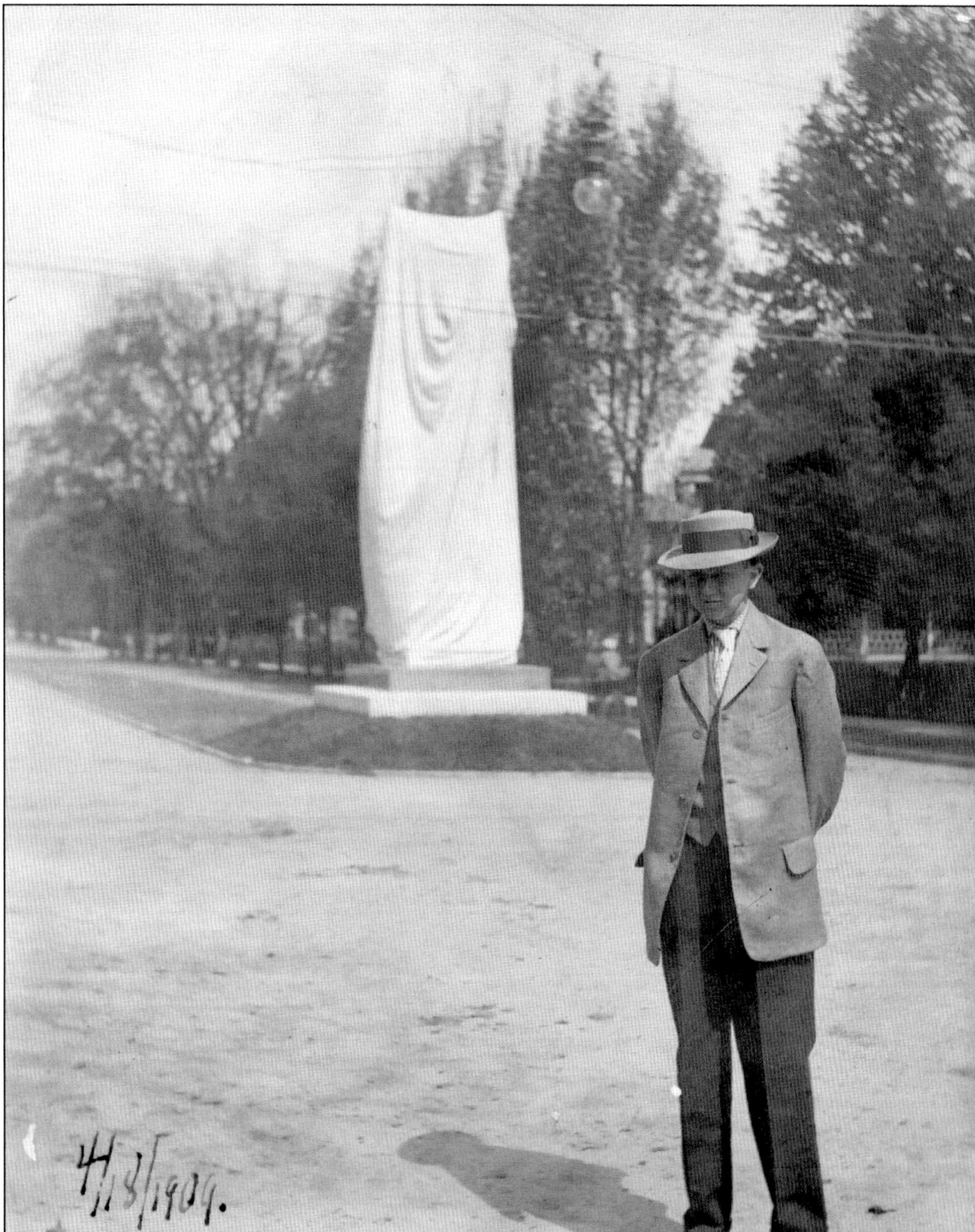

Local resident Thedie Brown stands in front of the covered Confederate monument on April 18, 1909. This statue, designed by Frederick W. RuckStuhl, is known as *Fame*. The pedestal is made of Rowan County pink marble, supplied by the Balfour Granite Company. (Courtesy Rowan Museum Collection.)

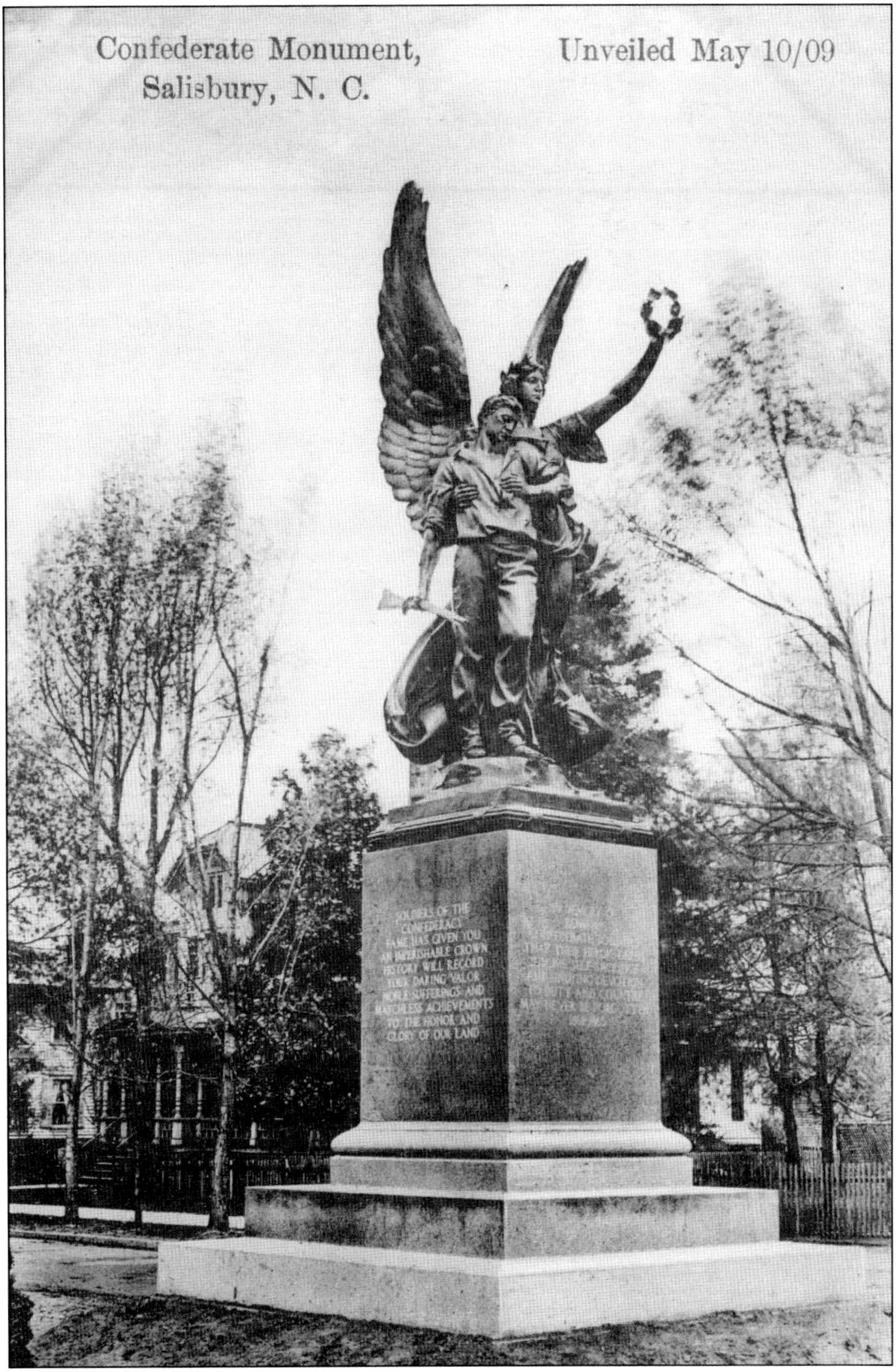

The monument was dedicated on May 10, 1909, Confederate Memorial Day. Along with local dignitaries and veterans, honored guests included Mary Anna Morrison Jackson, wife of Stonewall Jackson. The home of Theo Kluttz can be seen in the background. (Courtesy Rowan Museum Collection.)

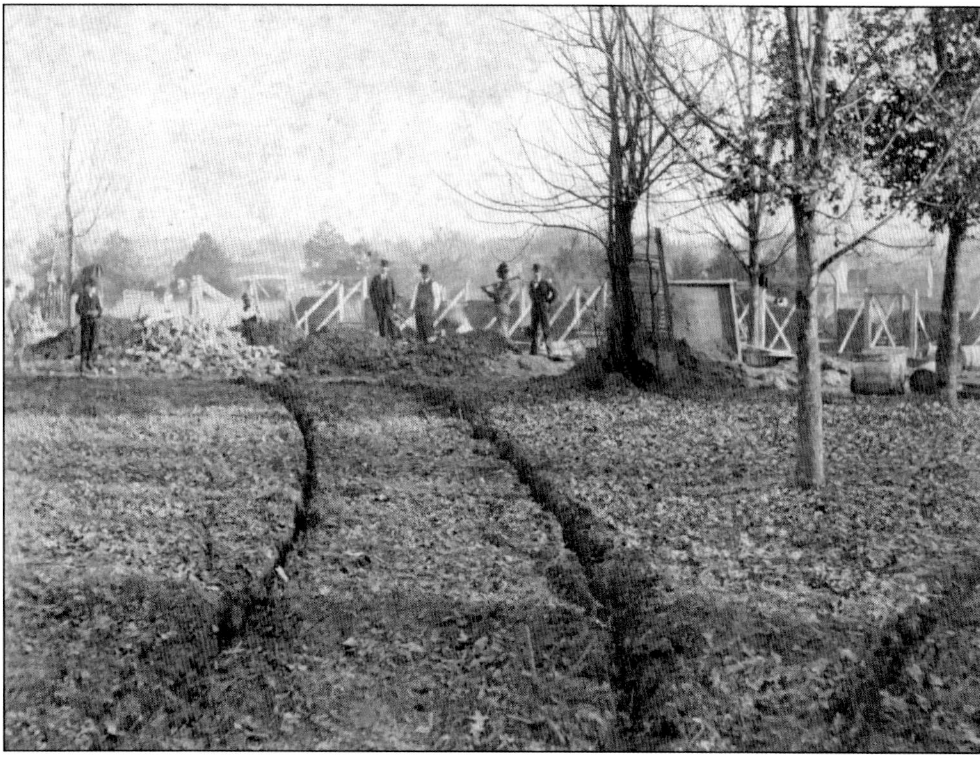

Construction is under way for the Whitehead-Stokes Sanatorium, which was located at the corner of Fulton and Liberty Streets. (Courtesy Rowan Museum Collection.)

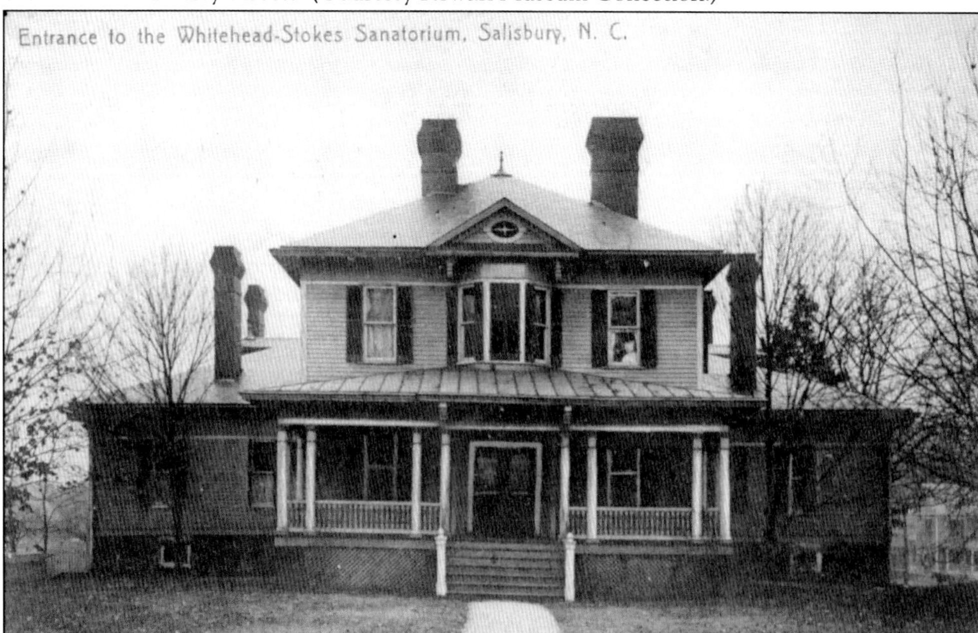

The 40-bed Whitehead-Stokes Sanatorium opened in 1899. The facility was under the direction of Drs. John Whitehead and J. Ernest Stokes with assistance from Ella Price Smith, who oversaw the nurses. (Courtesy Rowan Museum Collection.)

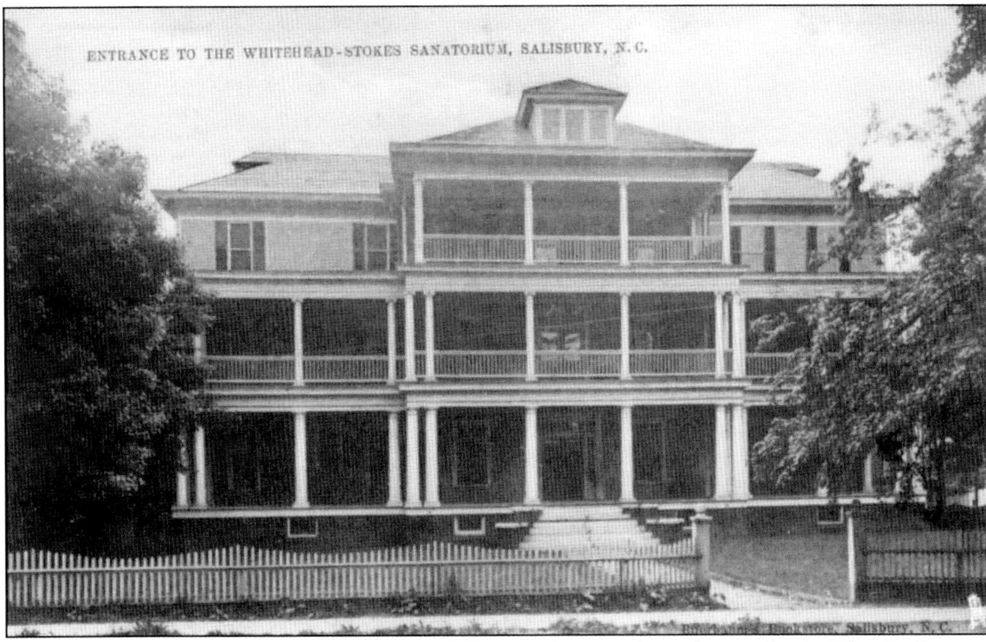

By 1907, the sanatorium had added a third floor and was enlarged to 60 beds. The facility was Salisbury's only hospital through the 1920s and 1930s. The Rowan Memorial Hospital was opened for patient care in July 1936 on the grounds of the current Rowan Regional Medical Center. Dr. Stokes helped the city start this new hospital, which benefited greatly from a Duke Endowment grant. (Courtesy Rowan Museum Collection.)

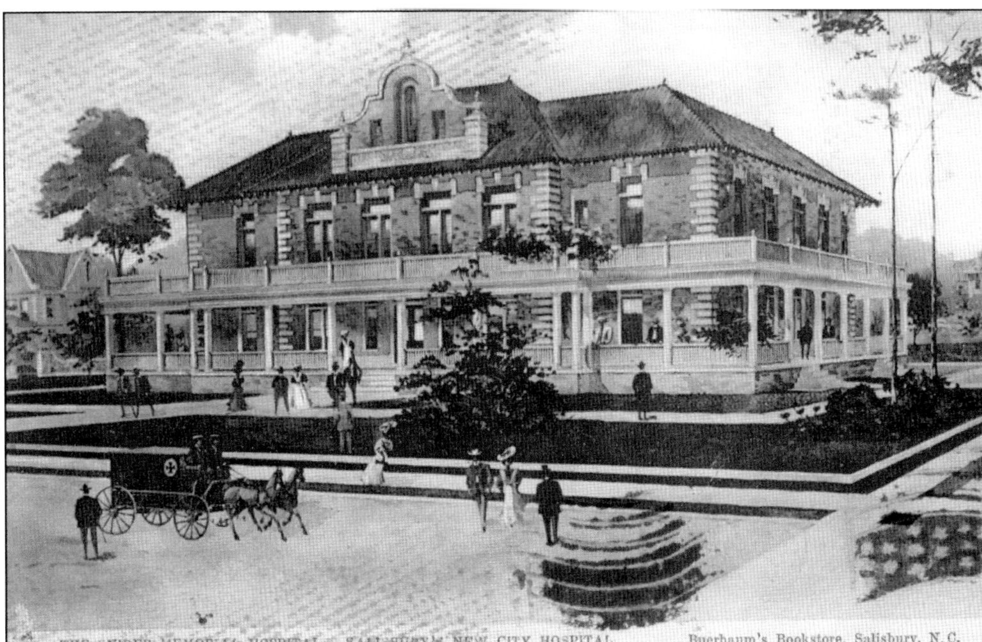

The Snider Memorial Hospital, designed by Frank Milburn, was never built even though drawings were made and circulated around Salisbury. (Courtesy Rowan Museum Collection.)

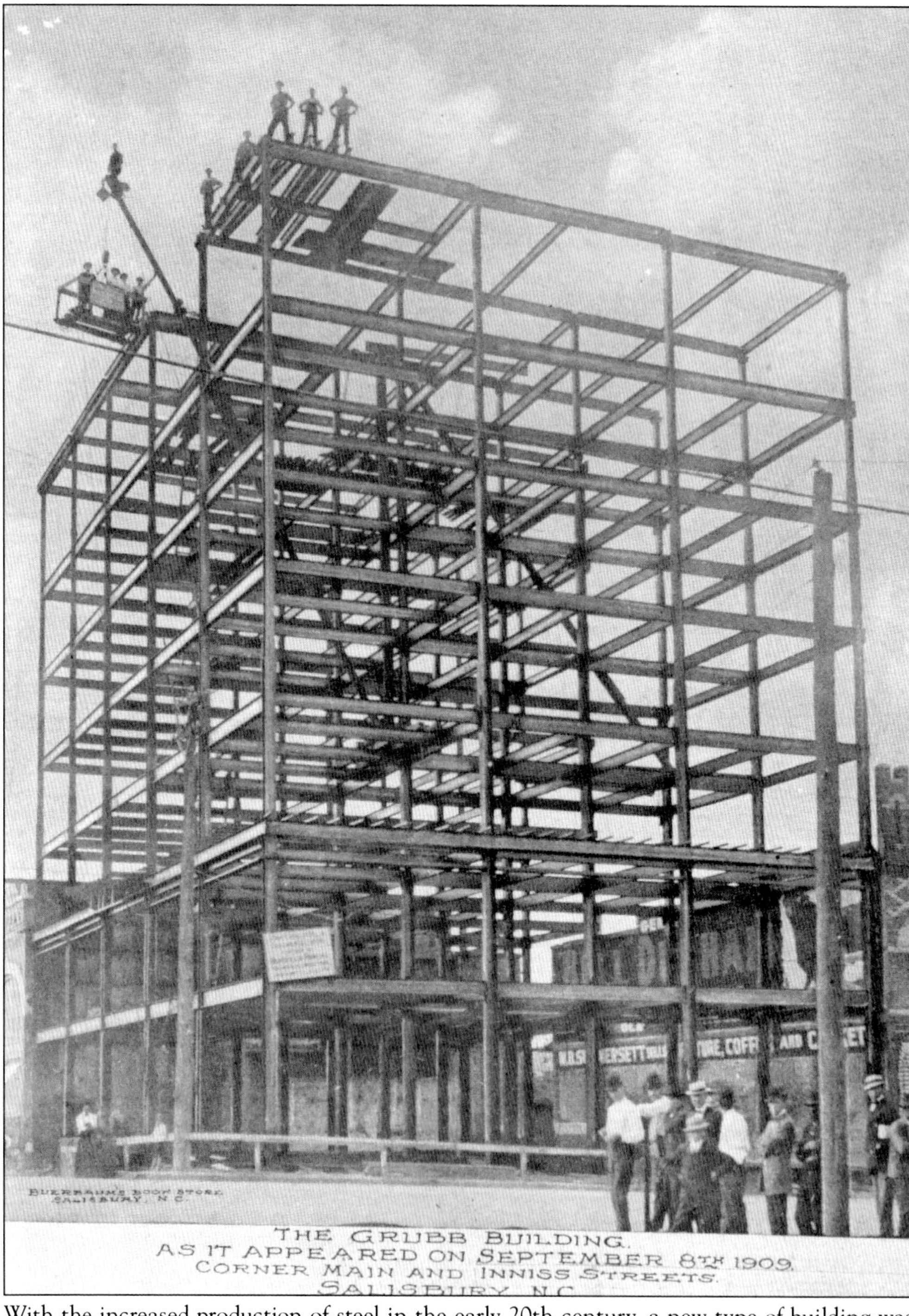

With the increased production of steel in the early 20th century, a new type of building was developed—the skyscraper. The Grubb Building (named for Henry Clay Grubb) was the first building in Salisbury constructed by this new method. Once completed, it was the tallest steel structure in North Carolina. As is evident by the onlookers in this postcard, the building was quite a novelty at the time. (Courtesy Rowan Museum Collection.)

Grubb died before his building could be completed in 1913. The structure, seven and a half stories tall, was designed by Frank Milburn, who also planned the Salisbury railroad depot. (Courtesy Rowan Museum Collection.)

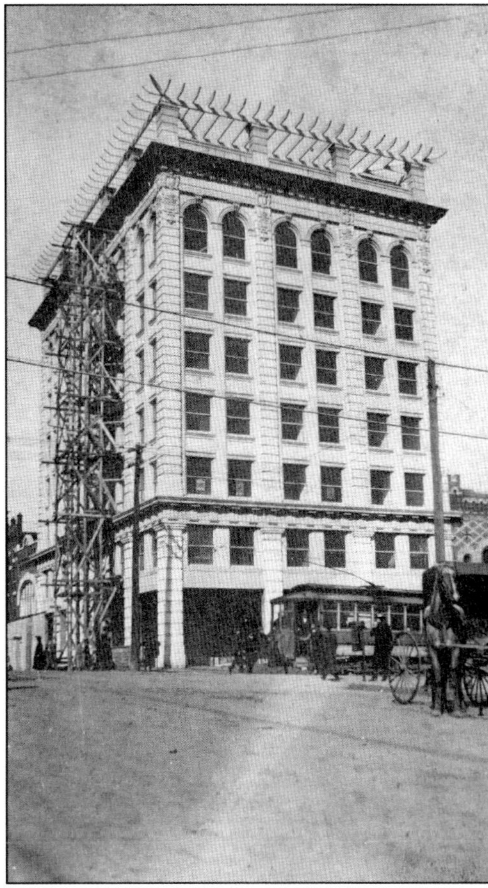

The Grubb Building in later years was purchased by the Wallace family, who sold real estate throughout Rowan County. Most people today remember this as the Wallace Building and, more recently, The Plaza, following a major renovation by Ralph and Anne Ketner. After the renovation, the building was donated to the City of Salisbury. (Courtesy Rowan Museum Collection.)

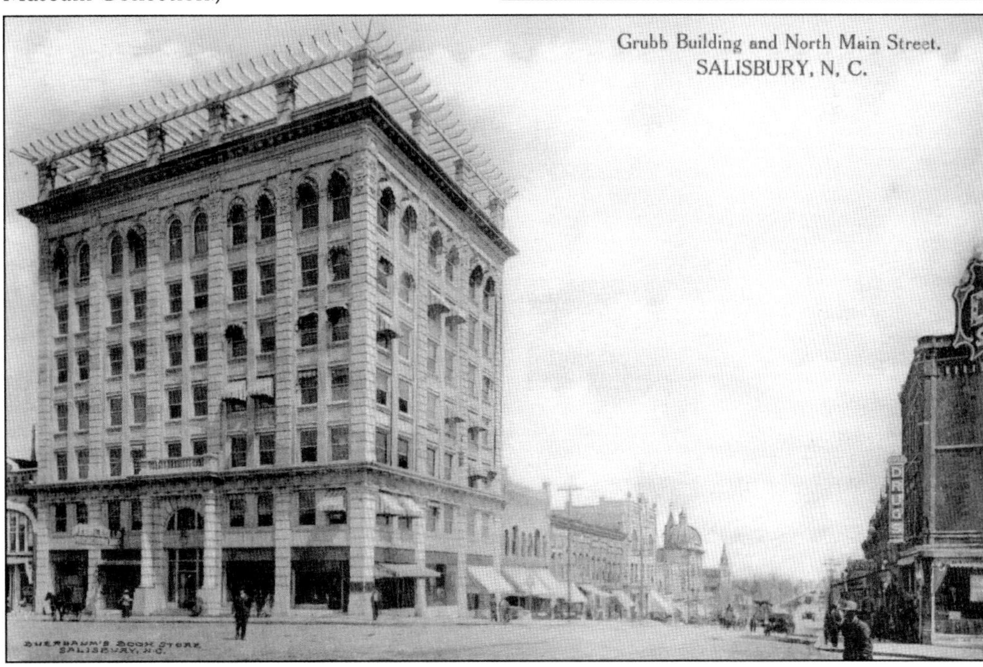

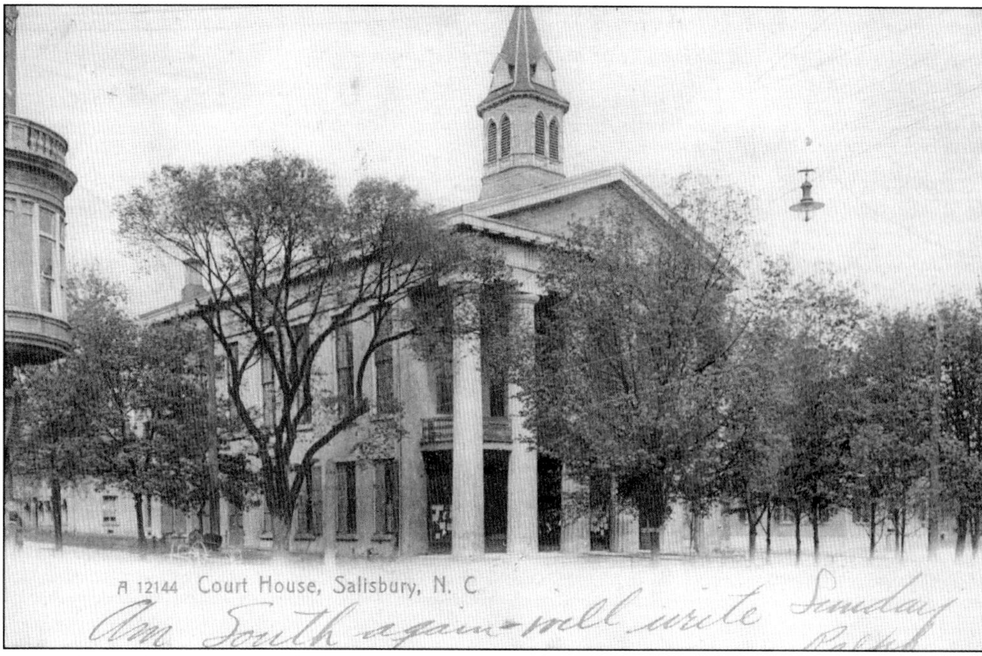

Shown here is Rowan County's third courthouse, completed in 1857. A clock was originally installed in the tower but was later replaced with a bell. Future governor John W. Ellis was the first superior court judge to hear a case in the building. The tower was removed by the early 1900s, giving the building an appearance similar to how it looks today. (Courtesy Rowan Museum Collection.)

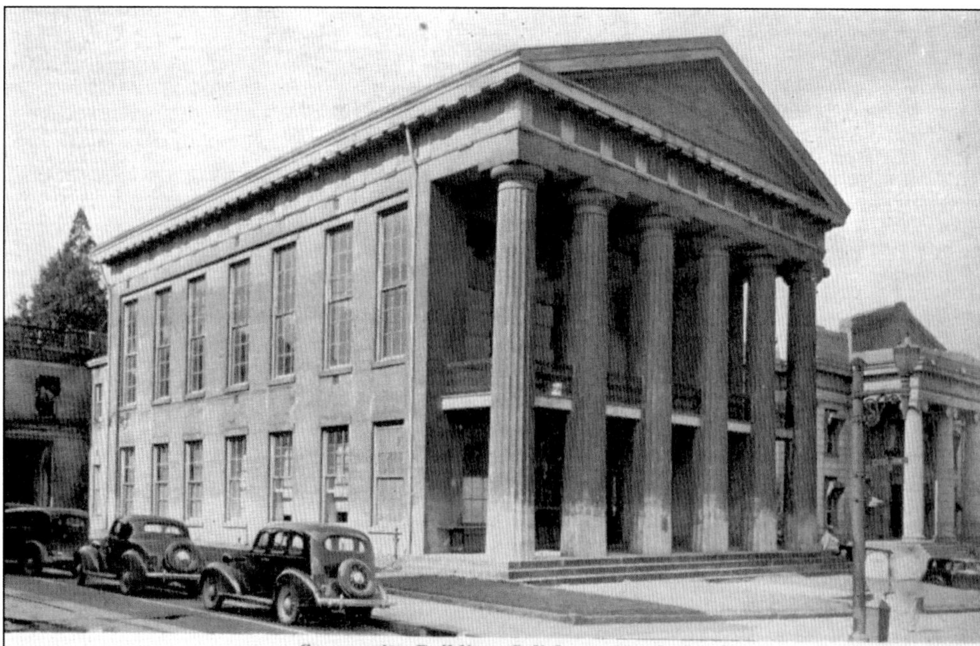

The old courthouse building is seen here in the 1930s or 1940s. It now houses the main offices of the Rowan Museum. On the right is the new court building. (Courtesy Rowan Museum Collection.)

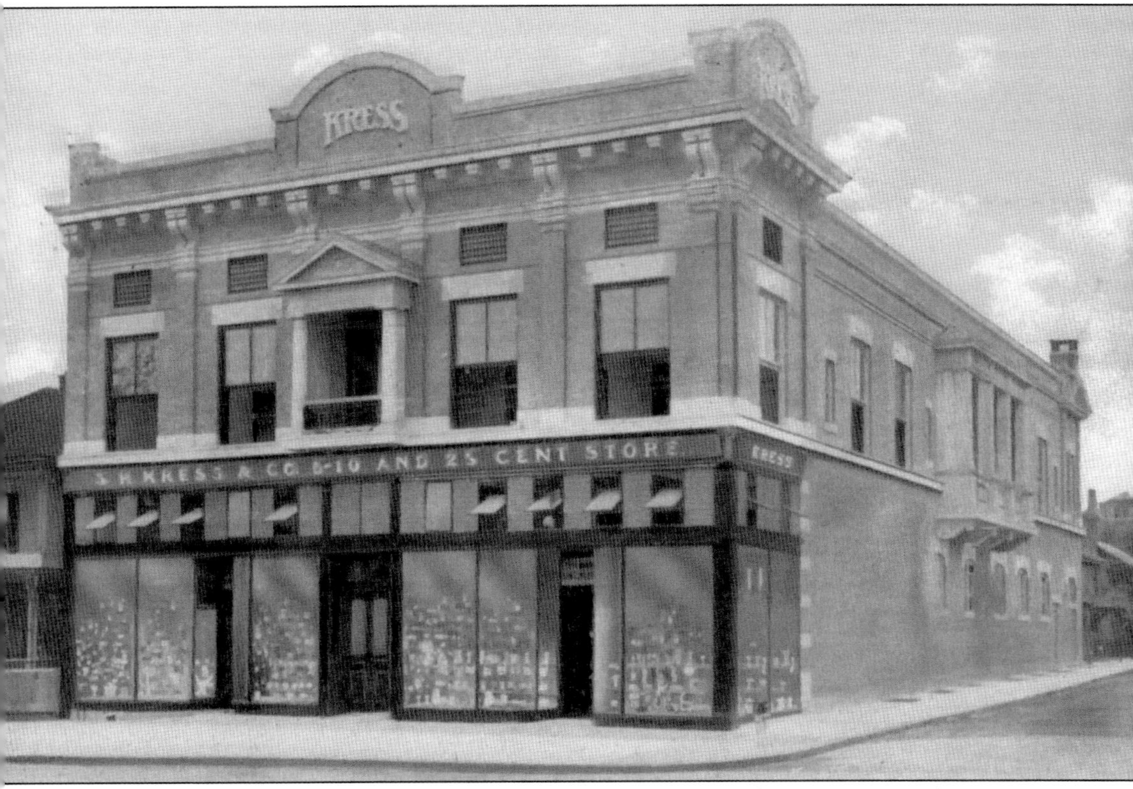

S.H. Kress and Company opened their store in Salisbury on September 17, 1910, on the corner of South Main and West Bank Streets. This building has now been preserved as the Kress Plaza with space for shops and loft apartments. (Courtesy Rowan Museum Collection.)

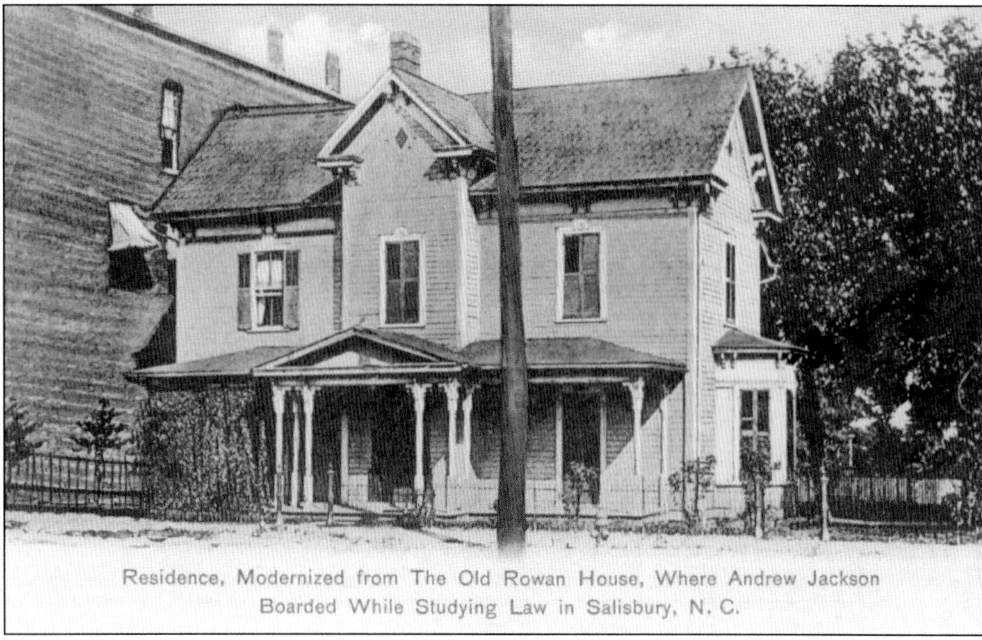

One of the famous residents of Salisbury was a future president, Andrew Jackson, who studied law under Judge Spruce Macay in 1784–1785. Jackson was later admitted to the Rowan County bar on November 6, 1787. (Courtesy Rowan Museum Collection.)

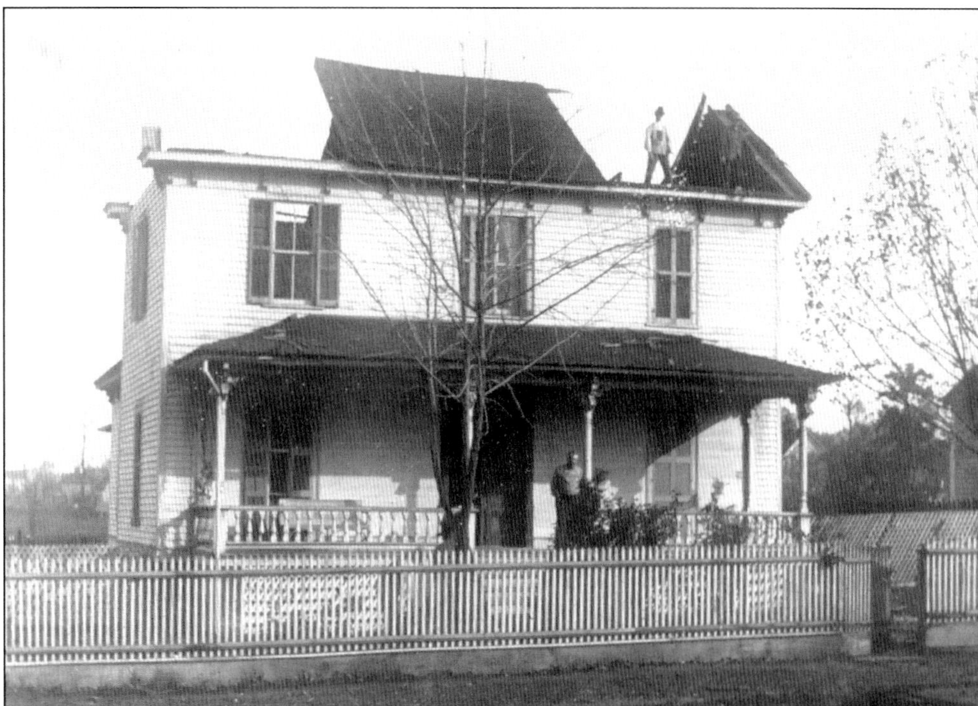

On April 5, 1905, a cyclone tore across parts of Rowan County. This house was lucky in that only the roof appears damaged. The storm affected Livingstone College first, then headed southeast toward downtown. (Courtesy Rowan Museum Collection.)

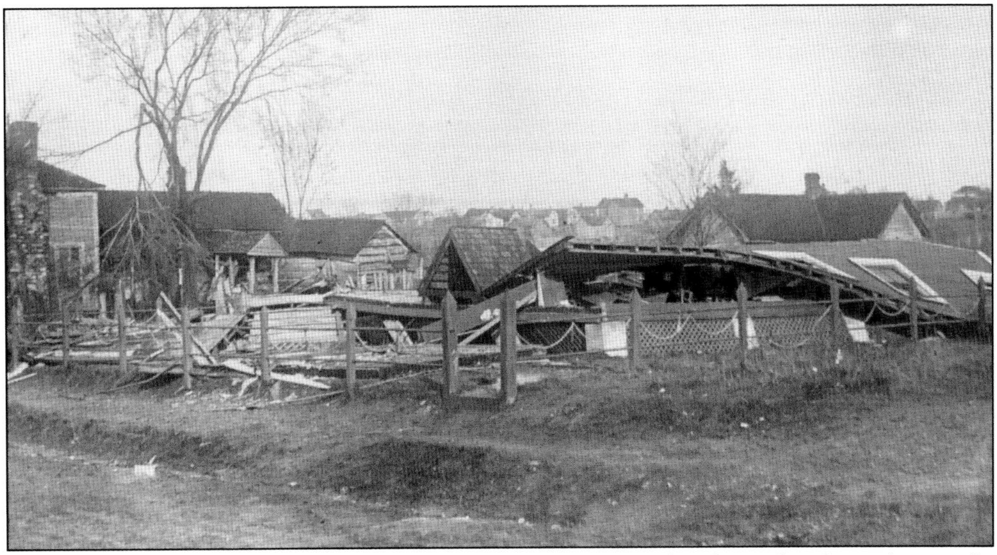

This structure was not as fortunate and may have received a direct hit from the winds. Tornadoes, though rare in Rowan County, have happened through the years. (Courtesy Rowan Museum Collection.)

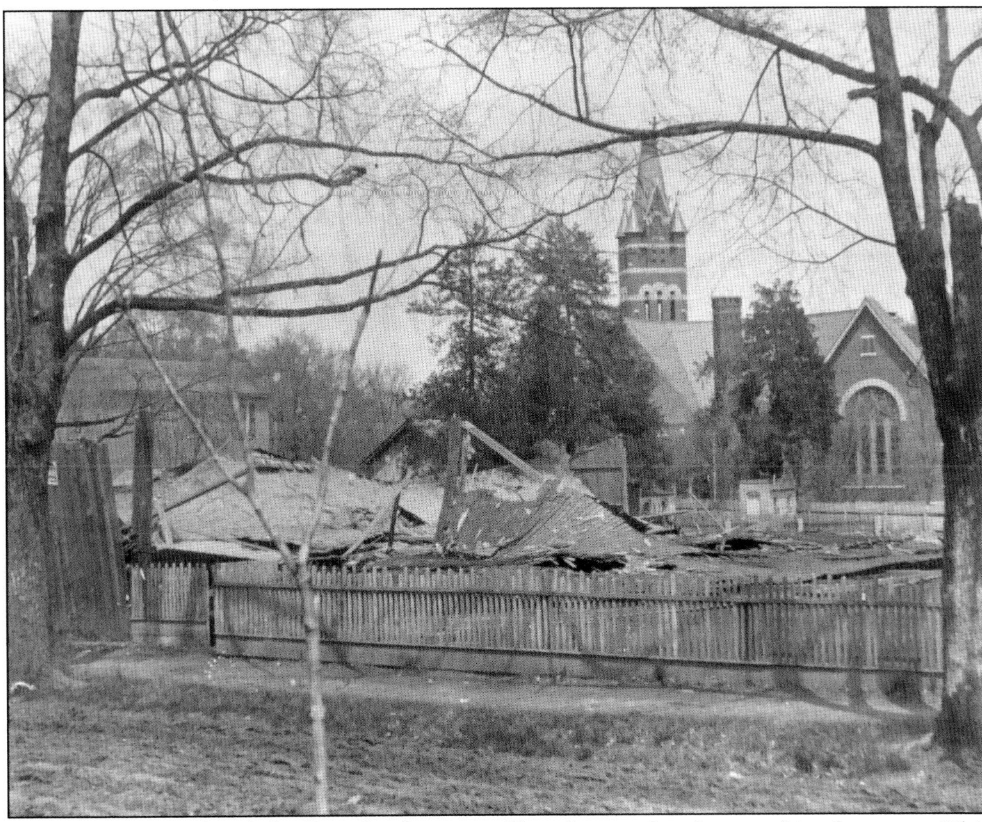

The tabernacle behind the First Presbyterian Church was also destroyed in the storm. This church was located on Innes Street between Church and Jackson Streets, only a few blocks from downtown. (Courtesy Rowan Museum Collection.)

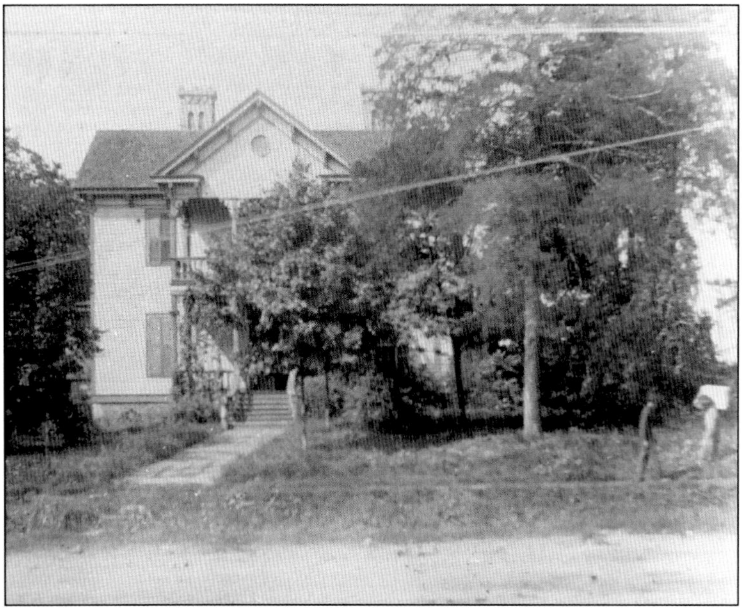

Dr. J.A. Caldwell resided at 125 East Innes Street. This location now houses the Nashville Nights Club. (Courtesy Rowan Museum Collection.)

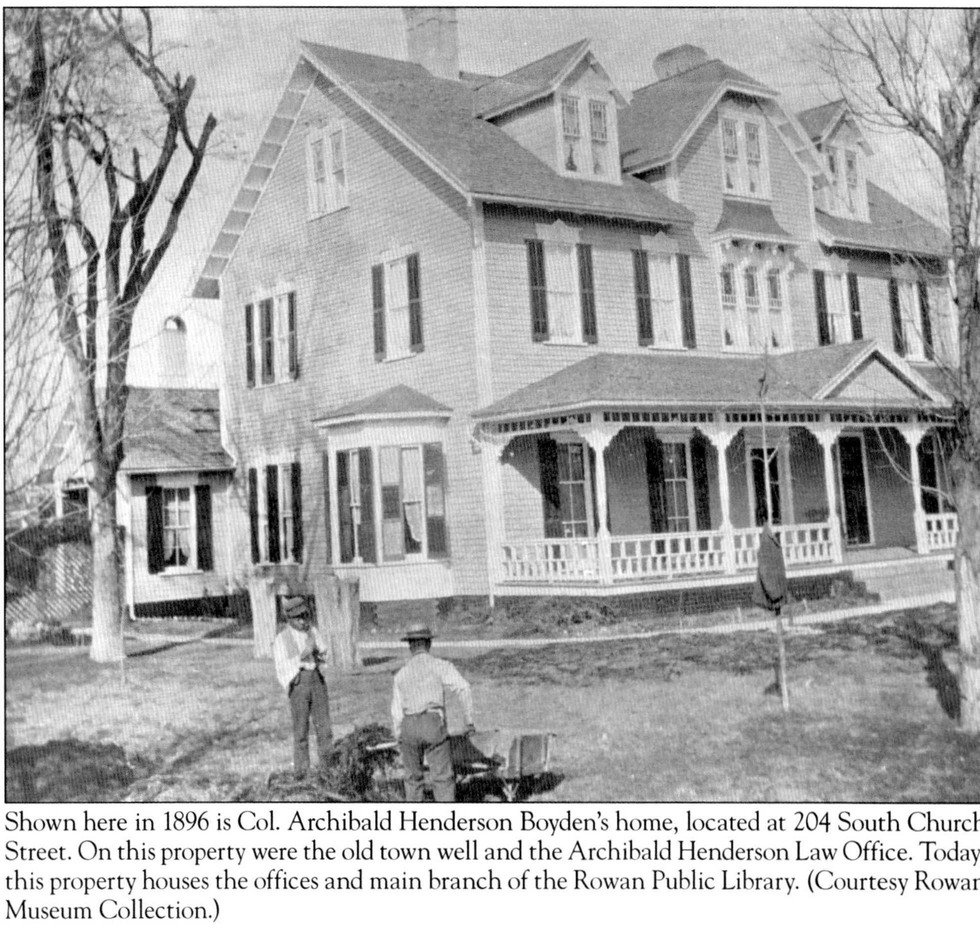

Shown here in 1896 is Col. Archibald Henderson Boyden's home, located at 204 South Church Street. On this property were the old town well and the Archibald Henderson Law Office. Today, this property houses the offices and main branch of the Rowan Public Library. (Courtesy Rowan Museum Collection.)

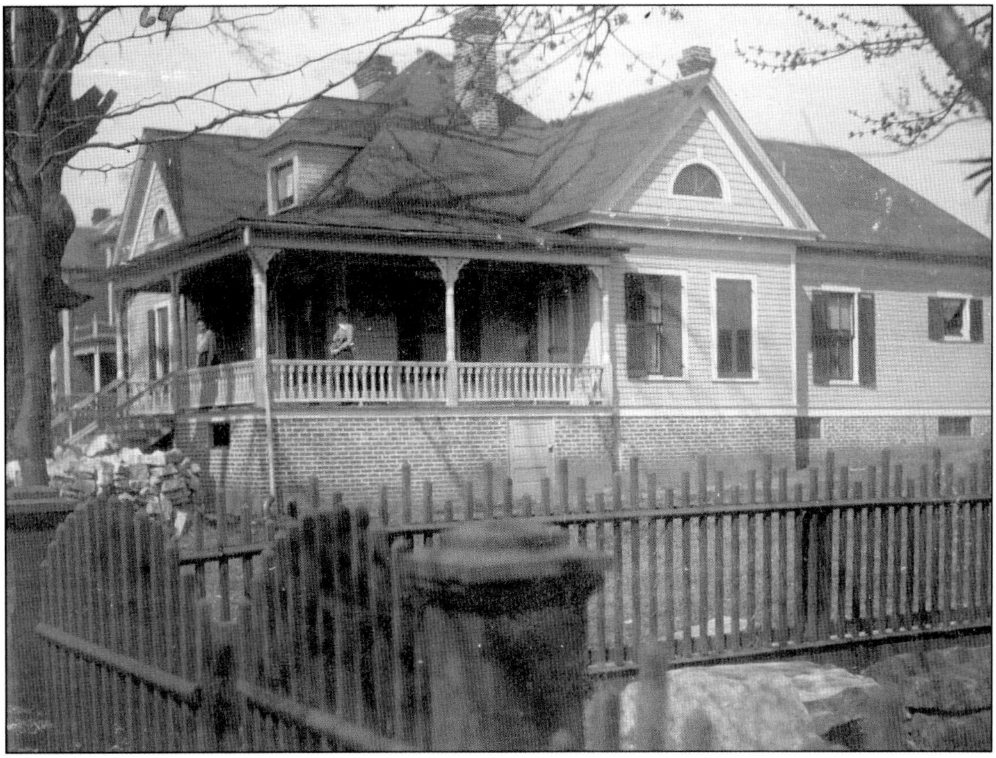

The home of Richard Eames, located at 212 West Bank Street, is pictured here. Eames was a mining engineer and the father-in-law of Theodore Buerbaum. (Courtesy Rowan Museum Collection.)

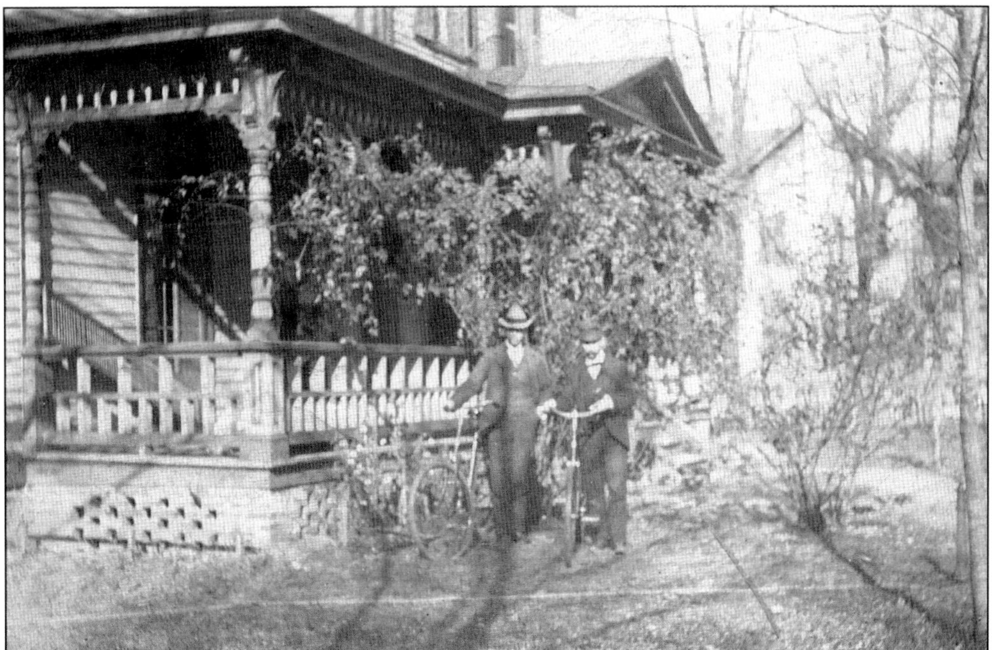

In this close-up photograph of the house at 202 South Fulton Street, the owners prepare to enjoy a bicycle ride through town. (Courtesy Rowan Museum Collection.)

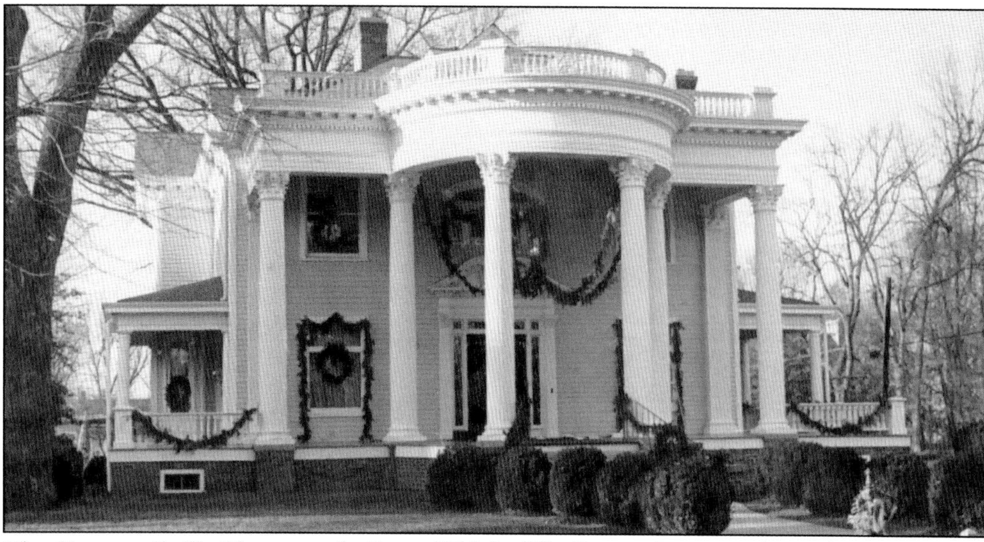

The Cannon-Guille Home was built in 1906 for Ella Brown Cannon, the widow of David F. Cannon, cofounder of Cannon Mills. The structure was designed by J.M. McMichael. (Courtesy Rowan Museum Collection.)

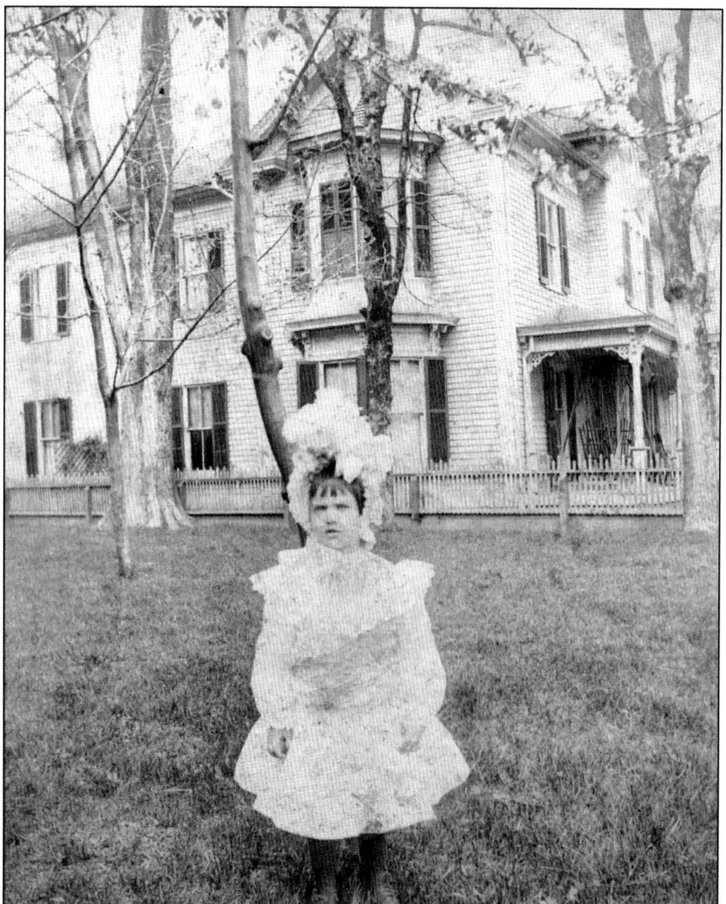

Alice Slater Cannon Guille poses for a photograph near the T.C. Linn Home at 120 South Fulton Street. Guille would become the first director of the Rowan Museum when it was established in 1953. (Courtesy Rowan Museum Collection.)

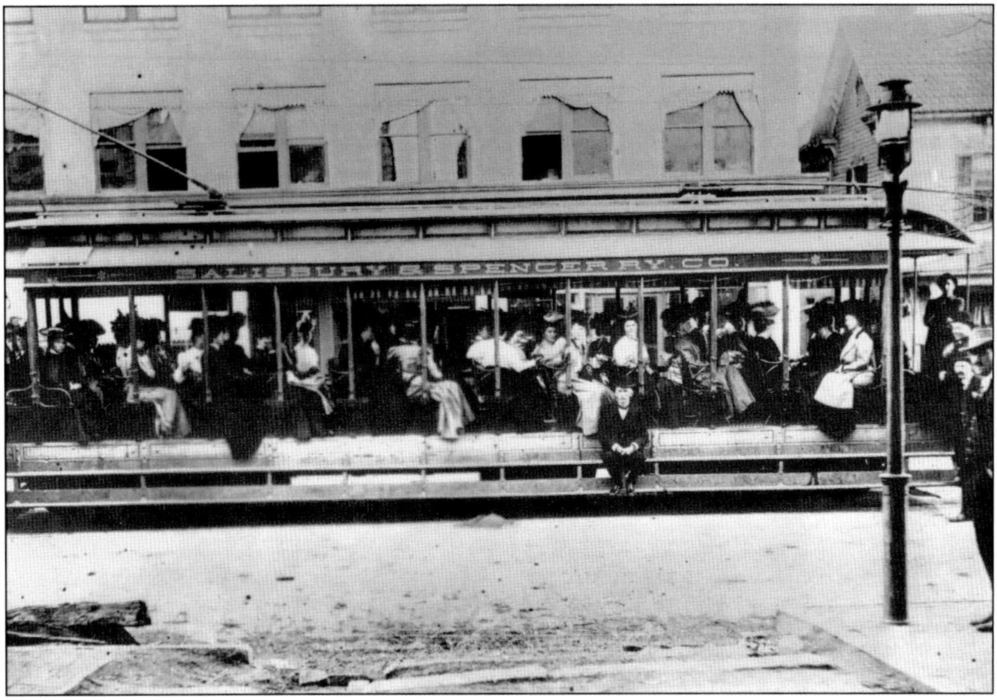

The Salisbury & Spencer Railway Company began operation in 1905 with service from the Fulton Heights neighborhood to Spencer Shops. The original cars were open but were soon changed to standard streetcars. The photograph below shows the railway company's headquarters, located in the Vanderford Hotel. (Both, courtesy Rowan Museum Collection.)

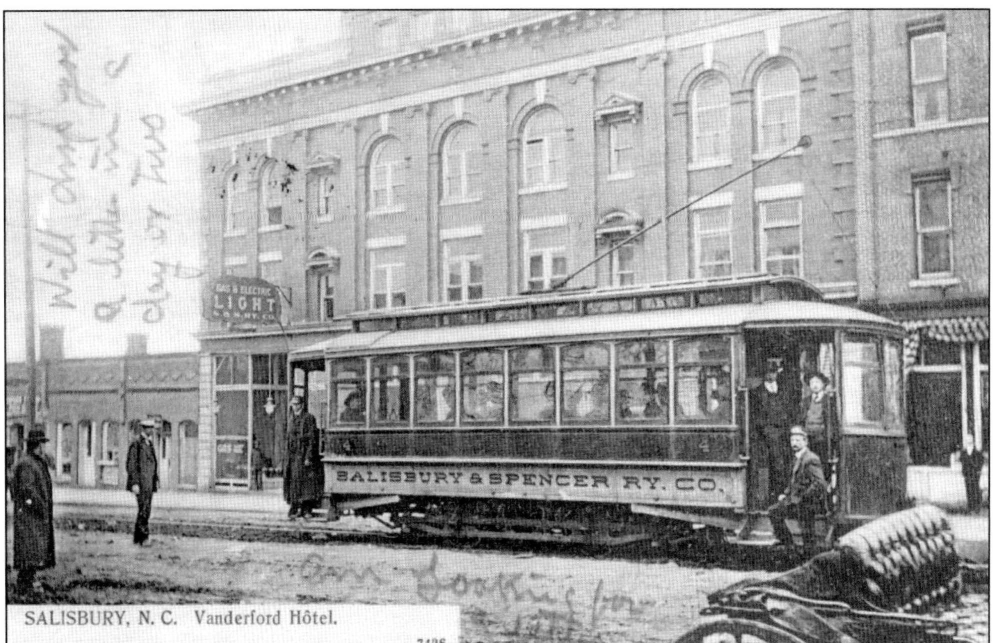

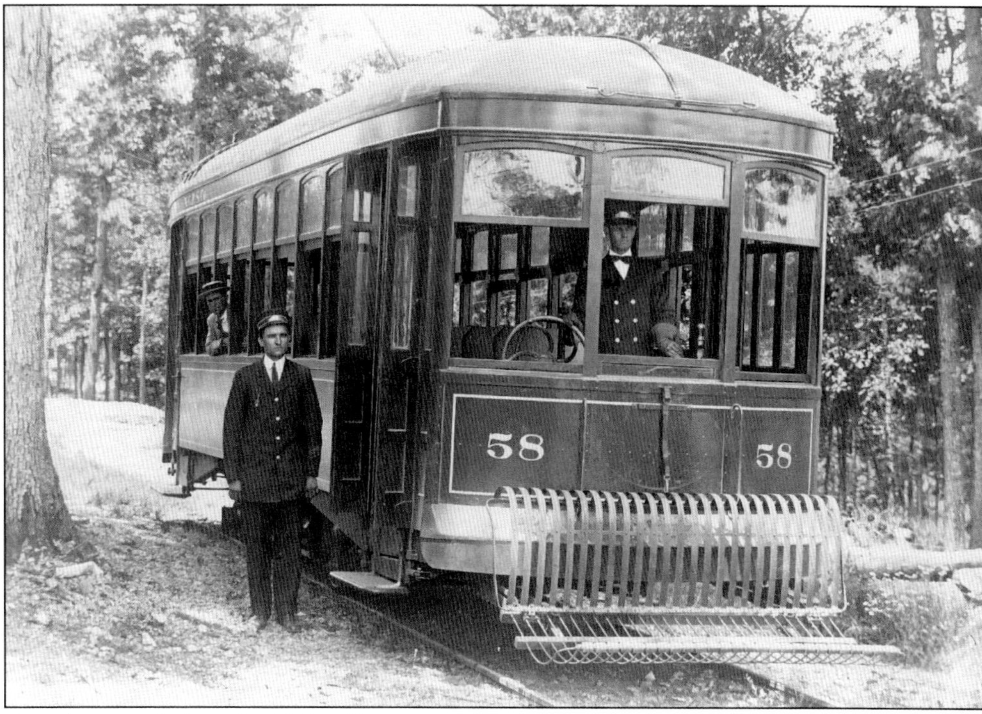

This photograph from the 1910s offers a typical view of a streetcar ready to start its route. Mitchell Avenue in the Fulton Heights area was unique, since the tracks ran through a center divider section, allowing the streetcar to safely operate between stops. The Salisbury & Spencer Railway Company shut down operations in 1938. (Courtesy North Carolina Division of Archives and History.)

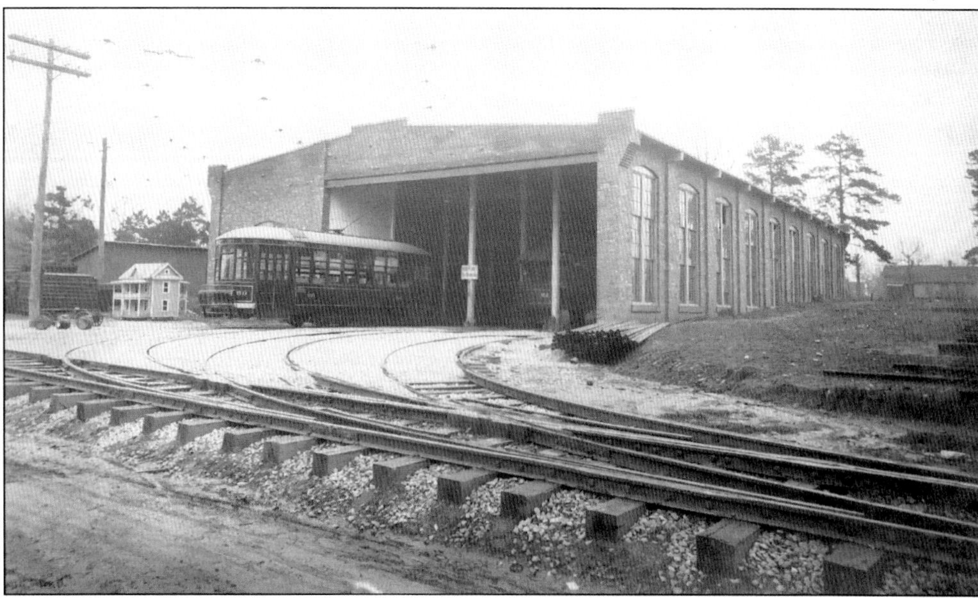

The main maintenance facility for the streetcars was located between Salisbury and Spencer off Salisbury Avenue. Southern Power Company, which was later renamed Duke Power, took over operation in 1924 and continued to use this building for various purposes after closure in 1938. (Courtesy North Carolina Division of Archives and History.)

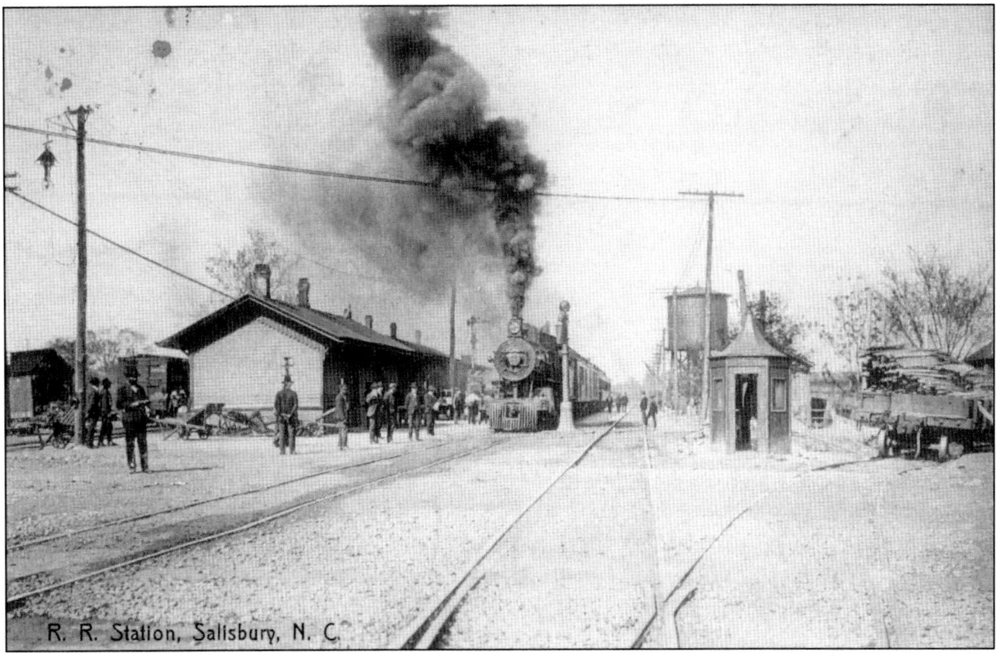

The original Southern Railway depot was a small building, located near the wye tracks connecting the North Carolina and Western North Carolina Railroads. The building was replaced by a large Spanish Mission structure in 1908. (Courtesy Rowan Museum Collection.)

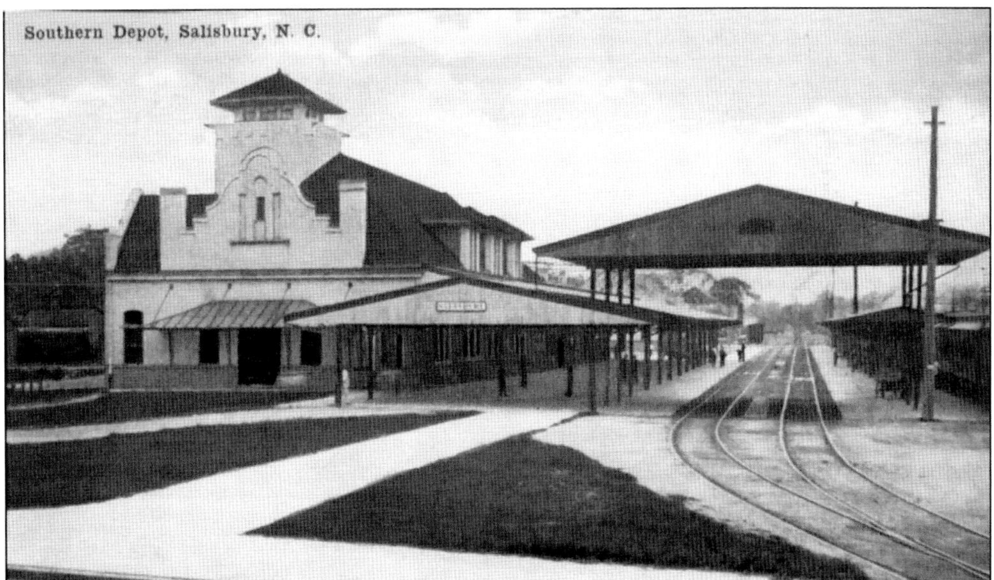

Frank P. Milburn designed a larger station, as Salisbury had established railroad connections to the north, south, east, and west. Southern Railway travelers headed to Washington, DC, or New Orleans had to travel through Salisbury. Connections could be made for Asheville and Goldsboro. (Courtesy North Carolina Division of Archives and History.)

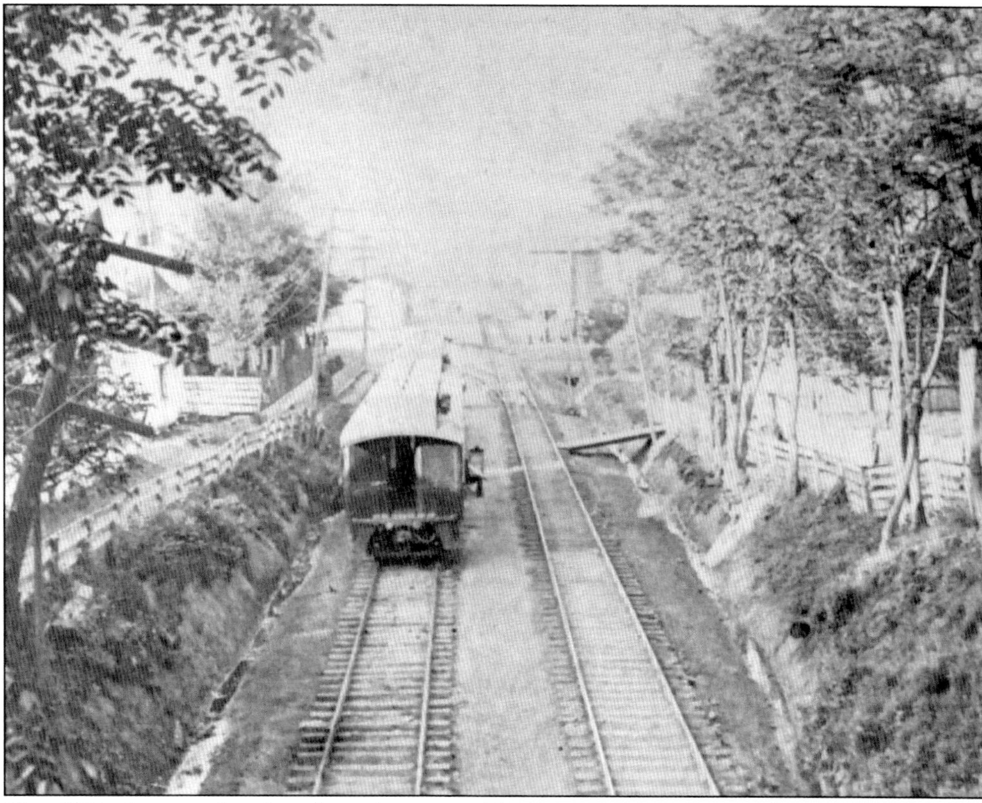

This 1888 photograph, taken from the covered bridge over Innes Street, shows a train heading into the old depot. The Richmond & Danville system operated the trains through Salisbury during this time, but soon, the Southern Railway would control all railroads lines through Rowan County. (Courtesy Rowan Museum Collection.)

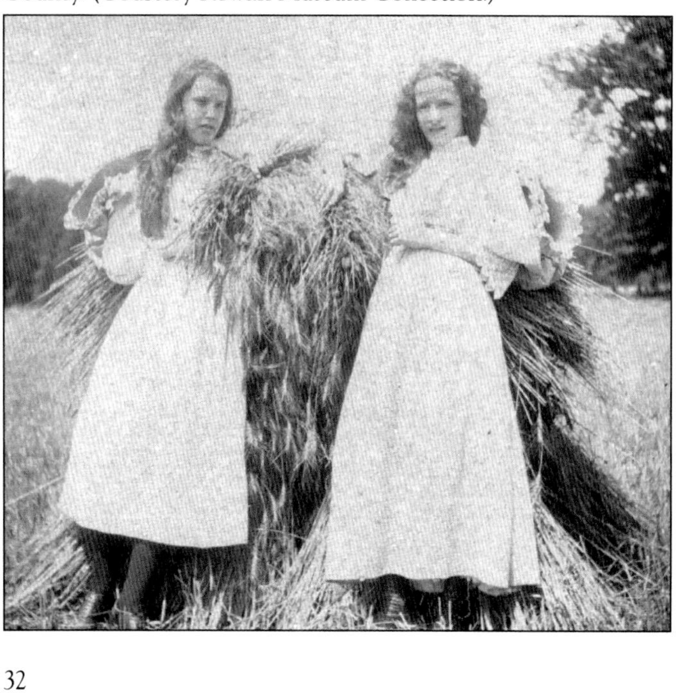

Two young ladies pose alongside a large hay bale in a field. Large farms still surrounded the city limits of Salisbury well into the 20th century. (Courtesy Rowan Museum Collection.)

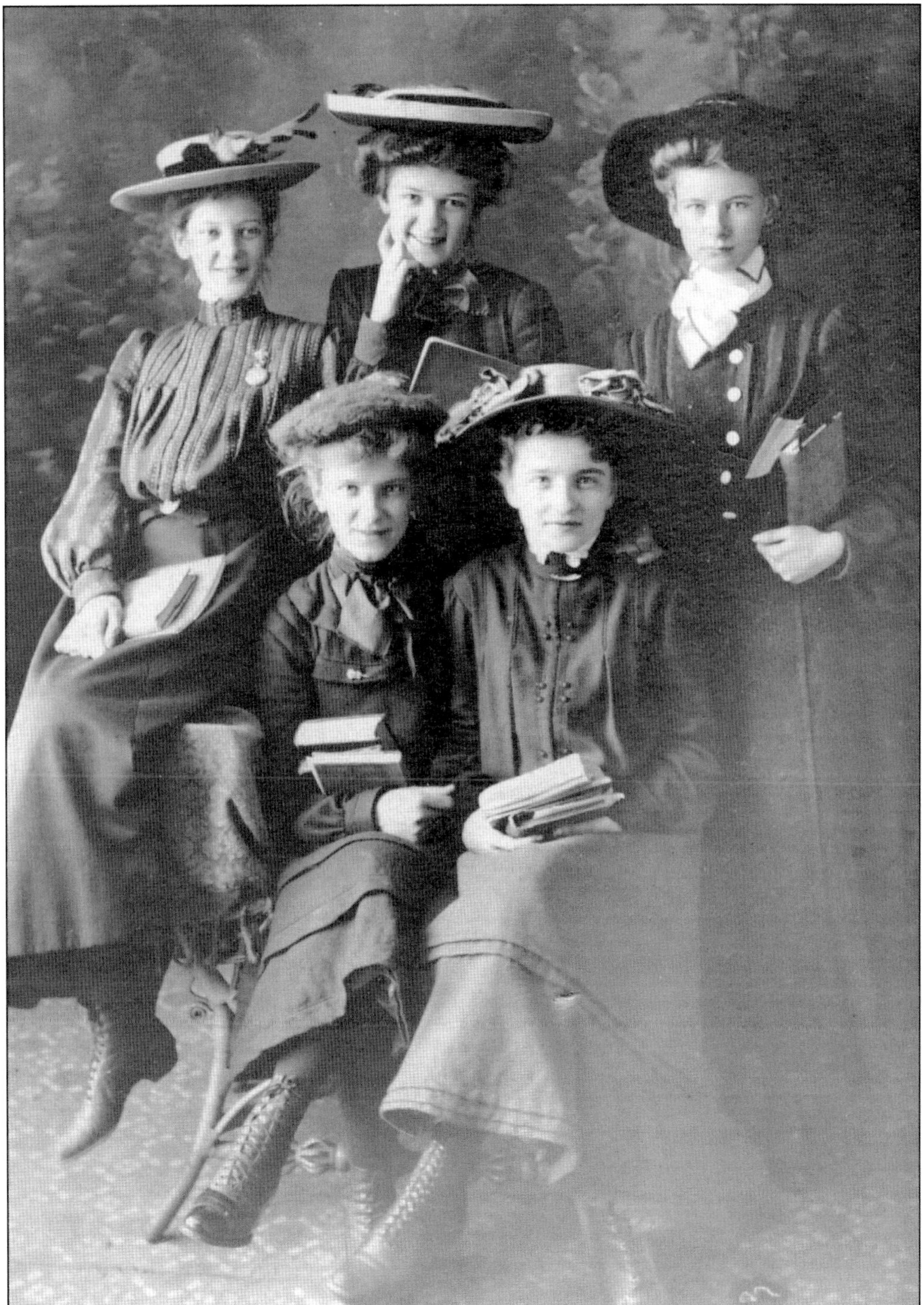

These young women are Sophie Kluttz and Mildred Brown (seated) and Mena Davis (on table) along with two other unidentified girls. Note the style of the dress from the 1890s, individualized with a distinctive hat. It is not clear why the girl in the second row did not smile. (Courtesy Rowan Museum Collection.)

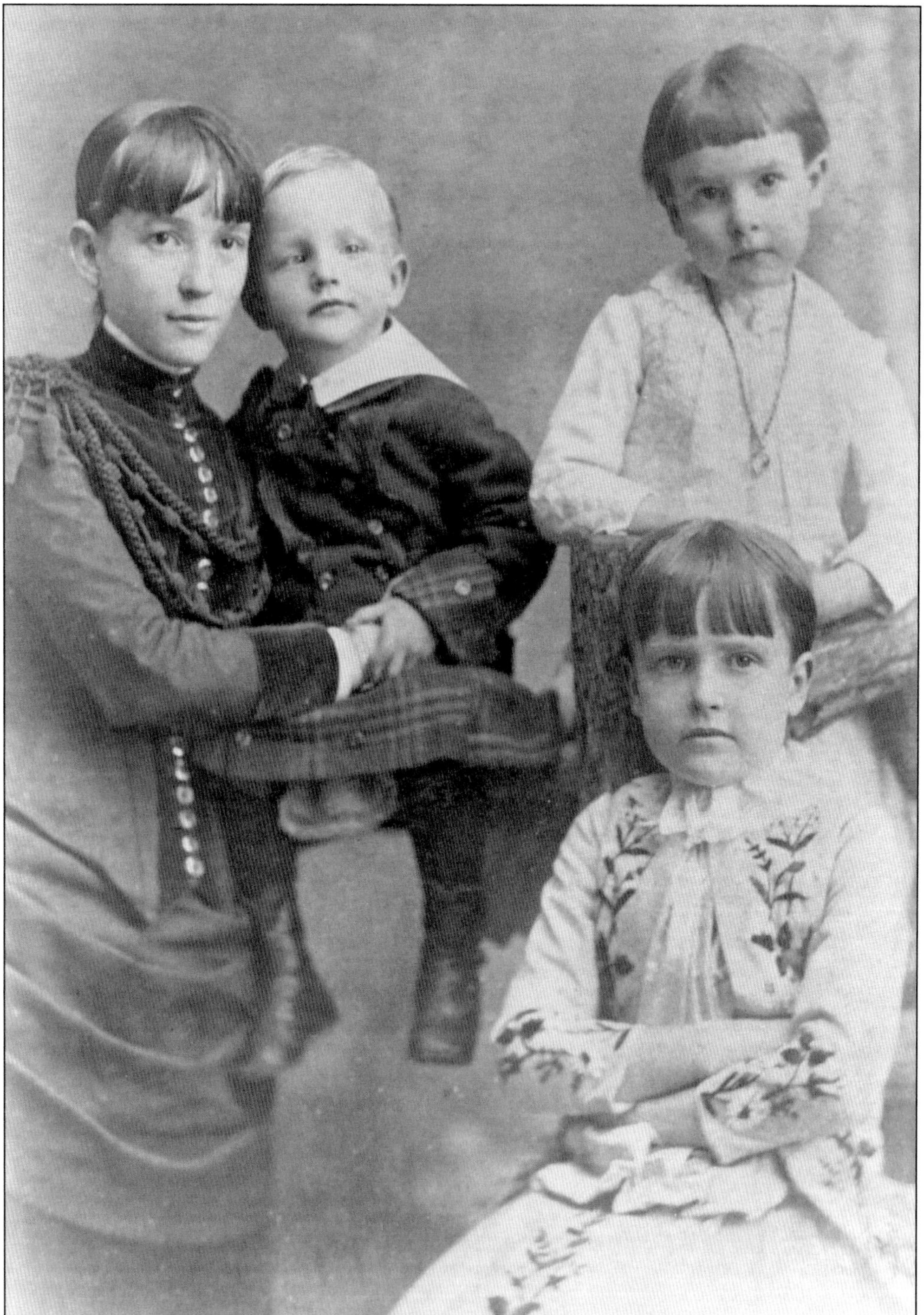

Four of the John Allen Brown children pose for a photograph during the mid 1880s. Bessie is holding Hargrave, Lila is standing alongside, and Jessie is seated. Lila and Jennie's dresses were preserved and are now on display at the Utzman-Chambers House. (Courtesy Rowan Museum Collection.)

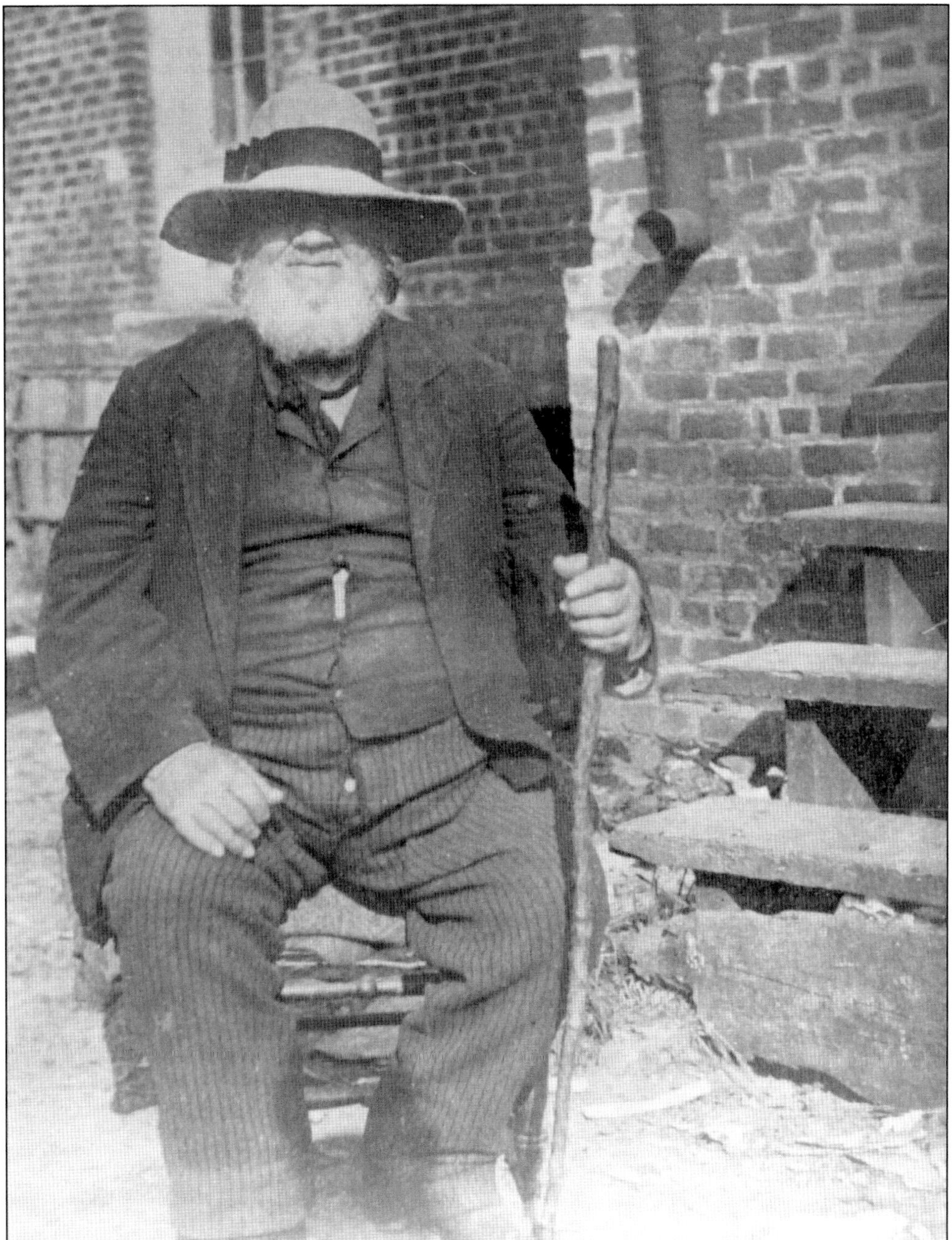

John Hedrick was 89 years old when this photograph was taken by Theodore Buerbaum in 1894. Hedrick, born at the start of the 19th century, must have experienced staggering changes. During his lifetime, he would have watched Salisbury grow into a modern city. (Courtesy Rowan Museum Collection.)

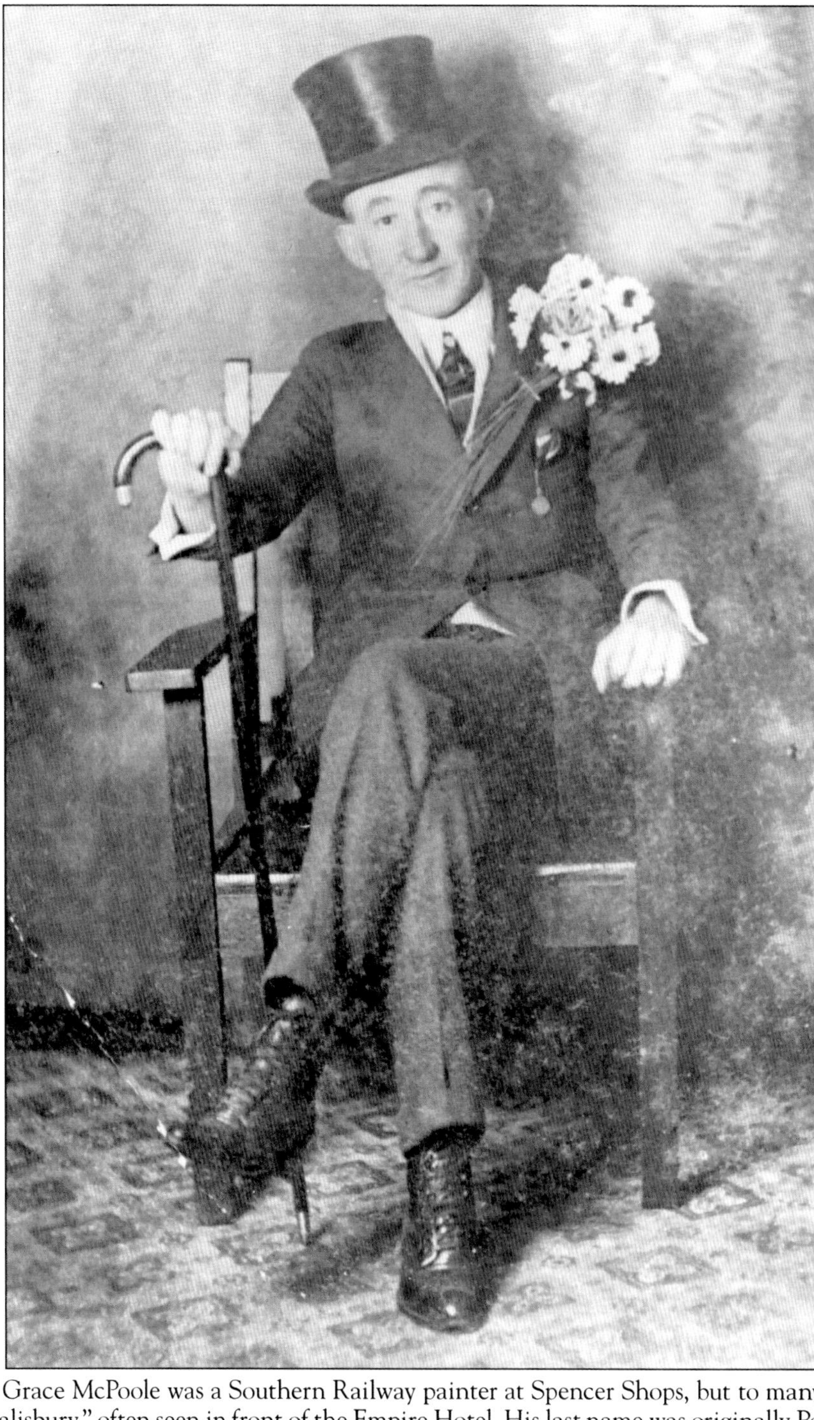

George Grace McPoole was a Southern Railway painter at Spencer Shops, but to many, he was "Lord Salisbury," often seen in front of the Empire Hotel. His last name was originally Poole, but, wanting to appear of higher caliber, he added the "Mc" after a cousin added "Van" to his name. As Lord Salisbury, he would dress in colorful clothes, hand out shiny pennies, and try to put a smile on everyone's face. He passed away in April 1951, and an estimated 10,000 people attended his funeral. (Courtesy Rowan Museum Collection.)

Two

Theodore Buerbaum

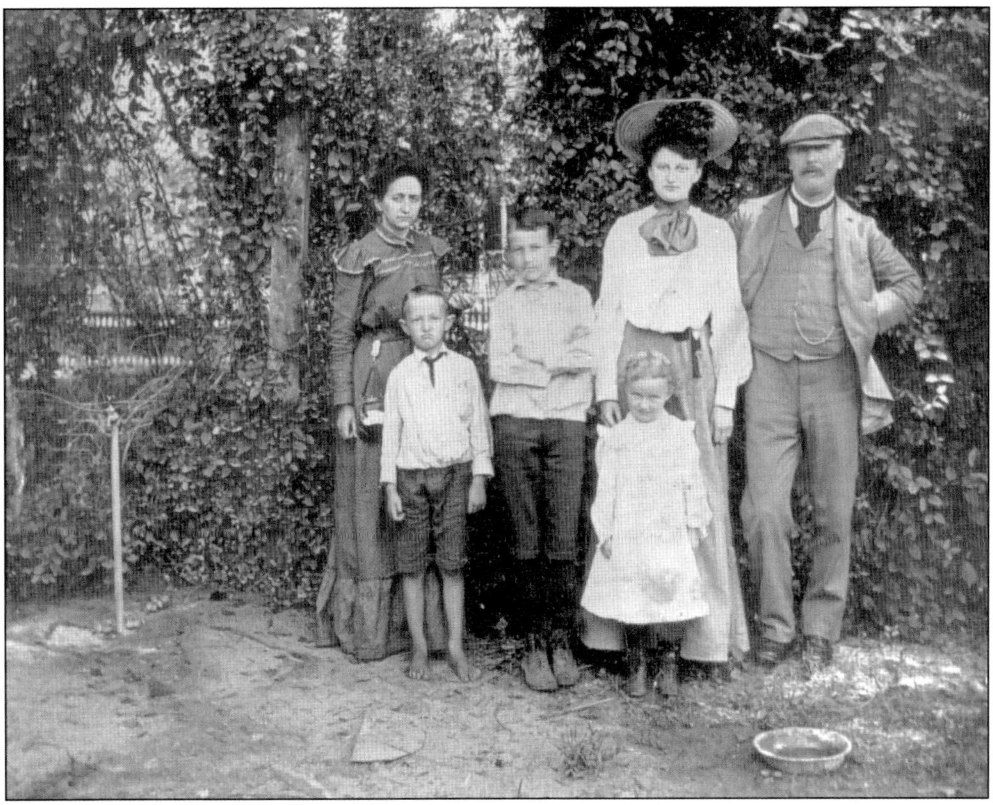

The Buerbaum family poses for a photograph in their backyard. Shown here are, from left to right, Jennie, Francis, Alfred, Minnie, Elizabeth, and Theo. In the 1880s, Theodore opened a general store in Salisbury, selling a wide variety of items. Most people, however, remember him for his postcards. He photographed Salisbury buildings, people, and street scenes and turned the images into postcards to attract shoppers to his store. He passed away on February 1, 1926, a half-century after he arrived in Salisbury from Germany. (Courtesy Rowan Museum Collection.)

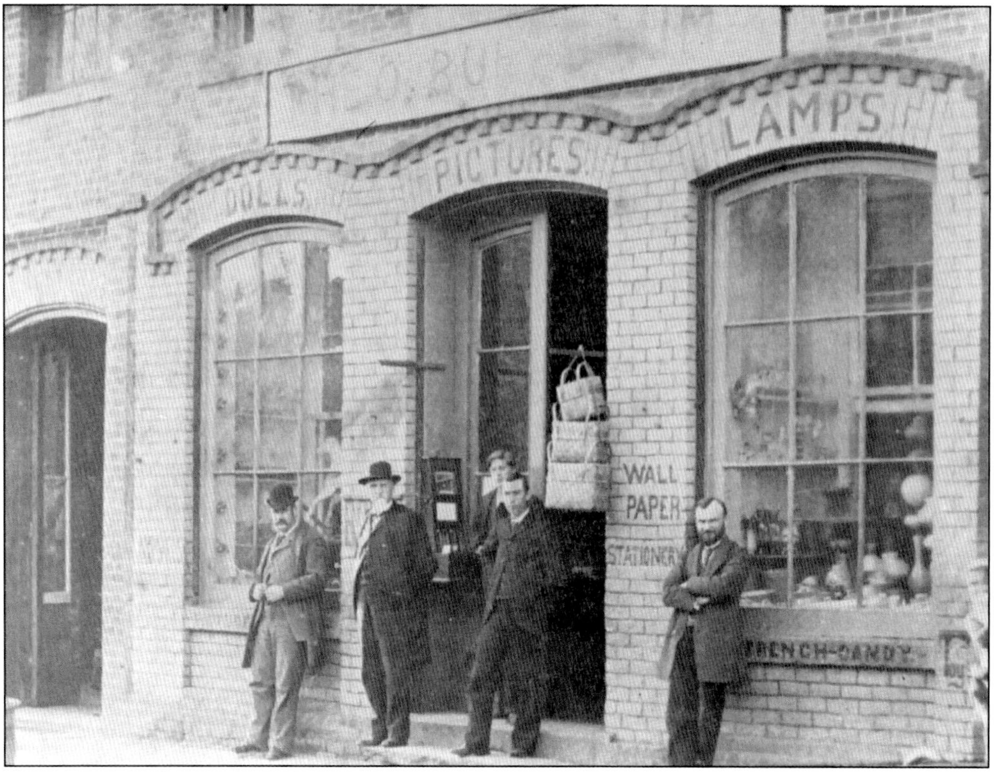

Theodore Buerbaum (far right) stands in front of his store in 1895. His establishment really was a general store, as evident by the variety of items advertised on the brickwork. (Courtesy Rowan Museum Collection.)

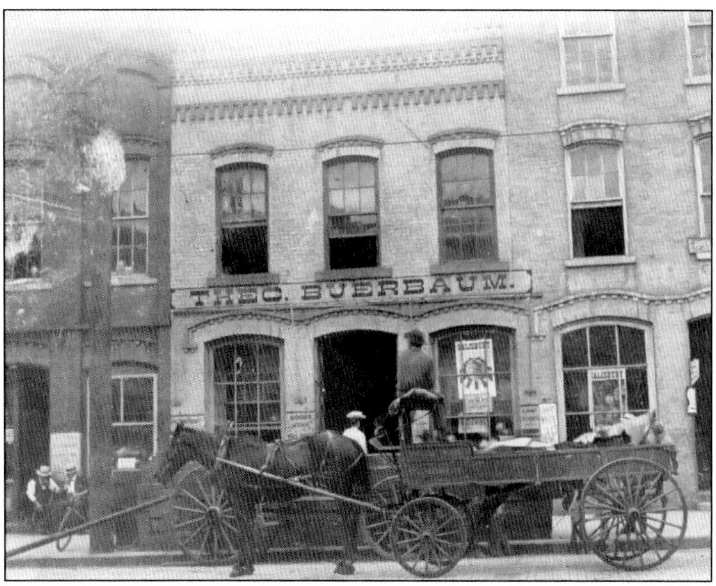

Buerbaum was planning a remodeling when this July 4, 1907, photograph was taken. (Courtesy Rowan Museum Collection.)

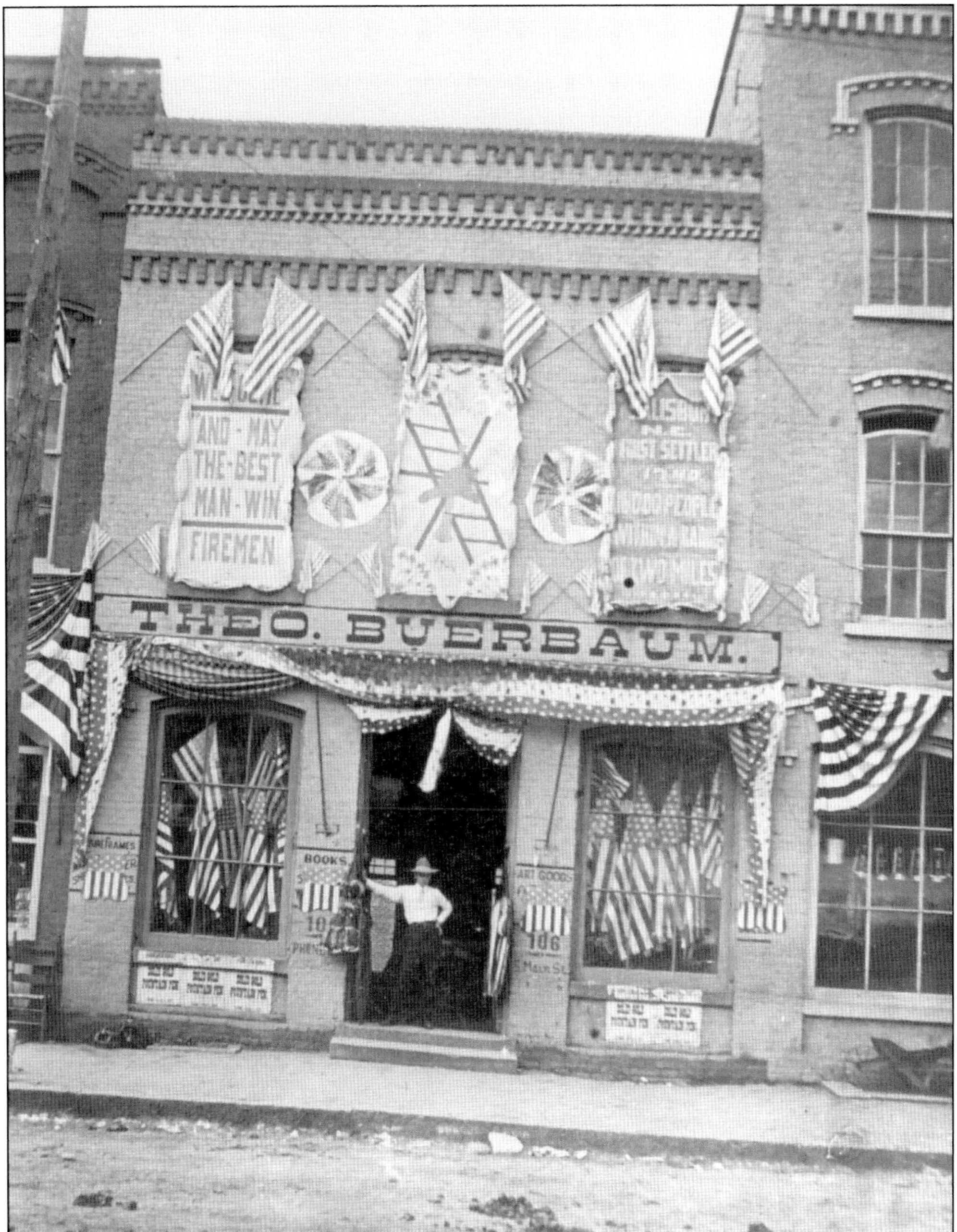

Buerbaum's store may appear to be decked out for the Fourth of July, but the occasion was the August 2–4, 1904, Fireman's Tournament. Each year, a different city in North Carolina hosted this competition to determine the best firemen in the state. (Courtesy Rowan Museum Collection.)

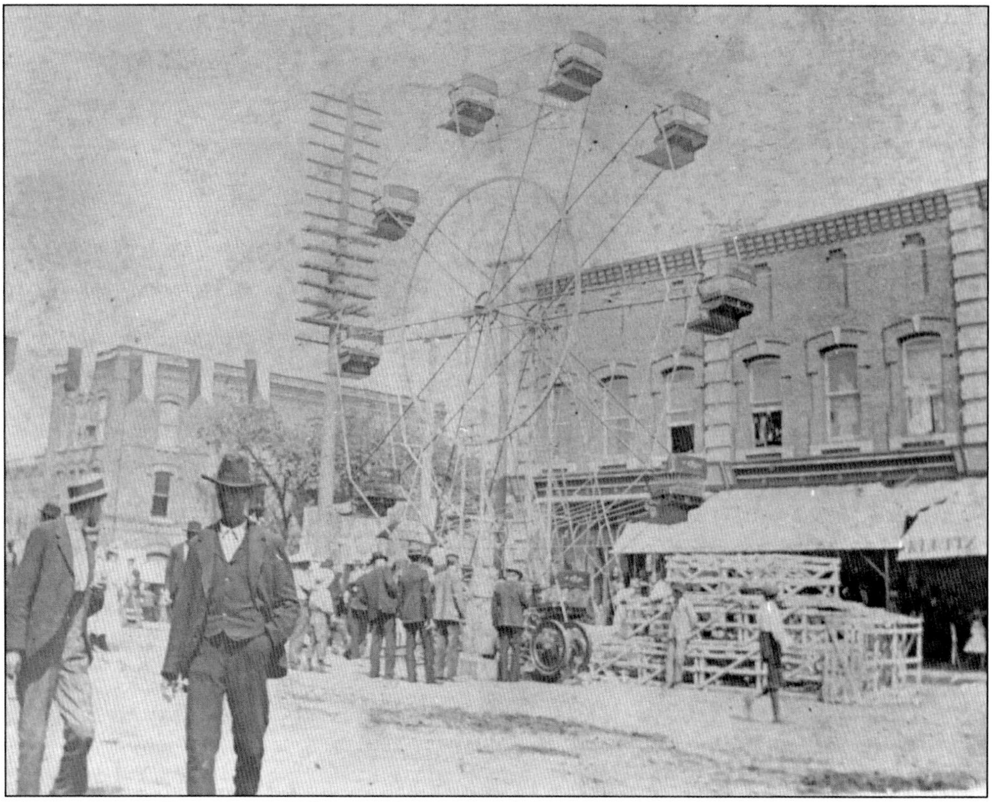

The Rowan Rifles was a Salisbury military unit that predated the Civil War. The local militia group became part of the 4th North Carolina, Army of Northern Virginia. In 1903, a carnival, complete with the large Ferris wheel seen here, was held to celebrate this unit. (Courtesy Rowan Museum Collection.)

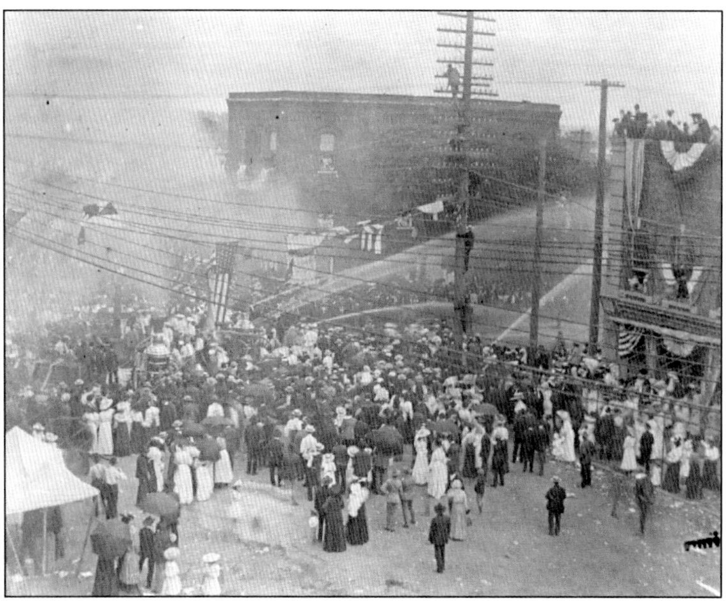

Salisbury hosted the North Carolina State Fireman's Tournament on August 2–4, 1904. This event showcased the best firefighters across the state. Here, some of the horse-drawn steam pumpers conduct a demonstration in the square. (Courtesy Rowan Museum Collection.)

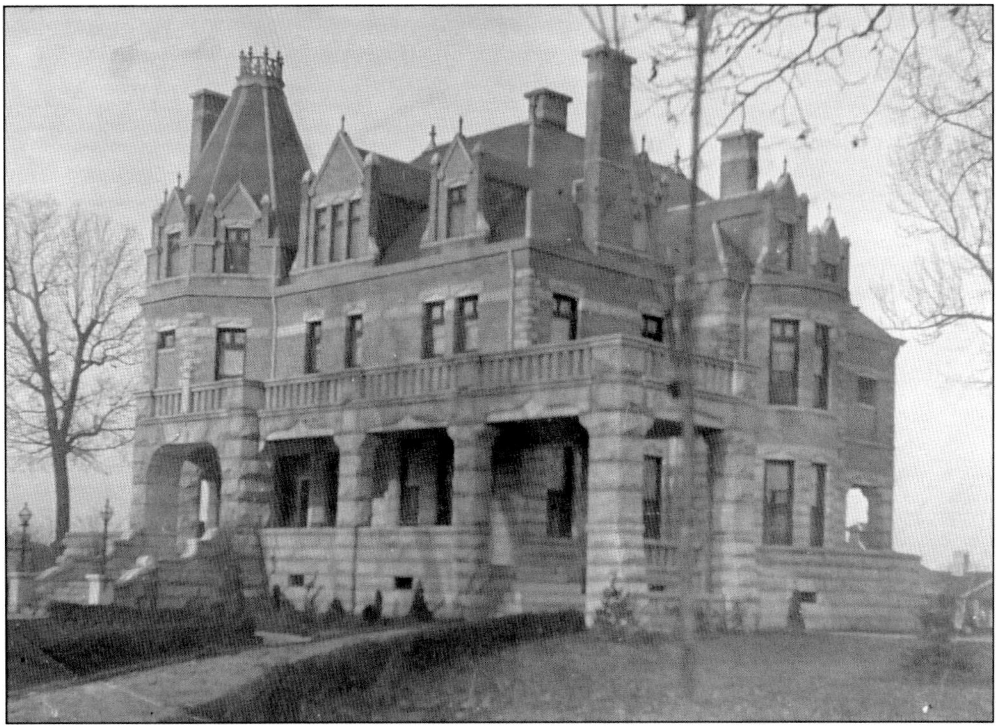

This large house was built for Egbert Barry Cornwell Hambley at 508 South Fulton Street. At the time, he was vice president of the Whitney Company, which was constructing a dam on the Yadkin River. Hambley was very prominent in the community, creating the Salisbury Gas & Electric Light Company and serving on several boards. The house, built in 1902, was designed by Charles Christian Hook. The above photograph was taken soon after the house was built. The postcard below was not issued until after Hambley's death in 1906. Today, most people know this as the Wallace House, since that family has owned the property since the 1930s. (Courtesy Rowan Museum Collection.)

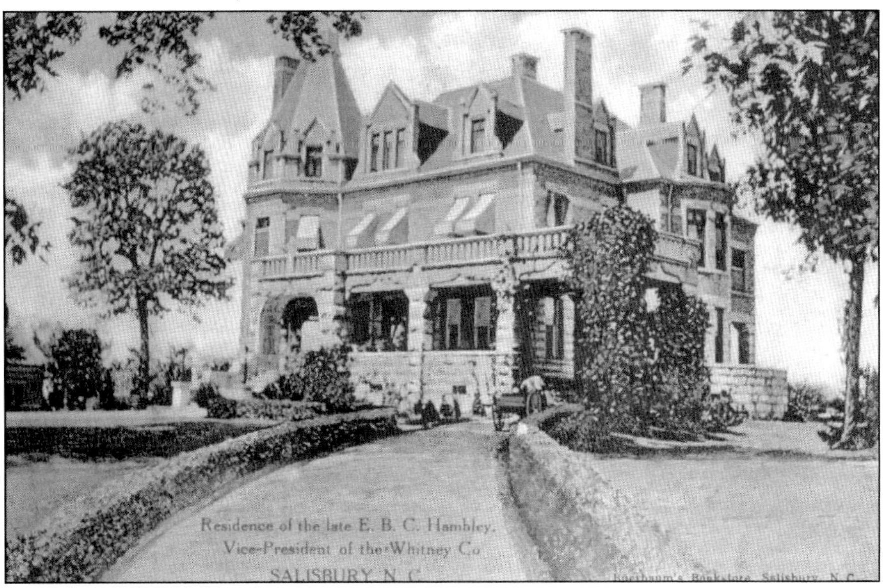

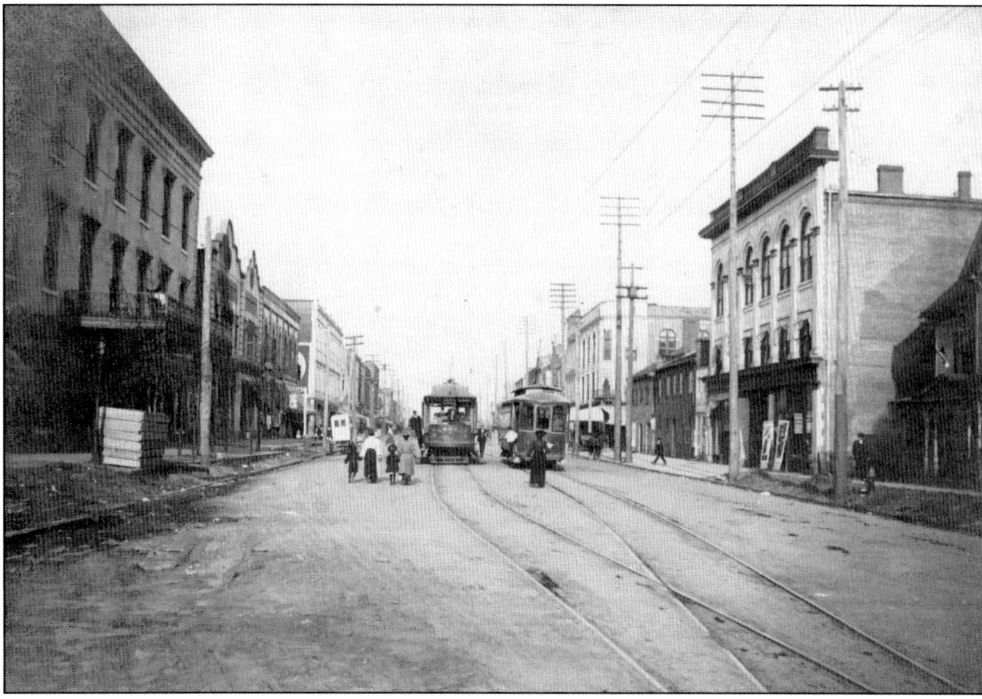

Street scenes were popular with Buerbaum, since they showed people in their daily lives. In the above photograph, two streetcars pass each other on Main Street while pedestrians wait their turn to ride. Taken sometime between 1905 and 1910, the photograph, looking northeast, illustrates that, despite Salisbury's growth into a viable city, the streets were still not paved. This would soon change, however, when automobiles replaced the buggies seen in the photograph below. (Both, courtesy Rowan Museum Collection.)

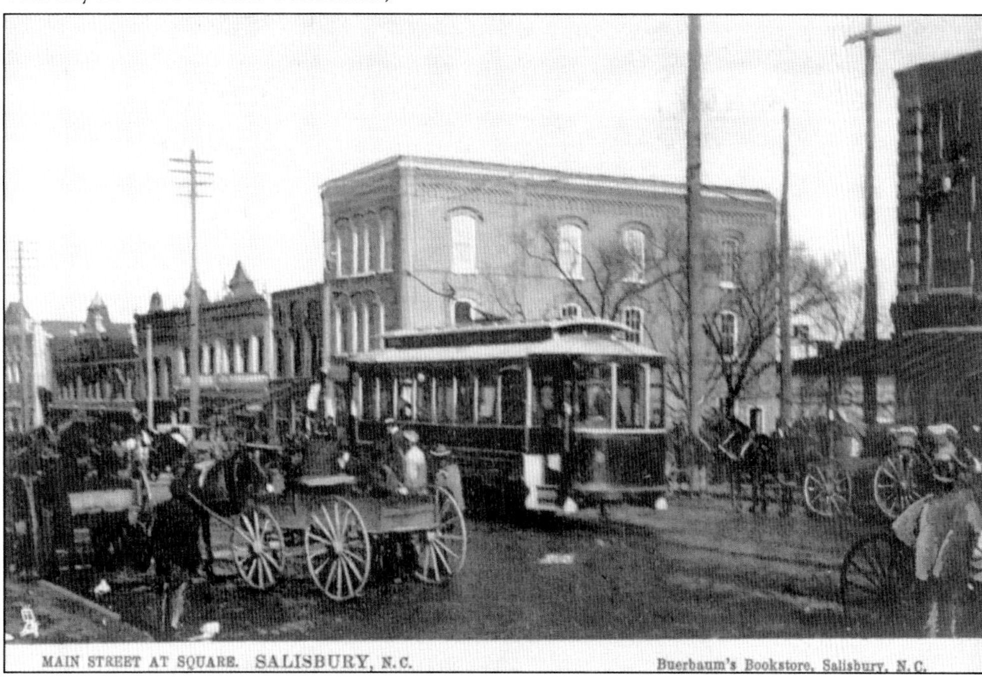

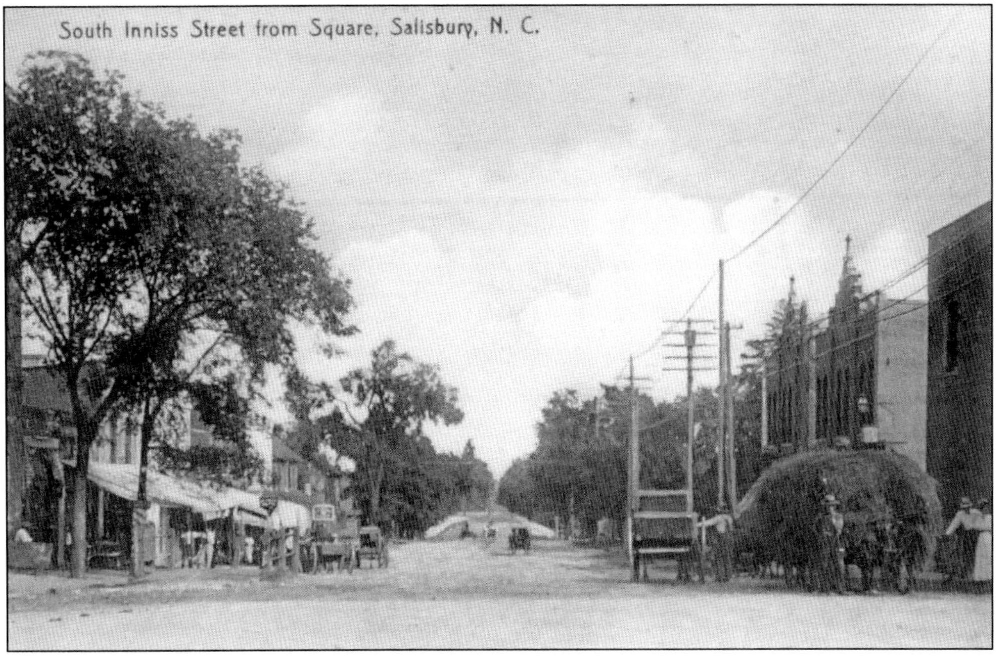

Buerbaum started taking photographs in the 1880s when horse-drawn buggies still ruled the dirt streets. At this time, the fountain was still in the center of the square, making it easy for Buerbaum to frame his prints based on direction. As seen in the labels on these postcards, Innes Street at the time was usually spelled "Inniss Street." The thoroughfare is named for James Innes, a land agent for Lord Granville during the Colonial period. (Both, courtesy Rowan Museum Collection.)

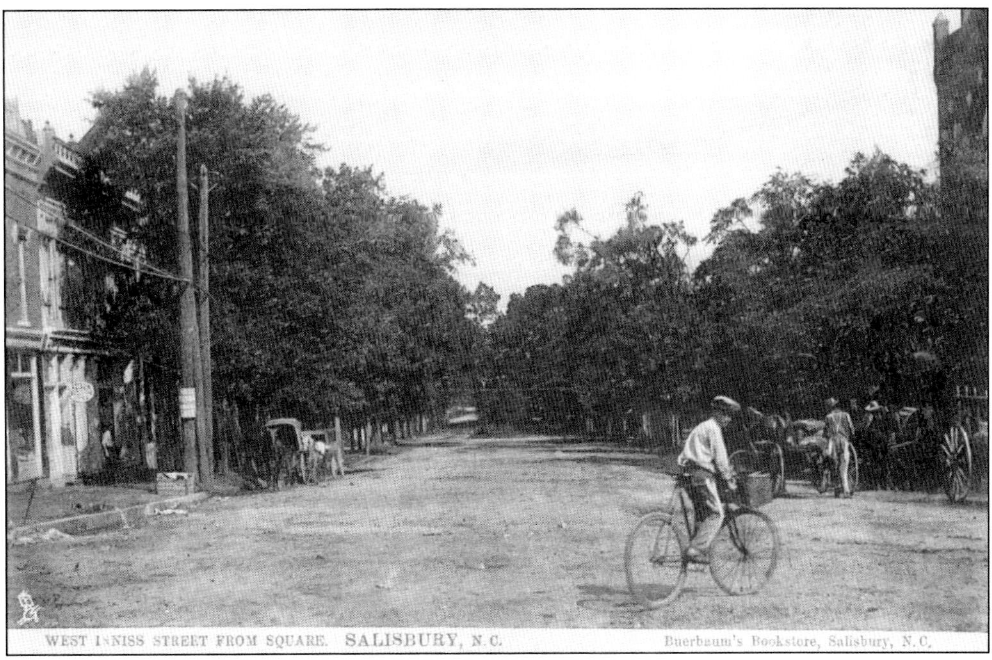

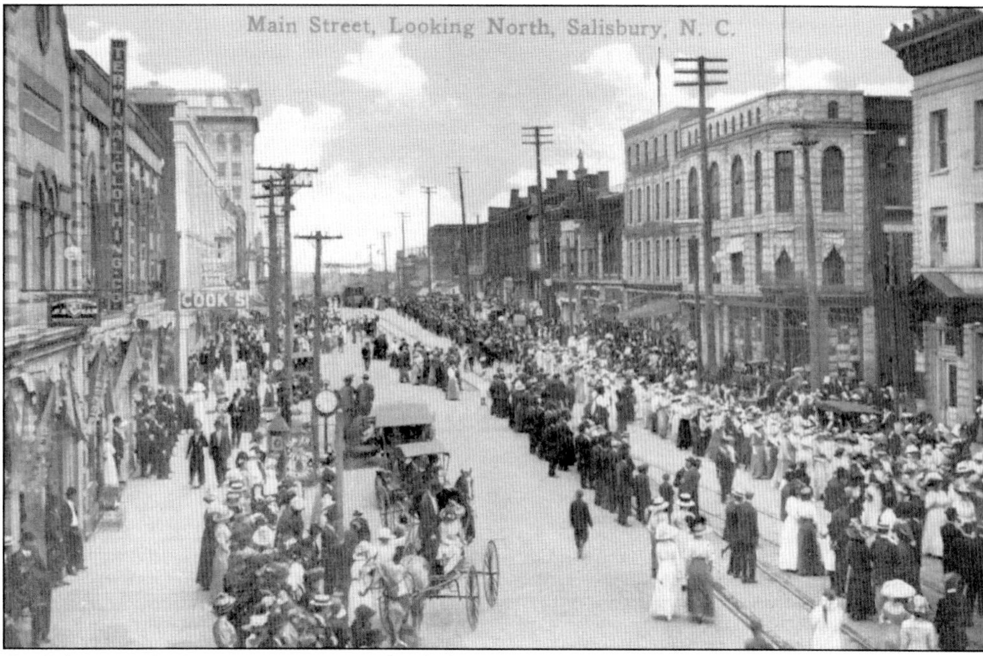

On July 4, 1907, Carrie Nation visited Salisbury to give a speech on the temperance movement. A member of the Women's Christian Temperance Union, Nation, shown in the photograph below, preached far and wide on the ill effects of alcohol. At events like these, she would sell souvenir hatchets, as she was known to hack open kegs while attacking bars. (Both, courtesy Rowan Museum Collection.)

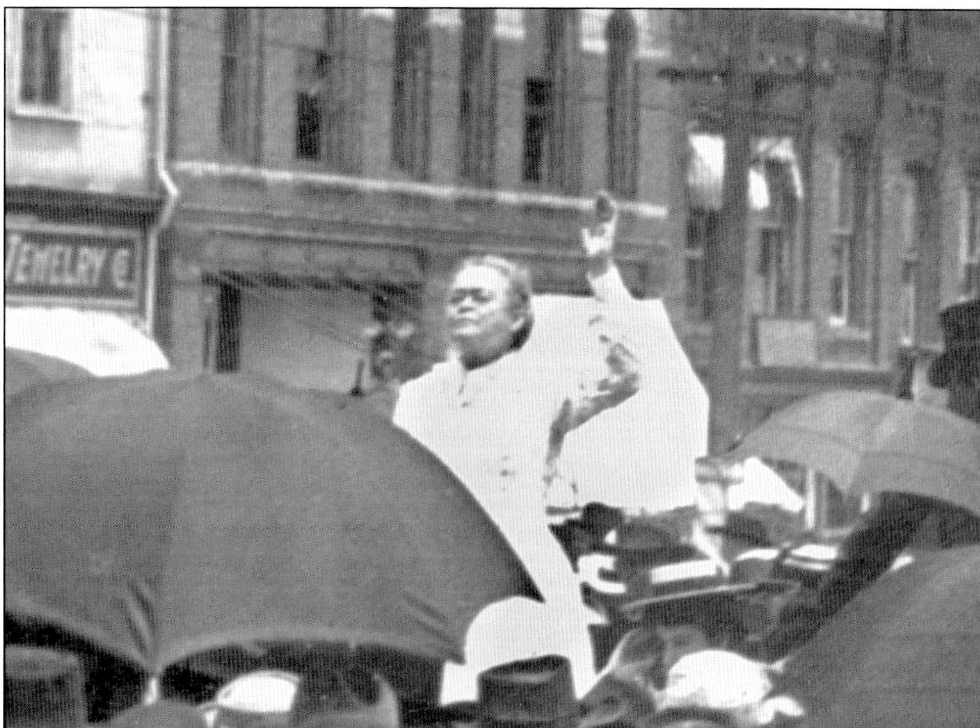

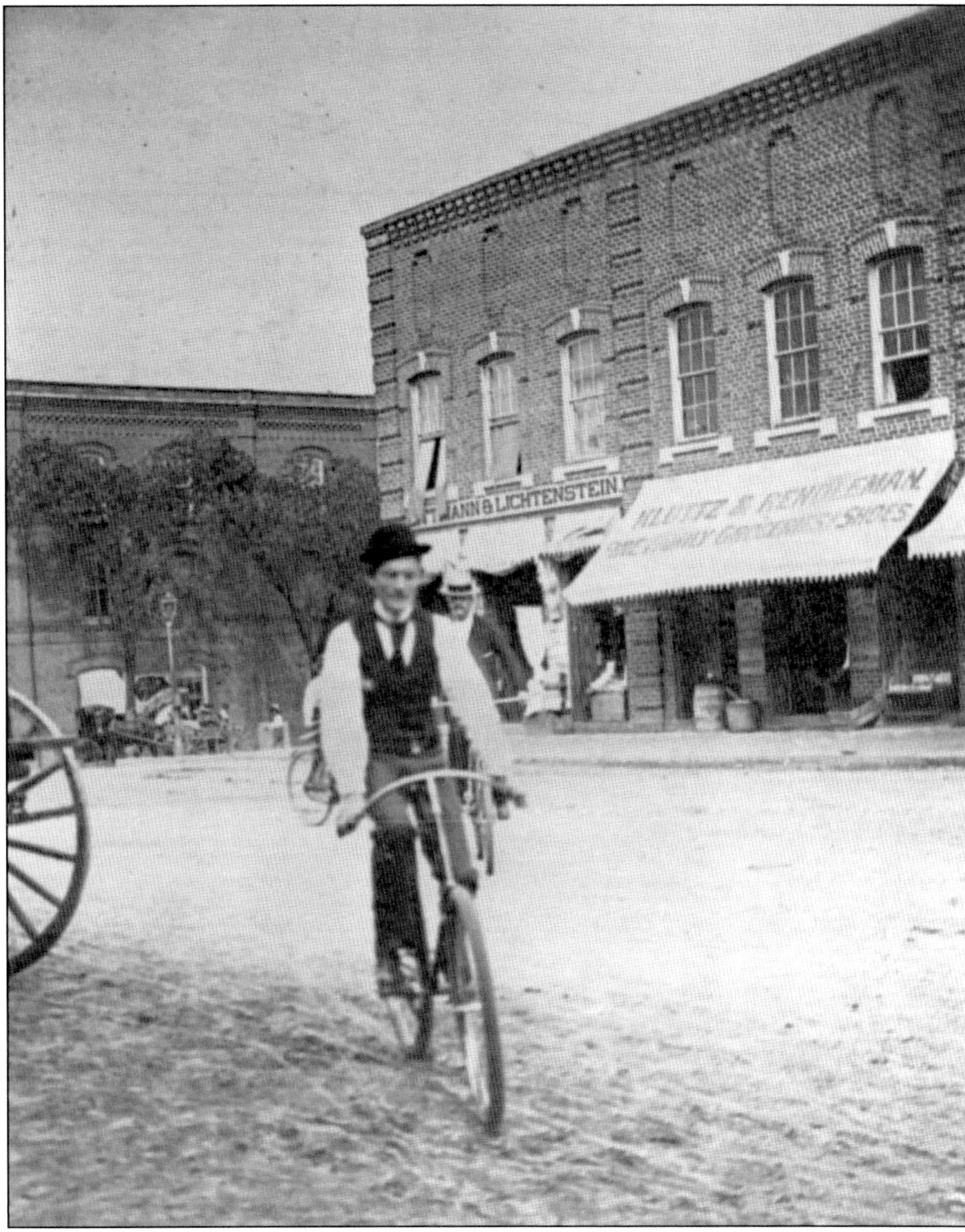

This 1893 photograph shows W.W. Krider (front) and I.H. Foust riding bicycles through town. The 1890s is considered the golden age of bicycles, due to the introduction of the safety bike, on which these men are riding. These bicycles were easier to ride and control than the big-wheeled versions of previous decades. (Courtesy Rowan Museum Collection.)

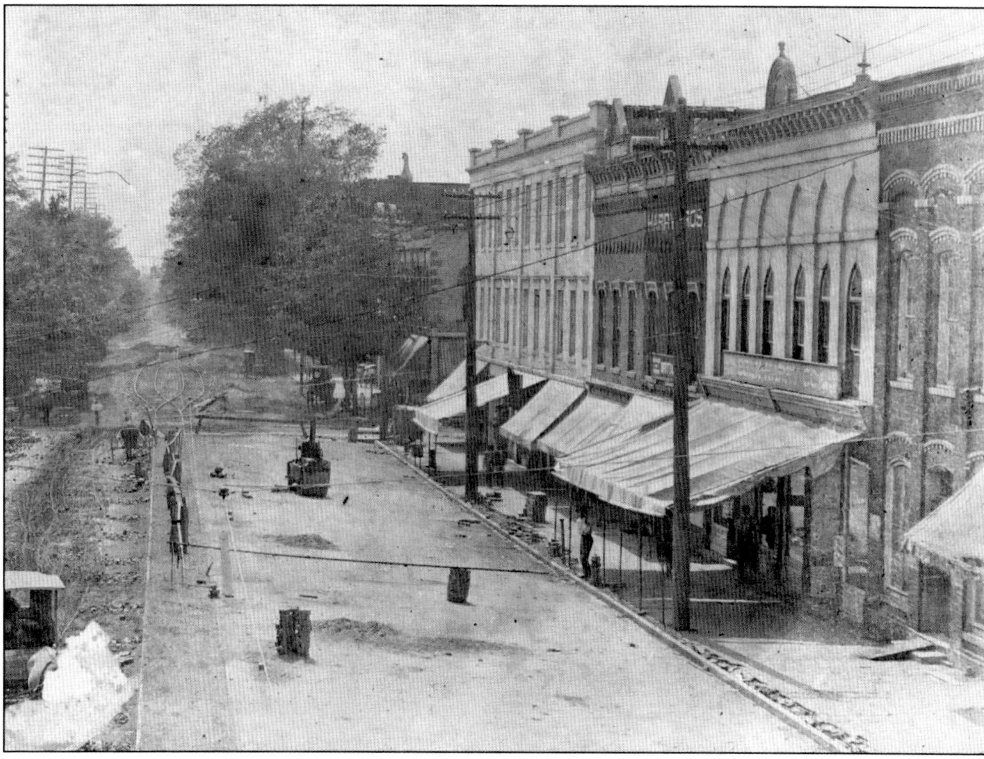

These photographs of Main Street, taken about six months apart, show the progress being made in the early 20th century. In the above photograph, streetcar tracks are being laid in the fall of 1905. The section being built includes a short pass track (upper left). The image below, from 1906, shows the streetcar in operation and bustling stores with their awnings stretched out. Note the lack of automobiles, which were still a novelty for many residents of Salisbury. (Both, courtesy Rowan Museum Collection.)

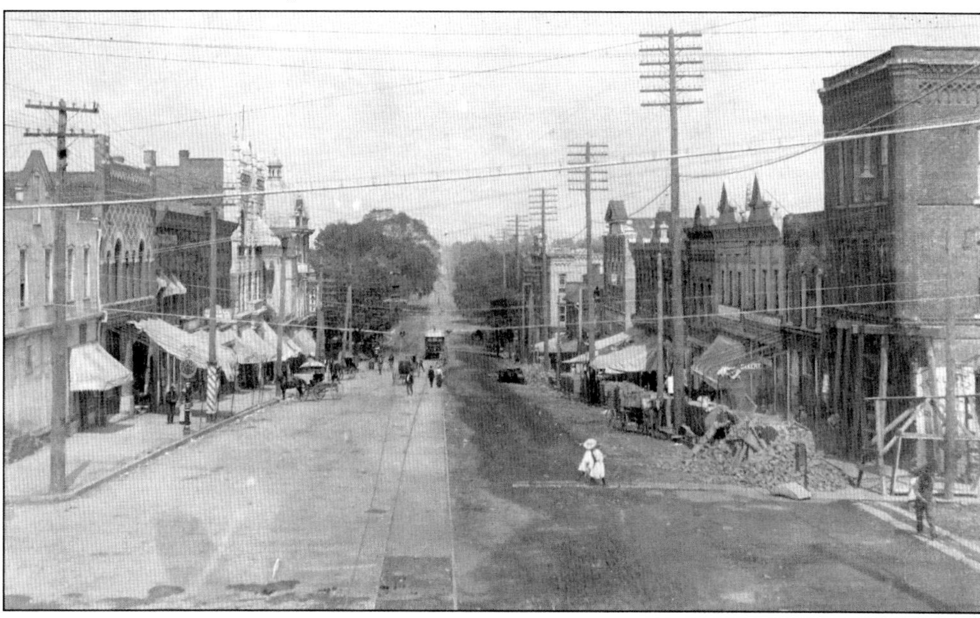

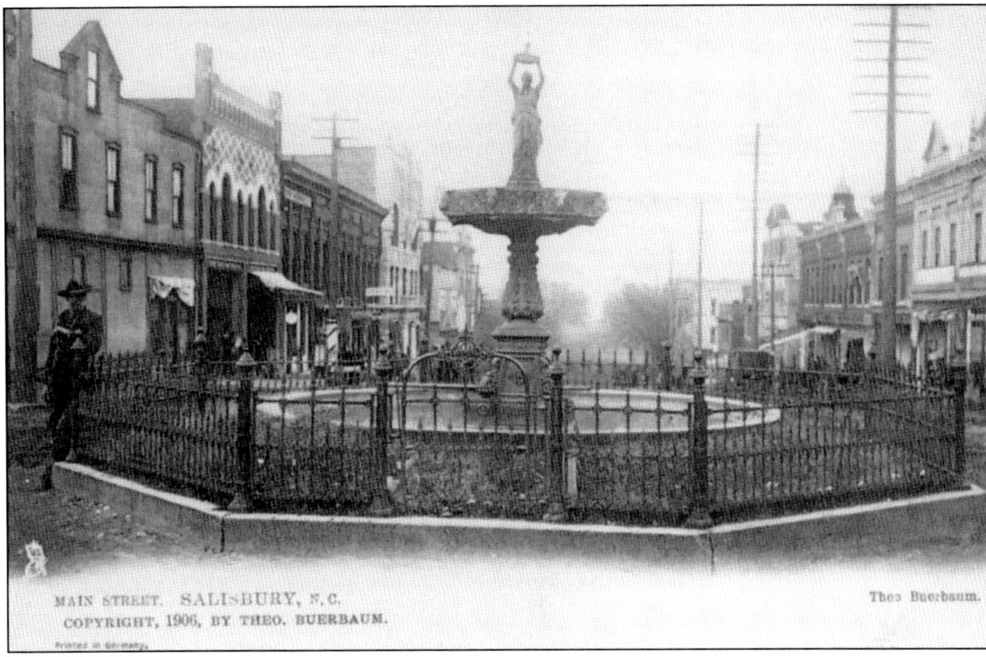

The fountain in the square, erected in 1888, remained a centerpiece in Salisbury until it was removed for the streetcar in 1905. To locals, the figure topping the fountain was known as "Rebecca of the Well." The fountain was later scrapped as part of the metal drives of World War II. Today, a replica, made from the original plans, serves to welcome visitors to Gateway Park and the city of Salisbury. (Courtesy Rowan Museum Collection.)

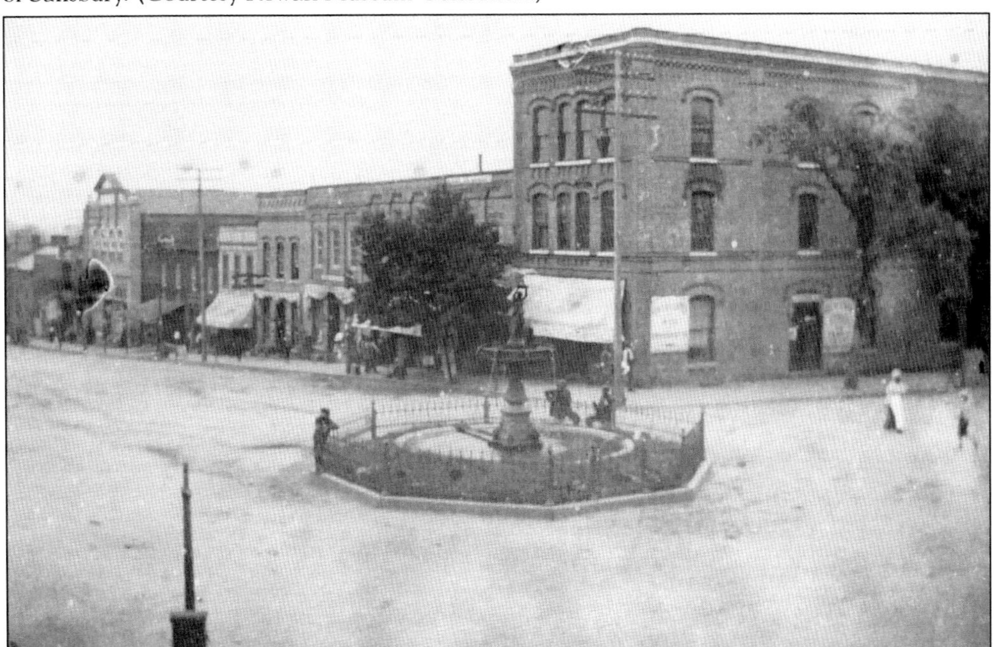

This photograph, taken from the east corner of the square and looking down North Main Street, provides a nice view of the fountain. The tall building on the corner currently houses Spanky's Homemade Ice Cream and Deli, a Salisbury favorite. (Courtesy Rowan Museum Collection.)

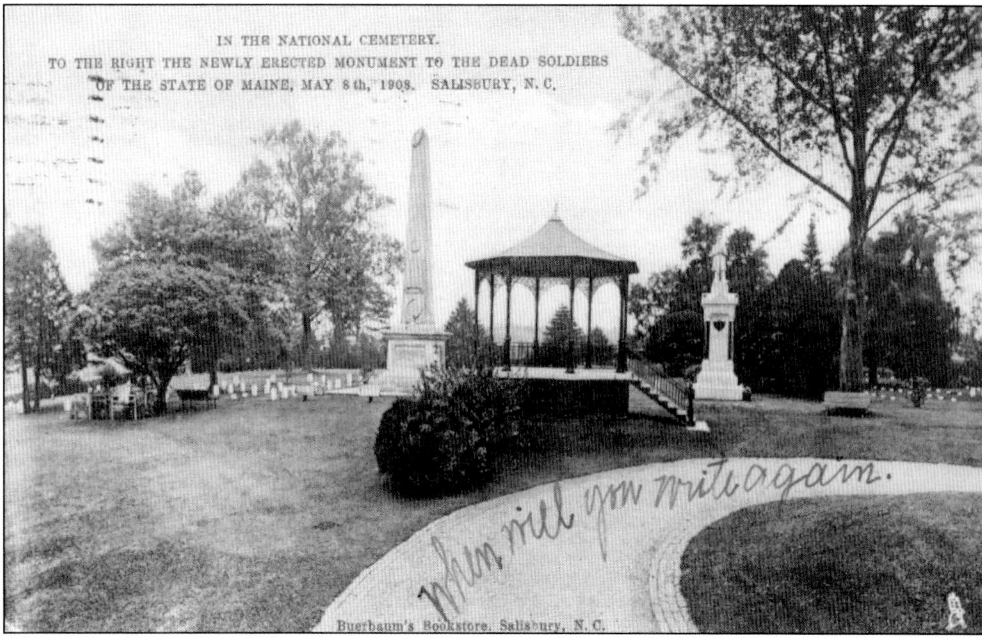

The original Salisbury National Cemetery was created in 1865 after the Union forces burned the Confederate prison. The original burials were in long, trench-like mass graves. Later burials included proper military headstones. The superintendent's house (below) looks very different from the building in place today. The original cemetery includes monuments erected by the states of Maine and Pennsylvania as well as one to the unknown dead. (Both, courtesy Rowan Museum Collection.)

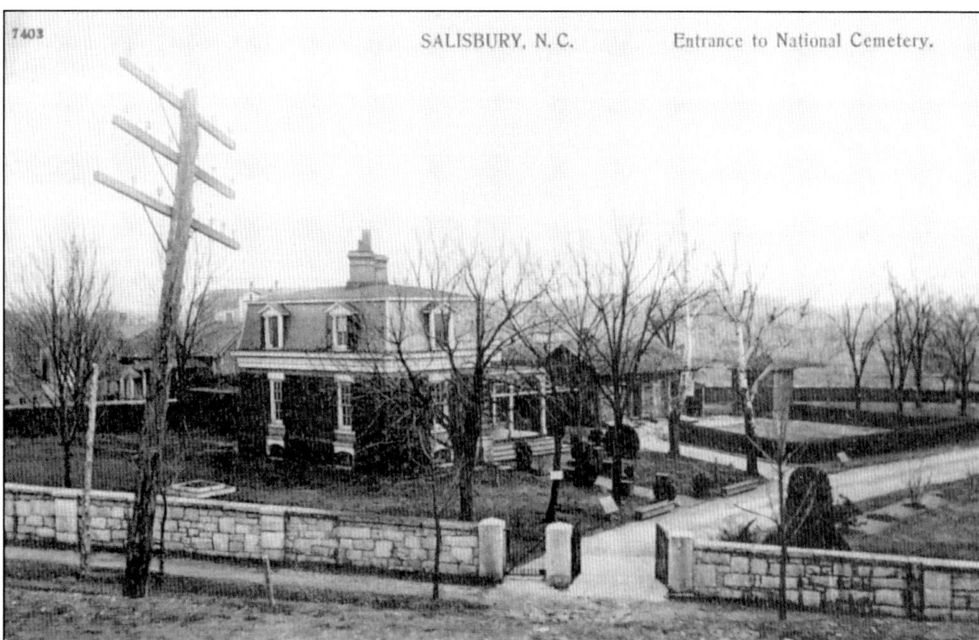

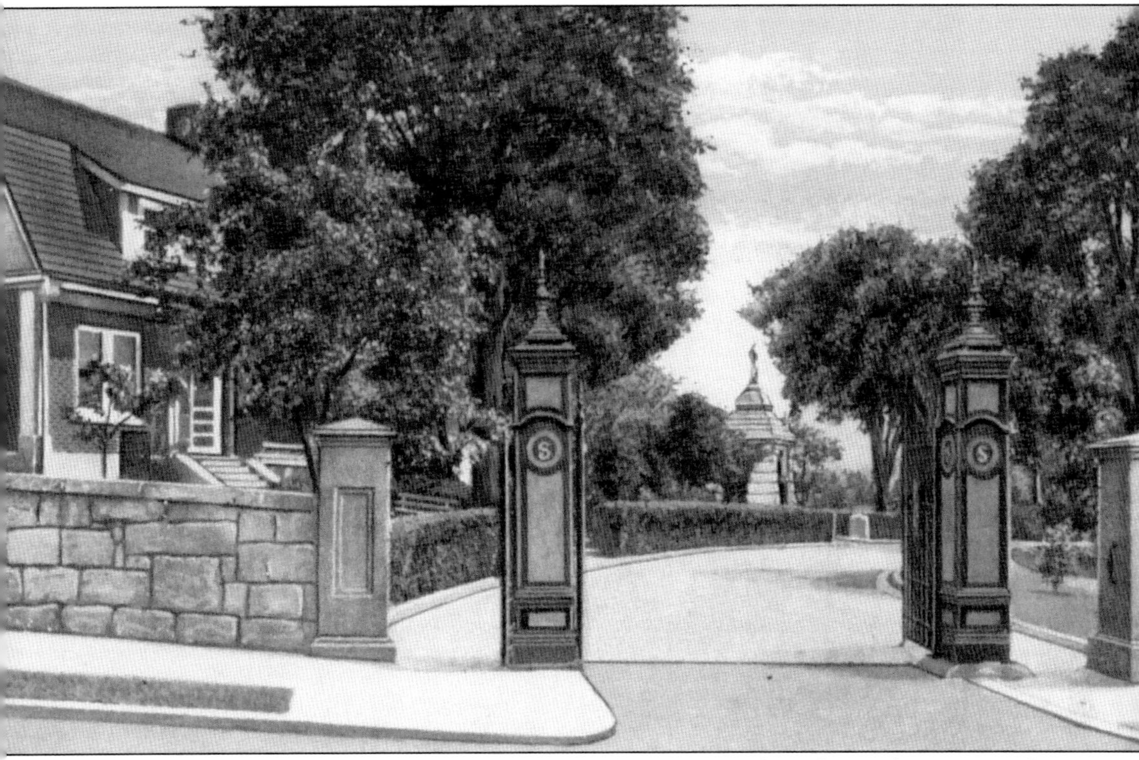

This view of the National Cemetery entrance includes the superintendent's house, front gate, and the wall constructed around the cemetery. Because of the need for more space, an annex to this cemetery was developed behind the William "Bill" Hefner Veterans Affairs building off Brenner Avenue. (Courtesy Rowan Museum Collection.)

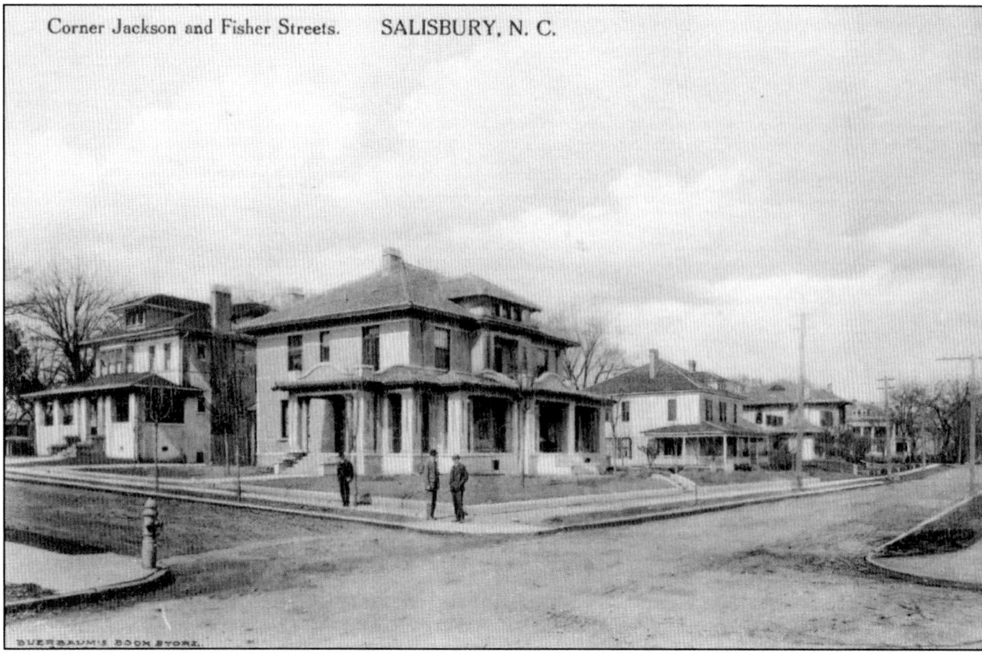

Streets lined with large houses defined Salisbury in the early 20th century. Neighborhoods were well kept, as is evident from the above postcard. New developments, like the one shown below near the National Cemetery, were built utilizing the open space that existed outside the center section of the city. (Both, courtesy Rowan Museum Collection.)

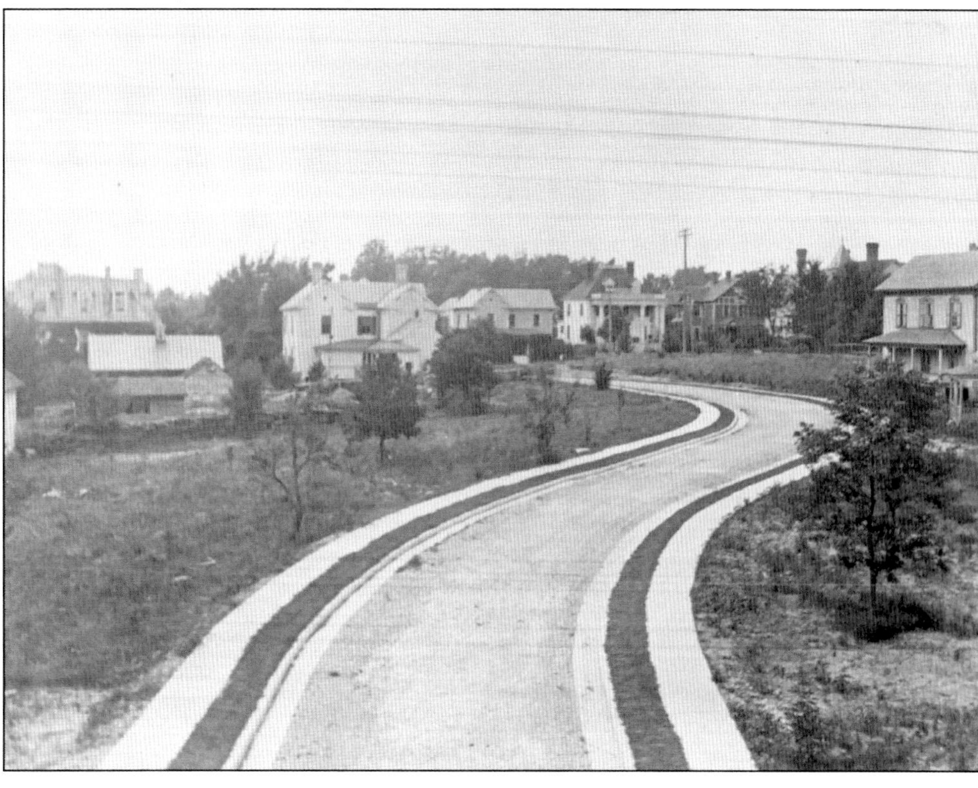

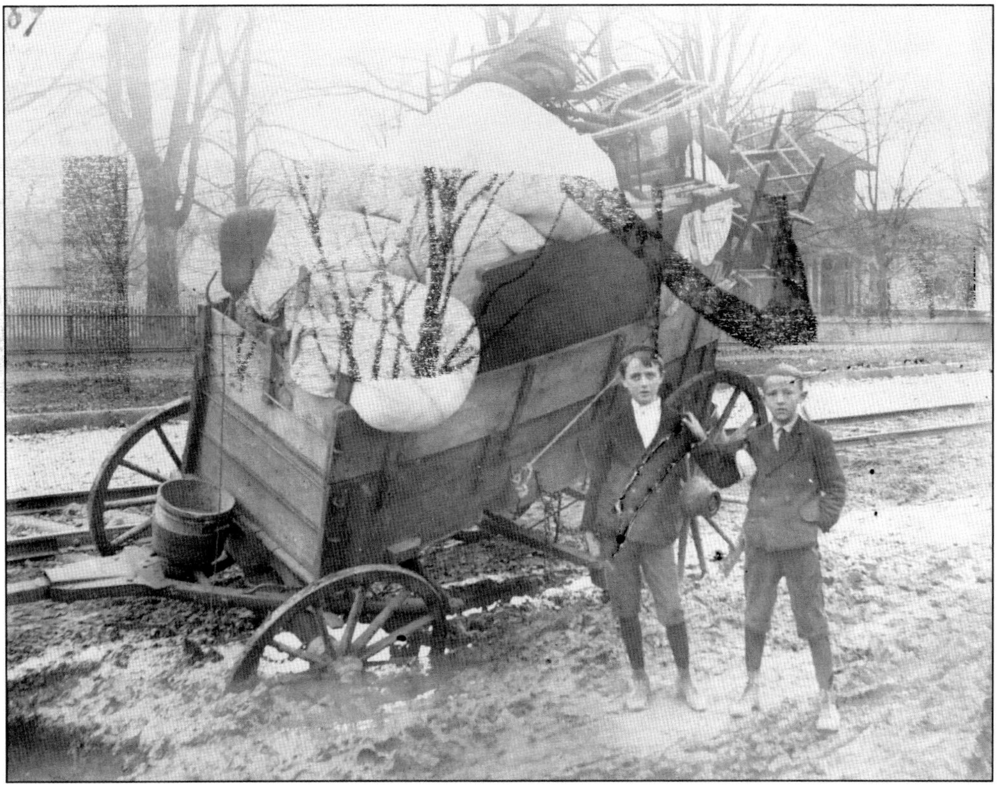

Sometimes, photographic opportunities present themselves right outside of one's front door. Buerbaum took this photograph in front of his home in November 1906, when the boys' wagon got mired in the mud beside the streetcar tracks. Such were the hazards of travel before the streets were paved. (Courtesy Rowan Museum Collection.)

In the horse-and-buggy era, people used what they had to pull their wagon into town. These two African American men are using a pair of oxen to pull their cart, instead of the usual horses or mules. (Courtesy Rowan Museum Collection.)

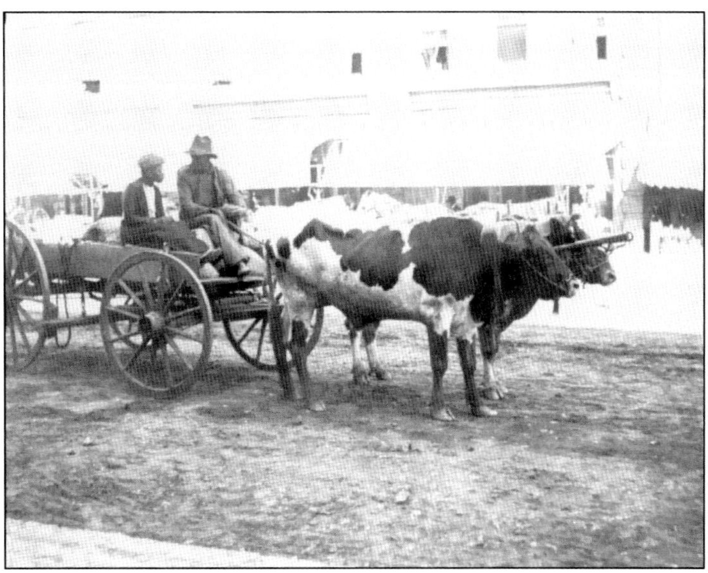

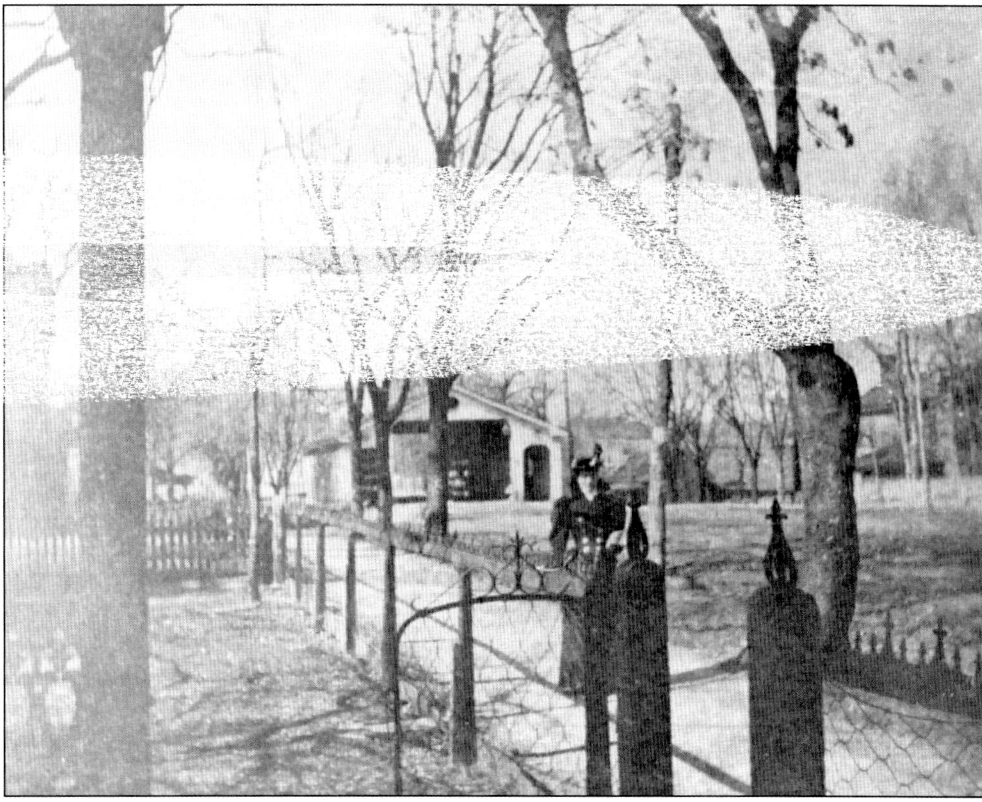

During the 1880s and 1890s, the railroad crossing for East Innes Street used this neat covered bridge, seen here from S.S. Cole's front porch. Innes Street was still a gateway for Salisbury with large trees and beautiful homes leading up to the square. (Courtesy Rowan Museum Collection.)

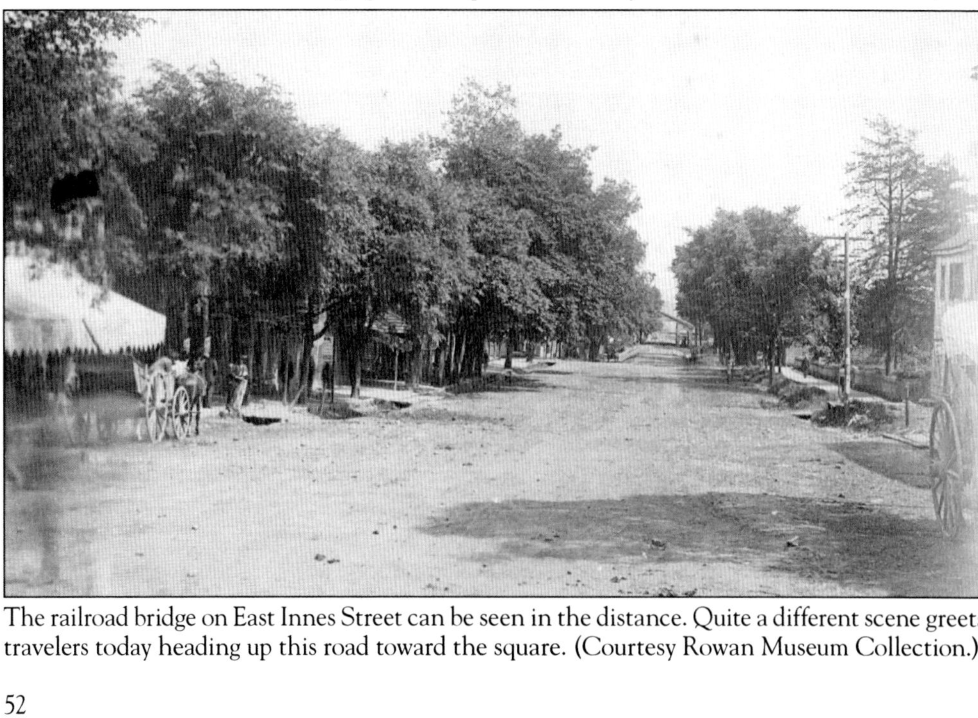

The railroad bridge on East Innes Street can be seen in the distance. Quite a different scene greets travelers today heading up this road toward the square. (Courtesy Rowan Museum Collection.)

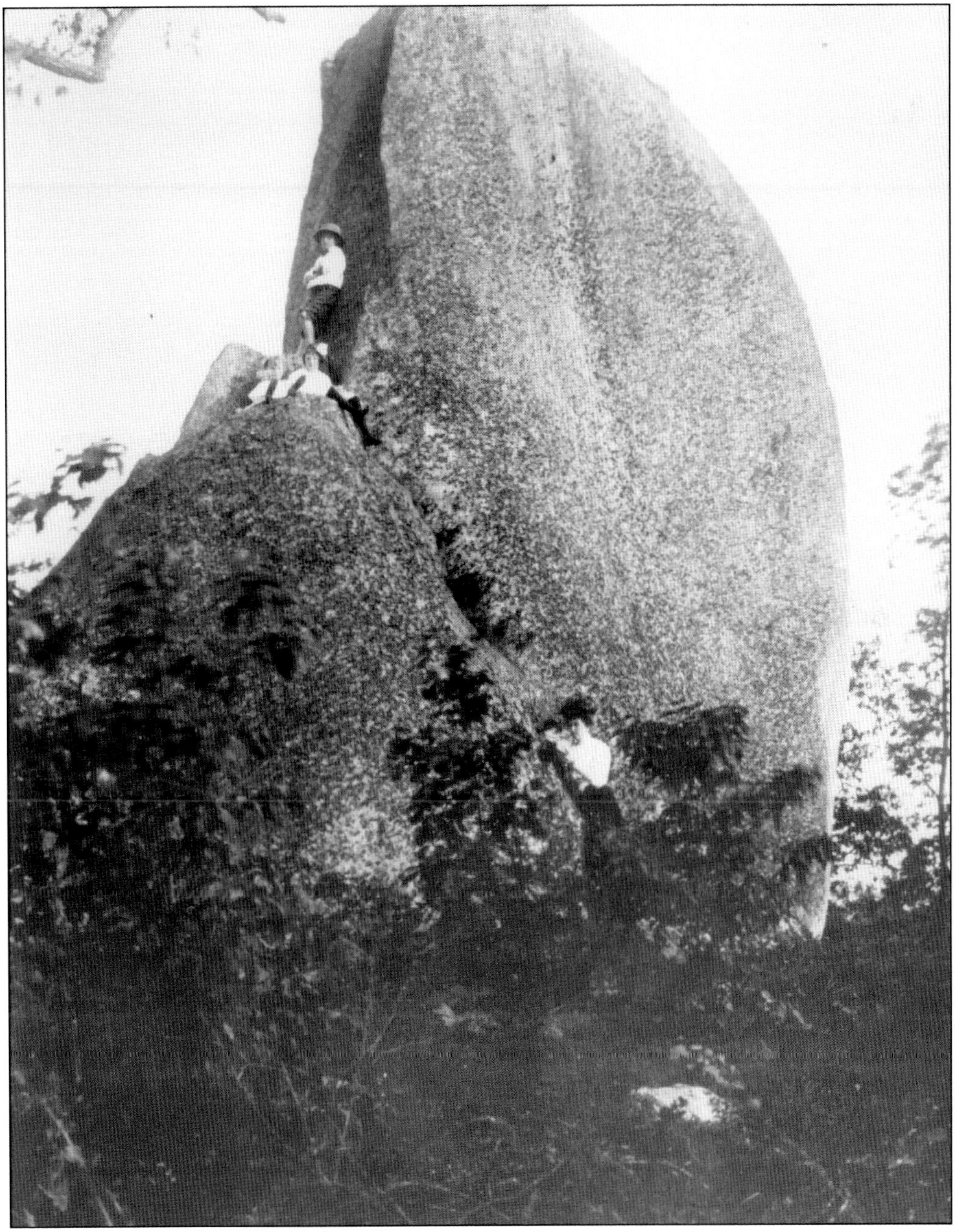

Buerbaum ventured out of Salisbury on occasion to photograph nearby attractions. On May 19, 1907, his family visited the Big Rock at Dunn's Mountain, located several miles east of Salisbury off Bringle Ferry Road. Today, there is a small park at the old quarry for people to safely visit the site. (Courtesy Rowan Museum Collection.)

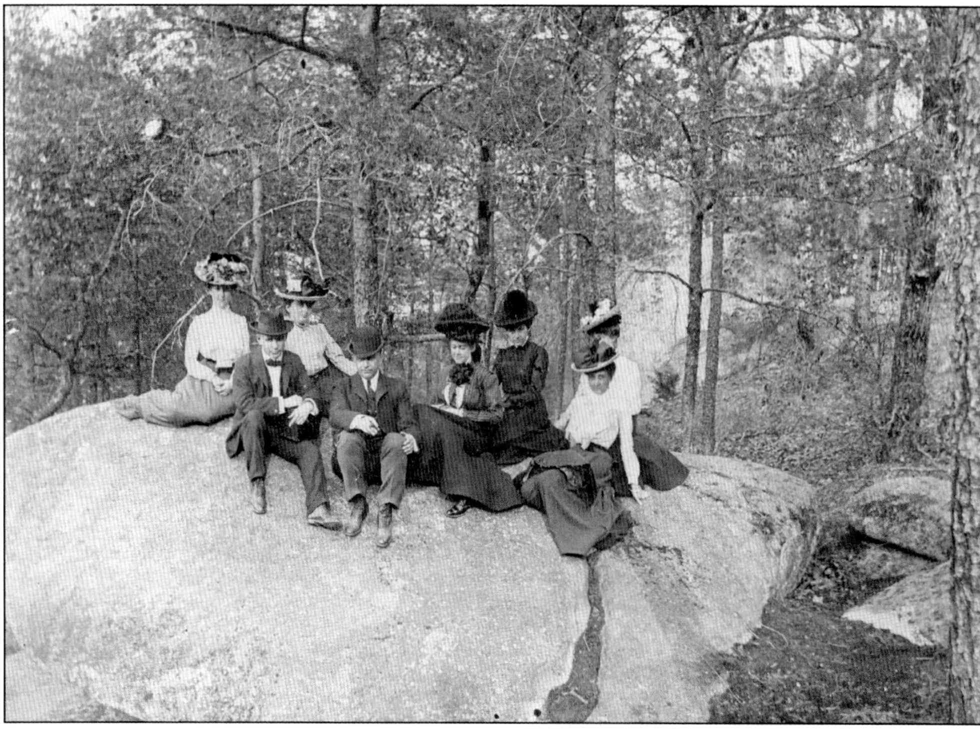

Some of Buerbaum's friends accompanied him on this trip, in part to pose for photographs at a popular picnic spot. Dunn's Mountain, with a peak elevation of 994 feet, promised visitors a steep climb to the top. In the photograph below, the rock to the left of the lady waving reveals holes left from drills used to break up the rock for building material. (Both, courtesy Rowan Museum Collection.)

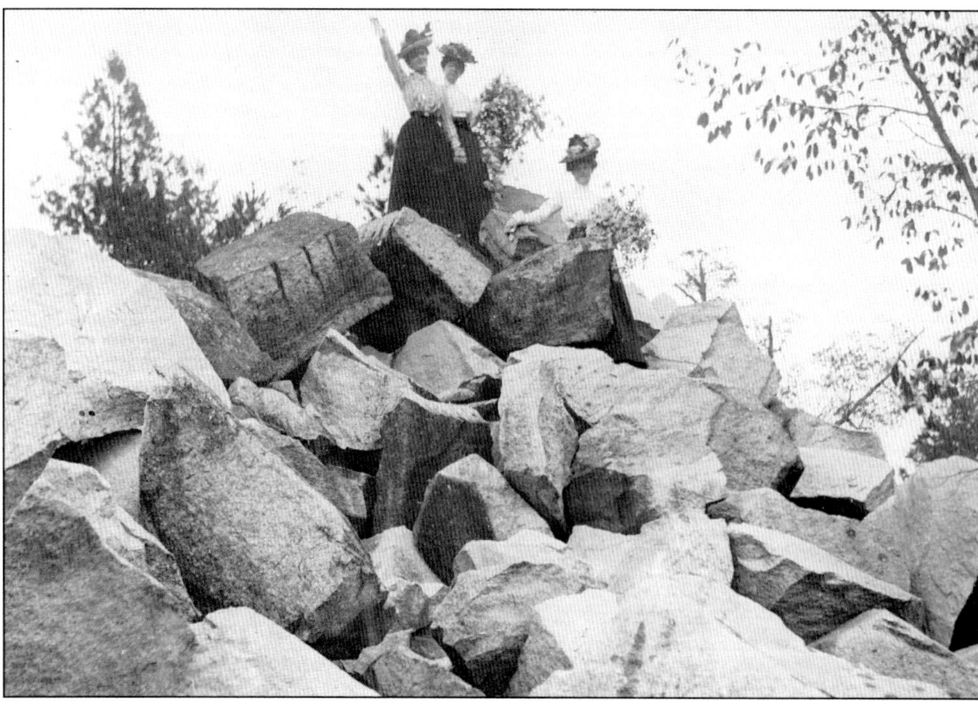

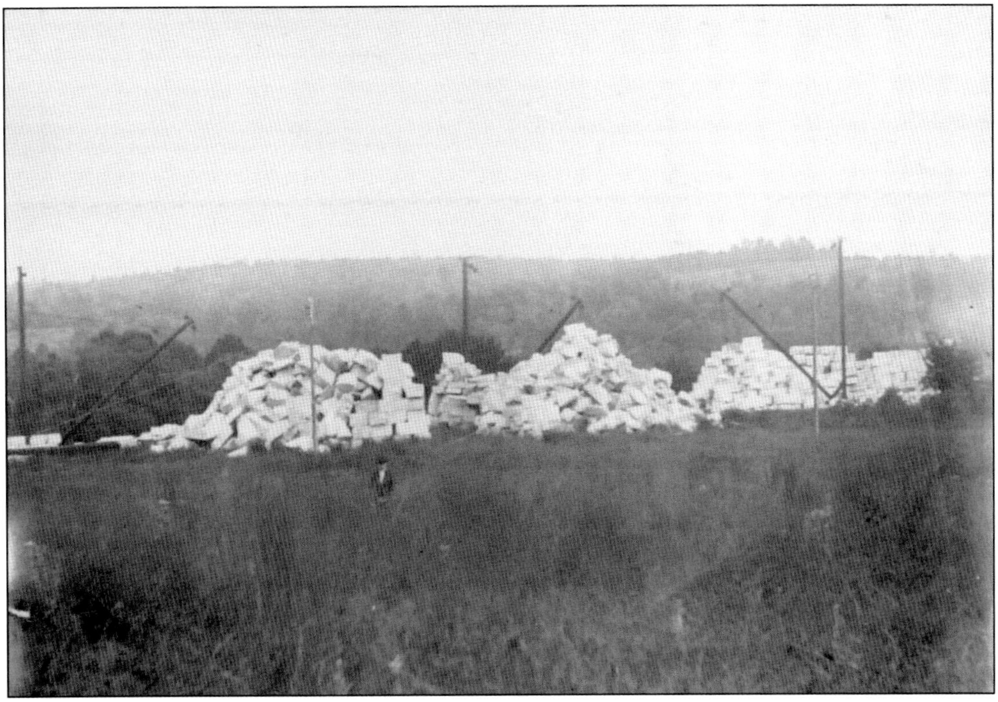

Buerbaum visited the Whitney Dam Project, which had begun in 1901. The project's aim was to build a dam in the Narrows area of the Yadkin River and construct a new town around the resulting lake. Work continued until 1907, and the project was bought out in 1912 by L'Aluminum Francais. ALCOA had purchased the property by 1915 and eventually constructed another dam and developed the town of Badin. (Both, courtesy Rowan Museum Collection.)

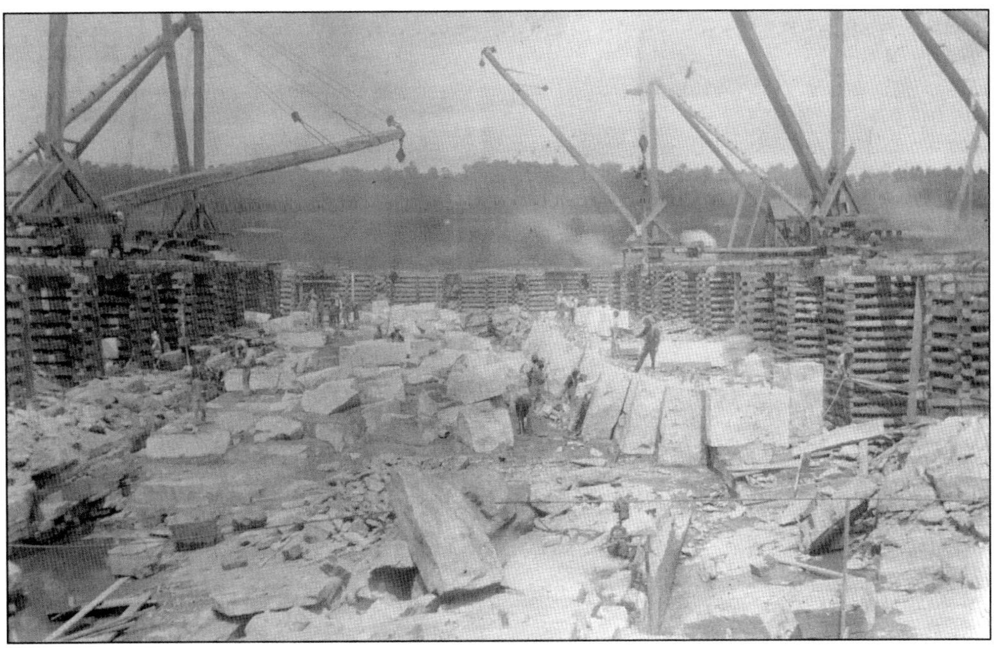

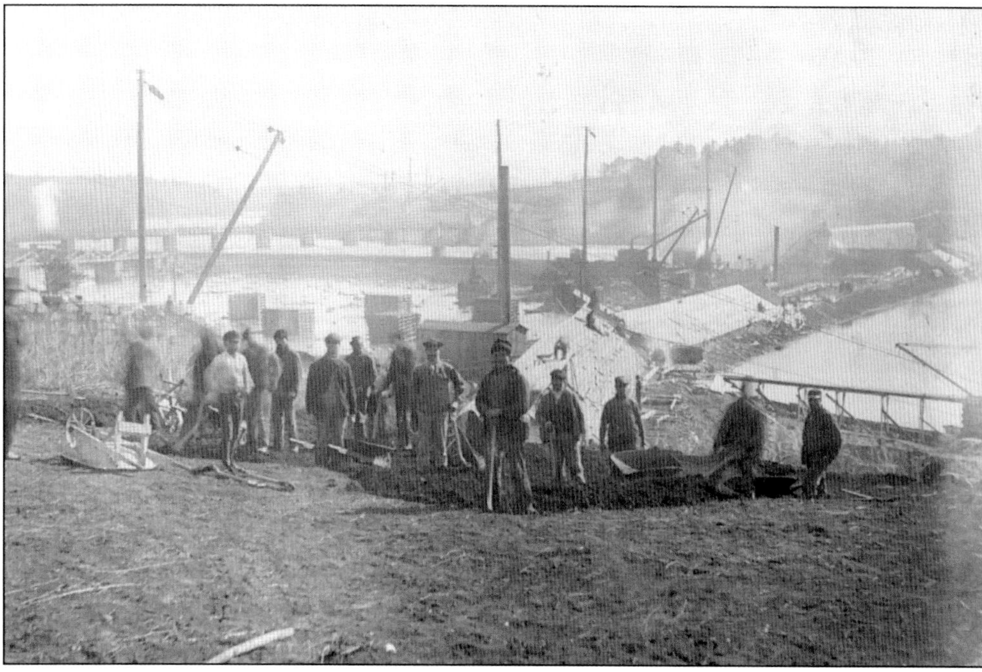

Dam construction workers take a short break for a photograph, but the numerous wheelbarrows show there is still plenty of work to be done. The completed work sprawls out behind them across the Yadkin River. (Courtesy Rowan Museum Collection.)

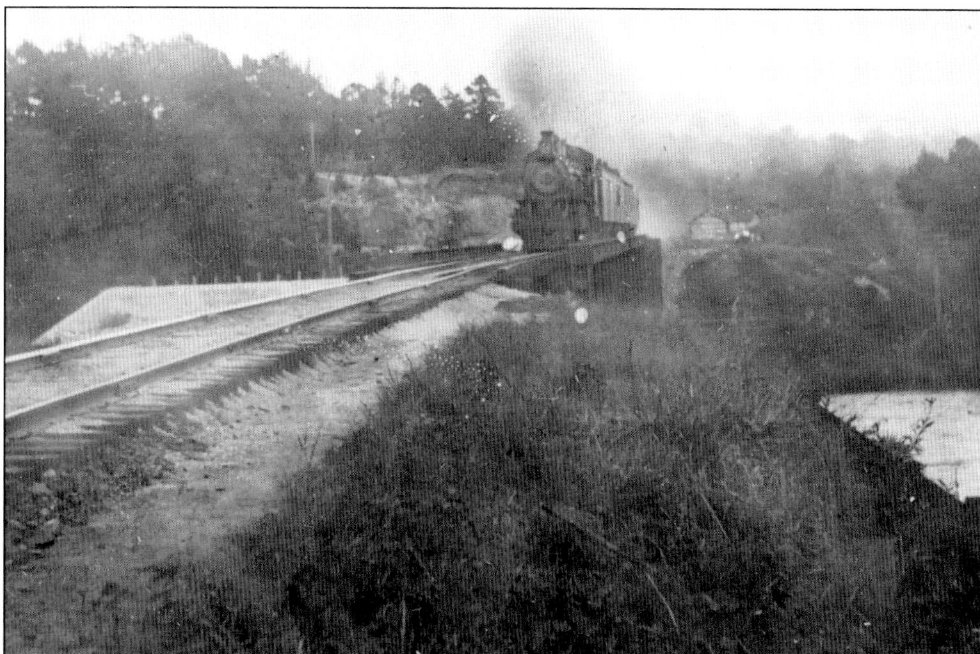

Along another part of the Yadkin River, the Southern Railway mail train speeds along its route to Spencer, three years after the famous wreck in Danville, Virginia. It was very important that the mail train be kept on time, as per the contracts awarded by the Post Office Department for railway mail service. (Courtesy Rowan Museum Collection.)

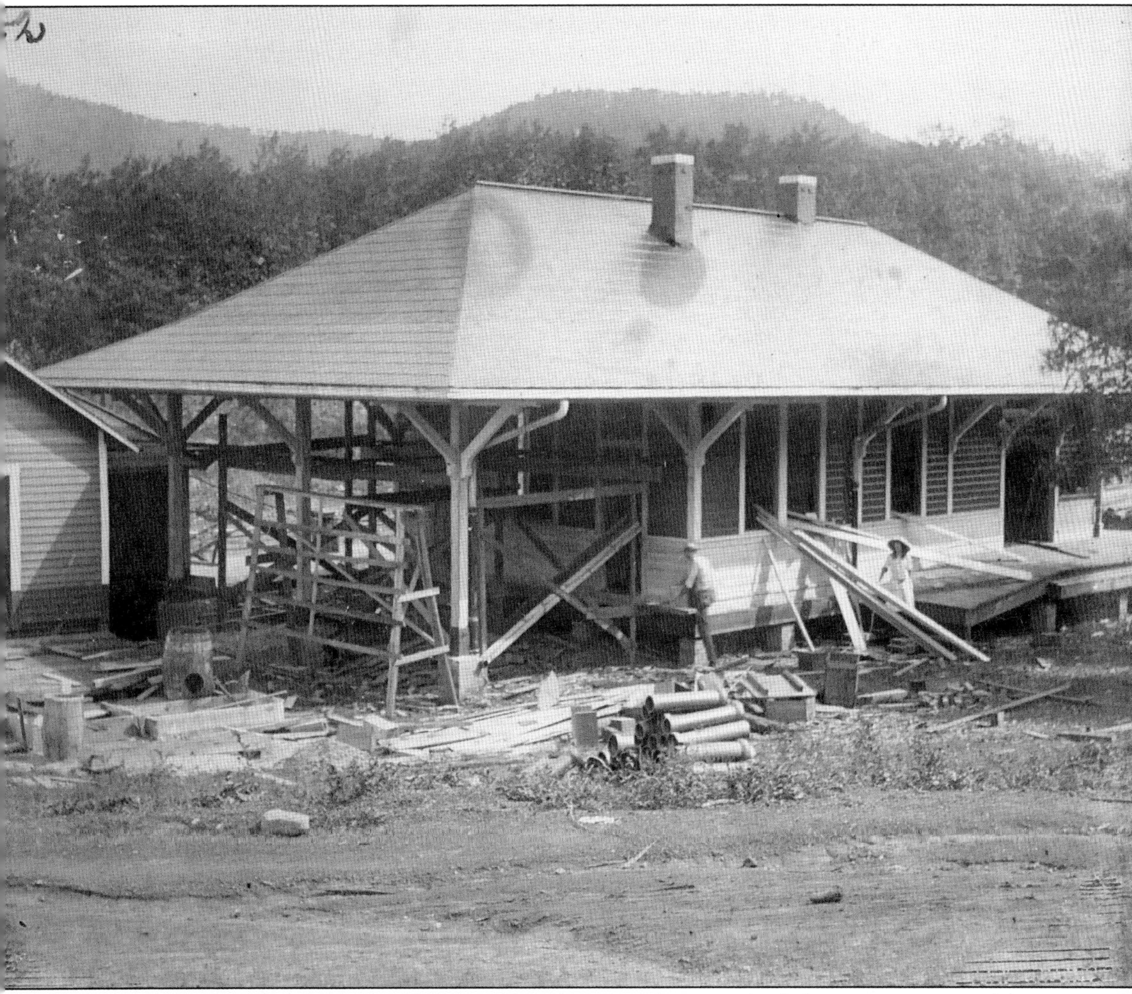

Buerbaum also traveled west toward Asheville, where he photographed the construction of the Ridgecrest depot in August 1912. Ridgecrest was the top of the grade for trains heading west to Asheville after traveling through the "Loops," a series of tunnels used to gain elevation. This building has been preserved and is in use today. (Courtesy Rowan Museum Collection.)

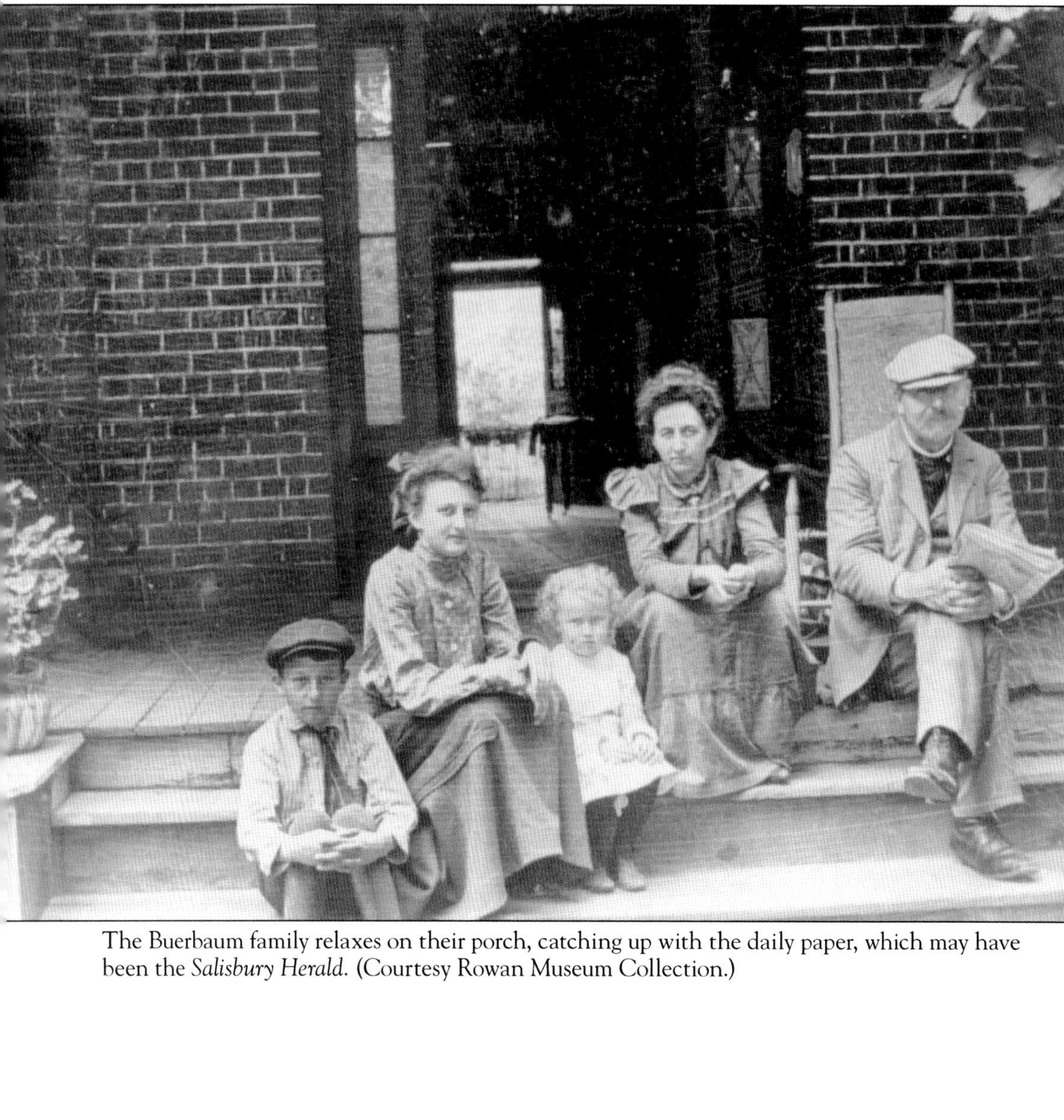

The Buerbaum family relaxes on their porch, catching up with the daily paper, which may have been the *Salisbury Herald*. (Courtesy Rowan Museum Collection.)

Three

SCHOOLS

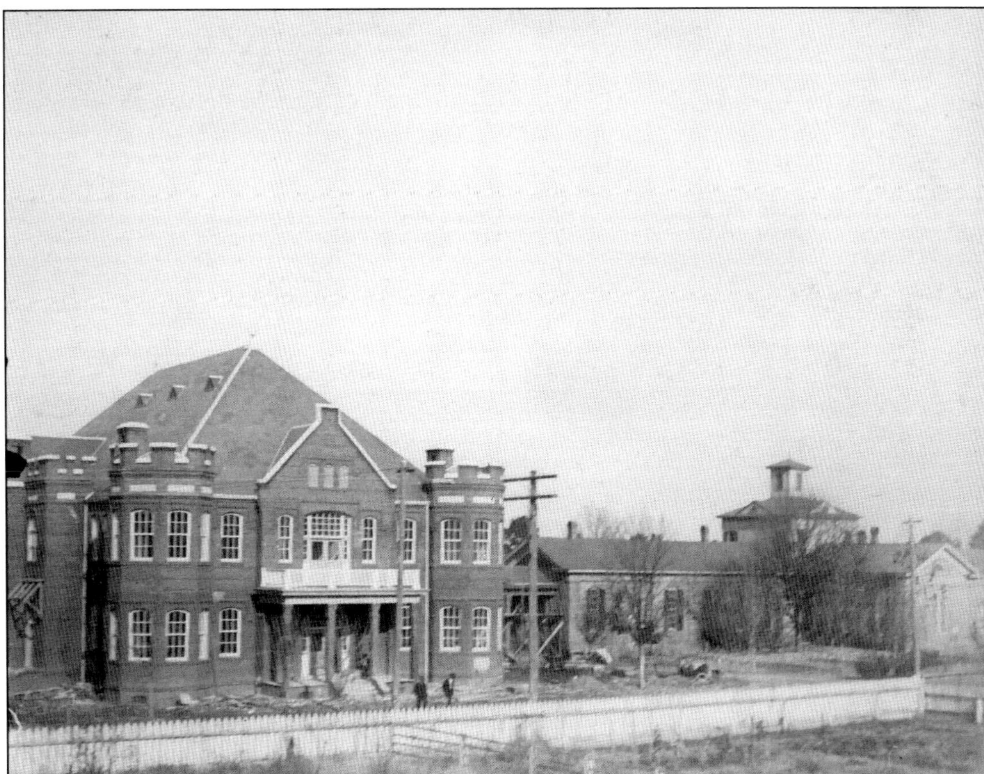

Salisbury Graded School was completed in 1904, but, as seen in this photograph taken that year, some work was still being done to the building. This was the second high school built in North Carolina and is shown here attached to the existing school, built in 1881. (Courtesy Rowan Museum Collection.)

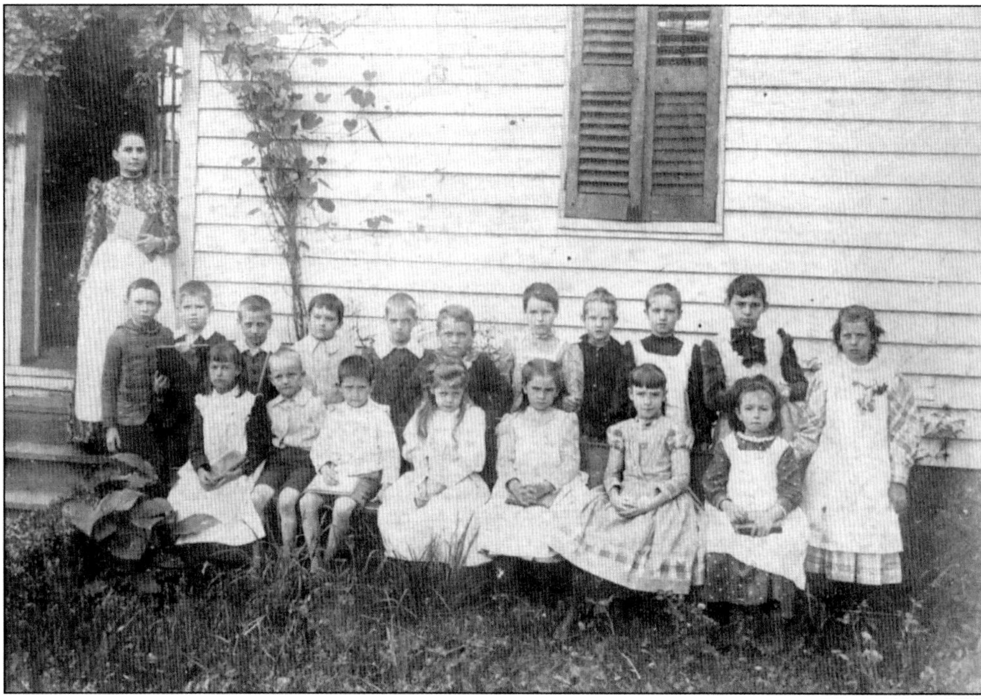

Two of Marie Coit's classes pose for photographs in the 1890s. The children are gathered at the corner of Fulton and Bank Streets, in the yard of the Summerell house. (Both, courtesy Rowan Museum Collection.)

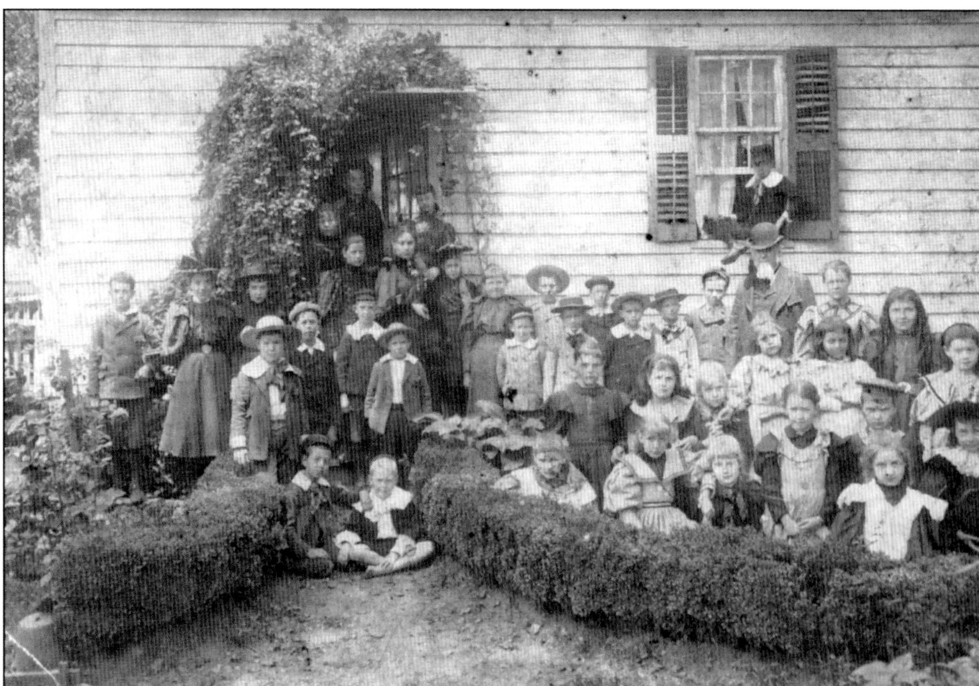

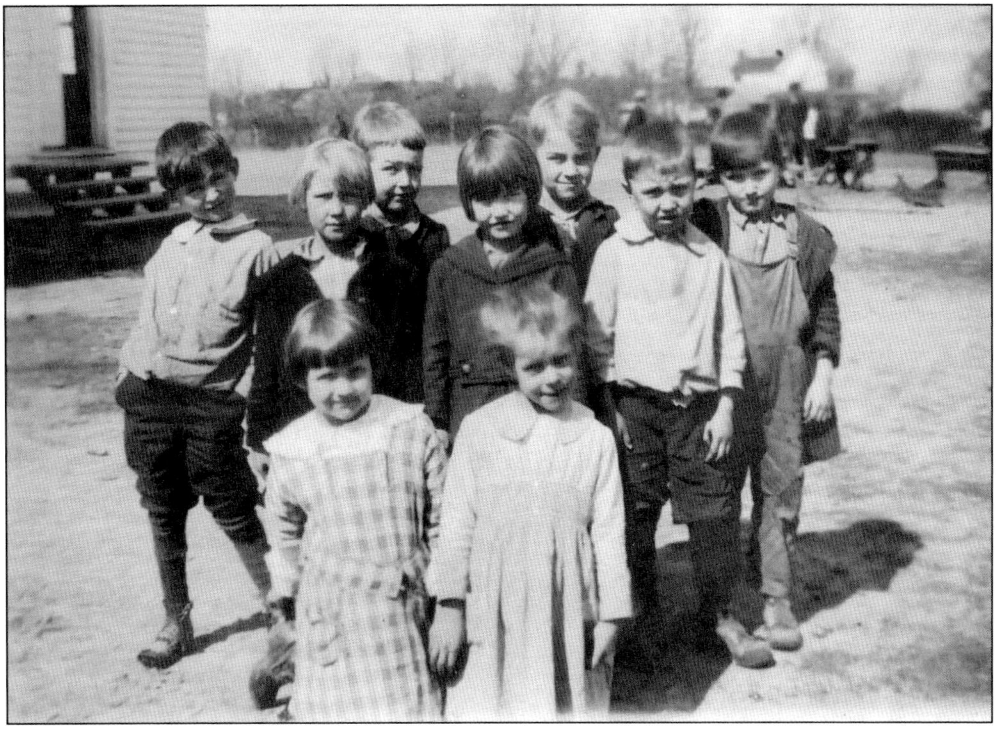

Ellis Cross Roads School was located off Old Mocksville Road, near the intersection with Ridge Road. The children in these photographs, apparently having fun during recess, take a moment to pose for the camera. Ellis remained a separate school until 1958 and the formation of North Rowan High School. (Both, courtesy Edith M. Clark History Room of the Rowan Public Library.)

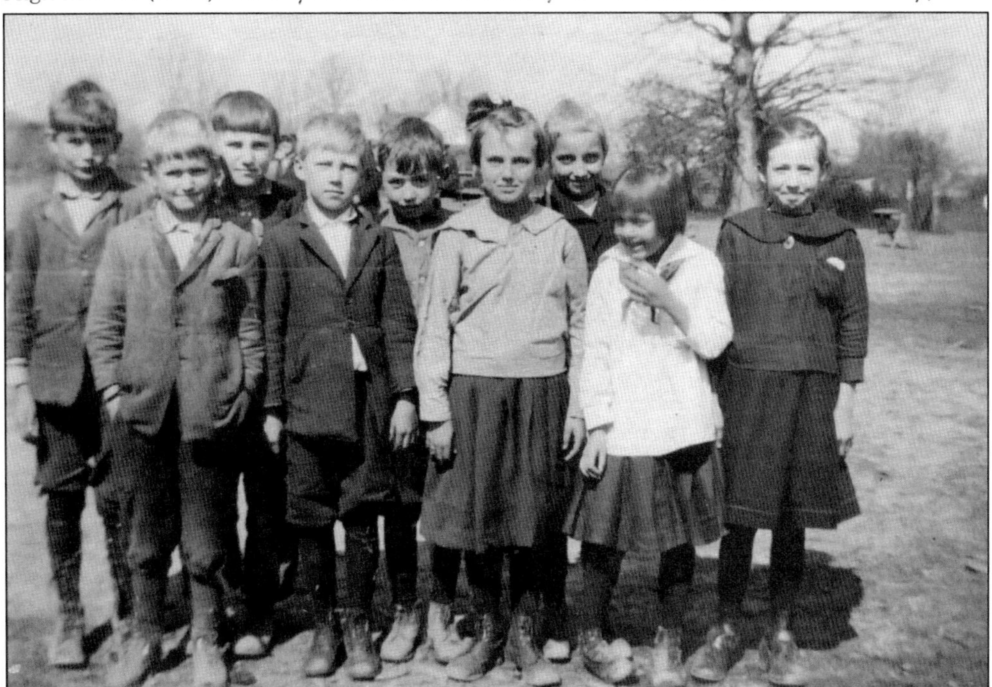

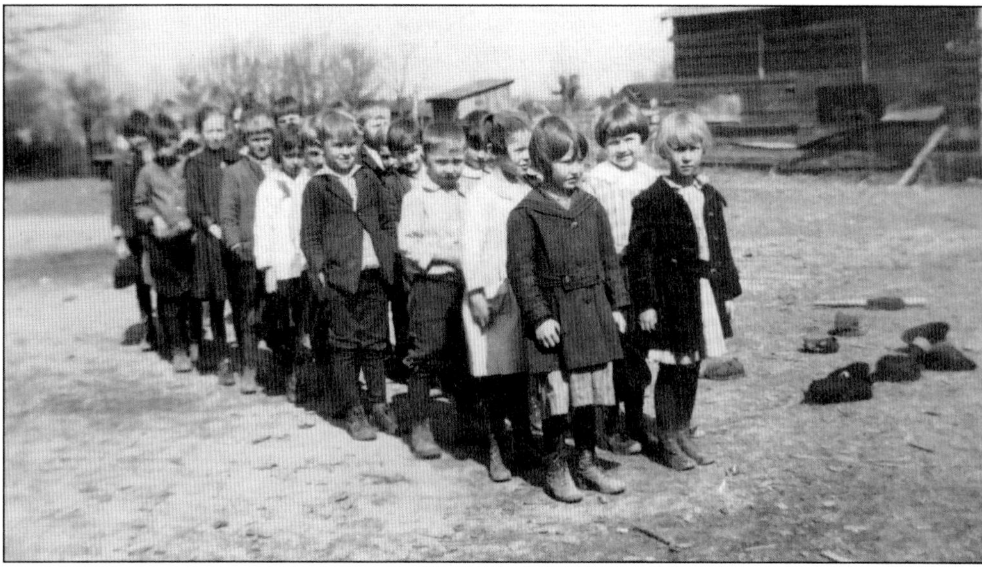

Recess must be over, for the children are lined up and ready to head back to class. Today, the school building and grounds are part of the Rowan County Parks and Recreation Department. An exhibit on the history of the school can be found inside the building. (Both, courtesy Edith M. Clark History Room of the Rowan Public Library.)

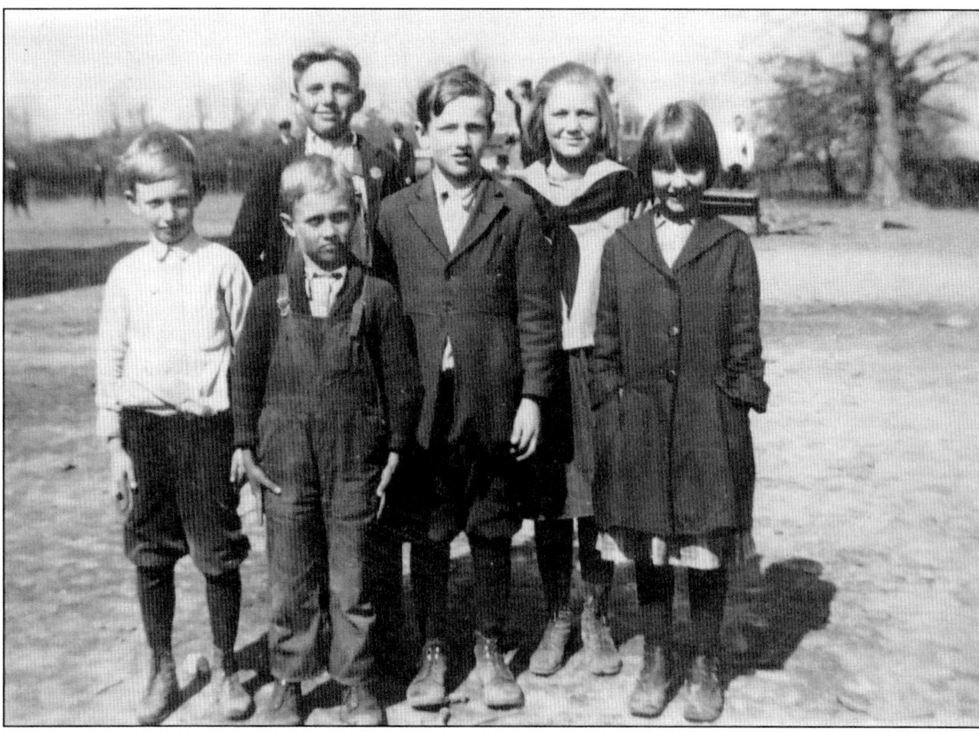

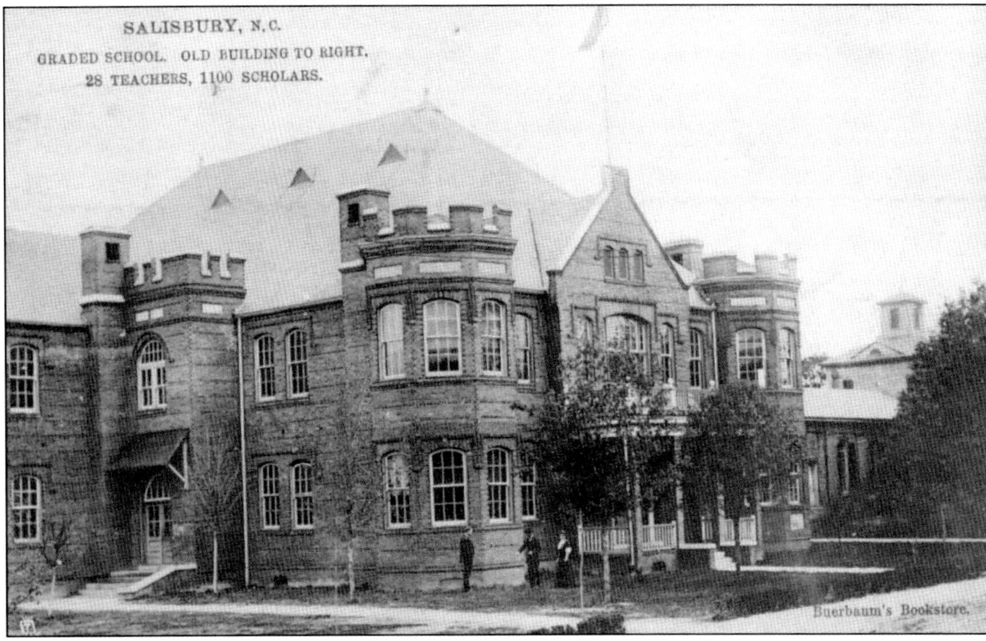

Salisbury Graded (High) School was located at 314 North Ellis Street, adjacent to the superintendent's residence. Eventually, 11 grades were offered, an increase from the nine offered when the school opened. This school eventually became Frank B. John Elementary after students transferred to Boyden High School in 1970 to comply with desegregation. Boyden was later renamed Salisbury High School. (Courtesy Rowan Museum Collection.)

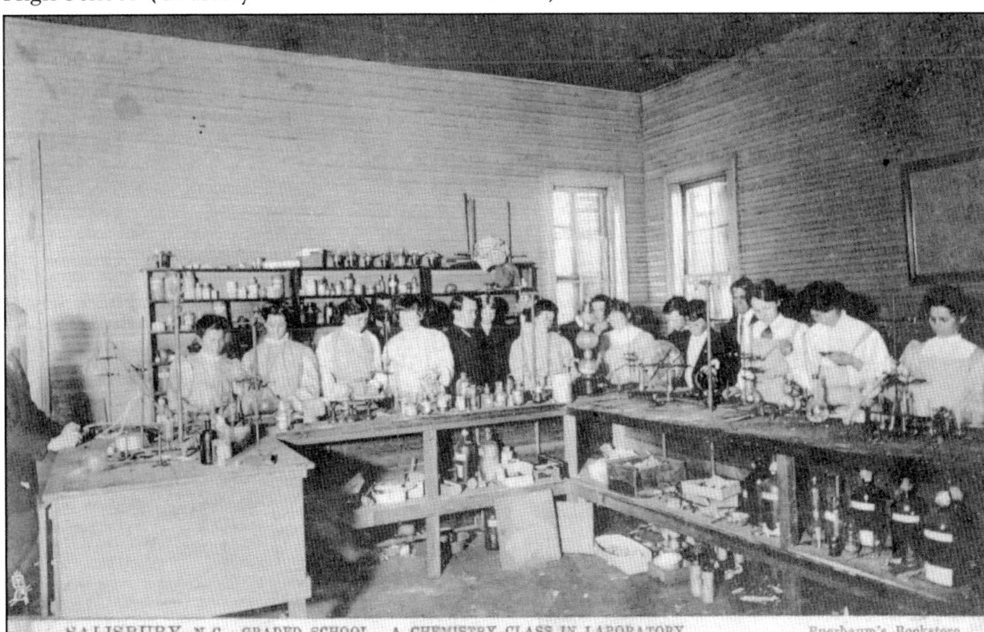

With all of the new technological innovations occurring at the beginning of the 20th century, science and mathematics became ever more important to seniors eager to graduate and begin working. This school, with modern chemistry and biology labs, was one of the most advanced graded schools in North Carolina. (Courtesy Rowan Museum Collection.)

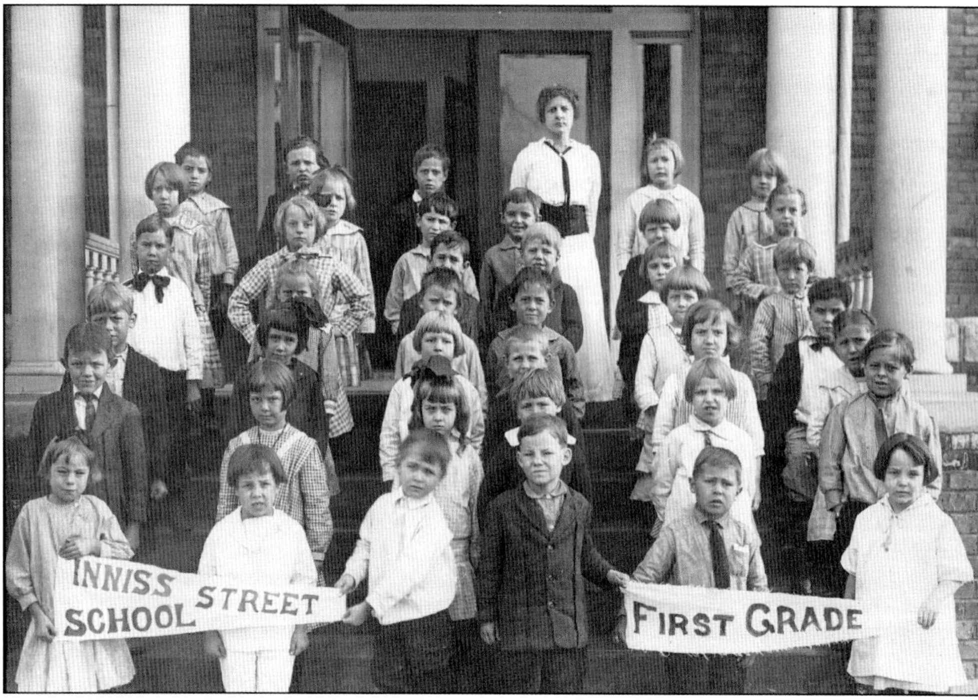

The Inniss Street School was located near the intersection of Inniss (Innes) and Long Streets. The original school was built in the early 1900s with an addition in 1922. This school was built following the development of land on Long Street and around Kesler Manufacturing Company. The above photograph was taken in 1914, and the photograph below was taken the following year. (Both, courtesy Edith M. Clark History Room of the Rowan Public Library.)

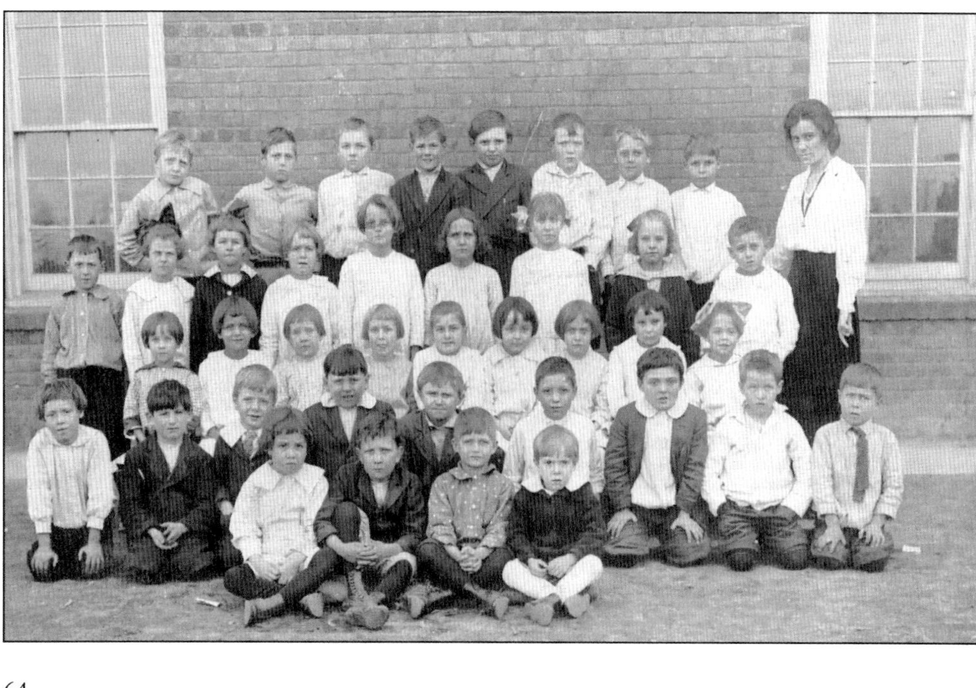

Upper-class students at Inniss Street School pose on a cold winter day in 1920 for their class photograph. (Courtesy Edith M. Clark History Room of the Rowan Public Library.)

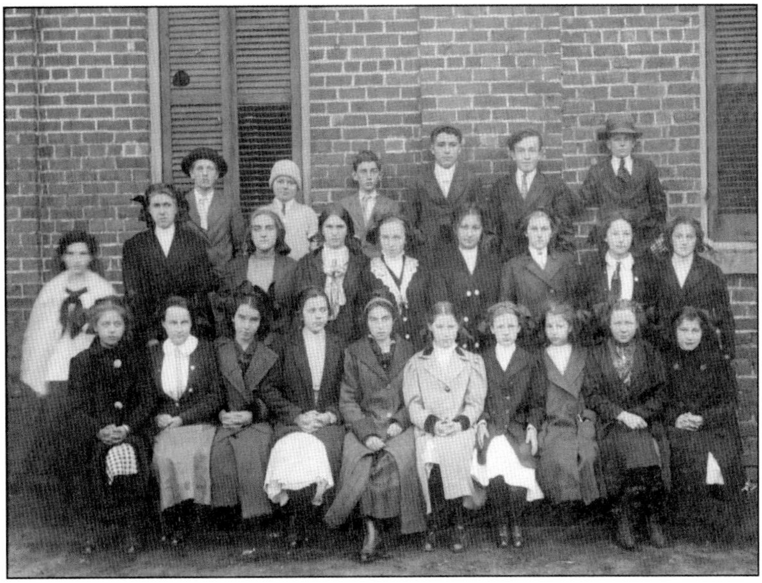

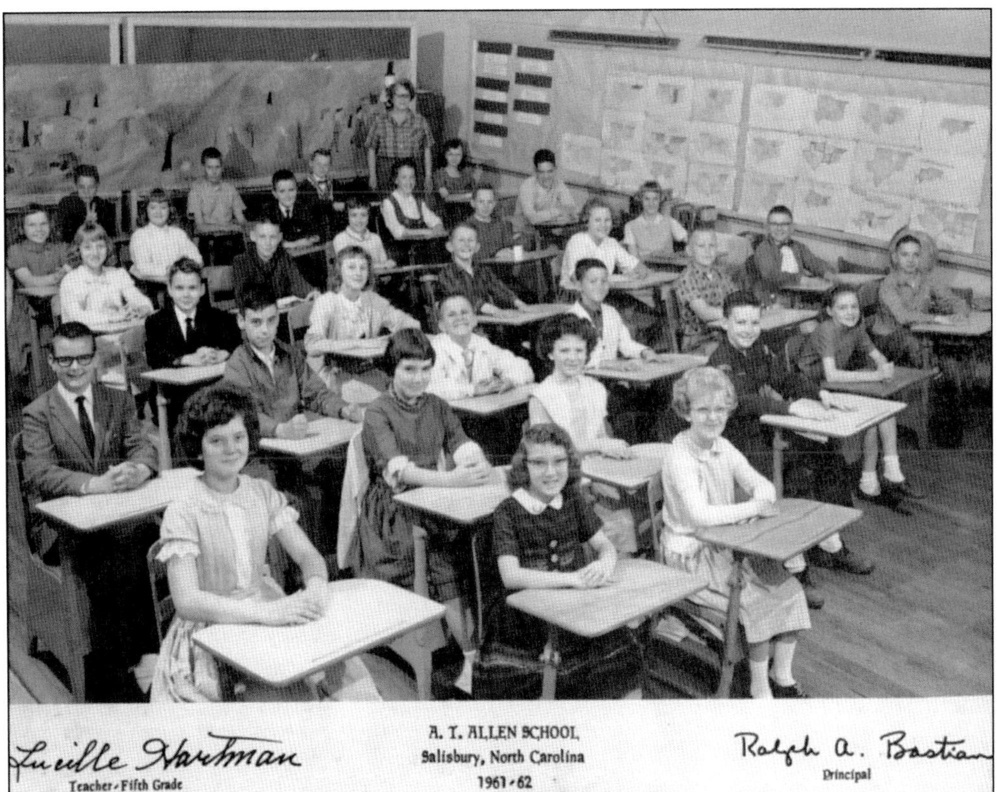

Inniss Street School, renamed A.T. Allen School in 1935, served students through the 1960s. The school was closed in the 1970s as new facilities were built. Today, these students would attend Koontz Elementary. (Courtesy Edith M. Clark History Room of the Rowan Public Library.)

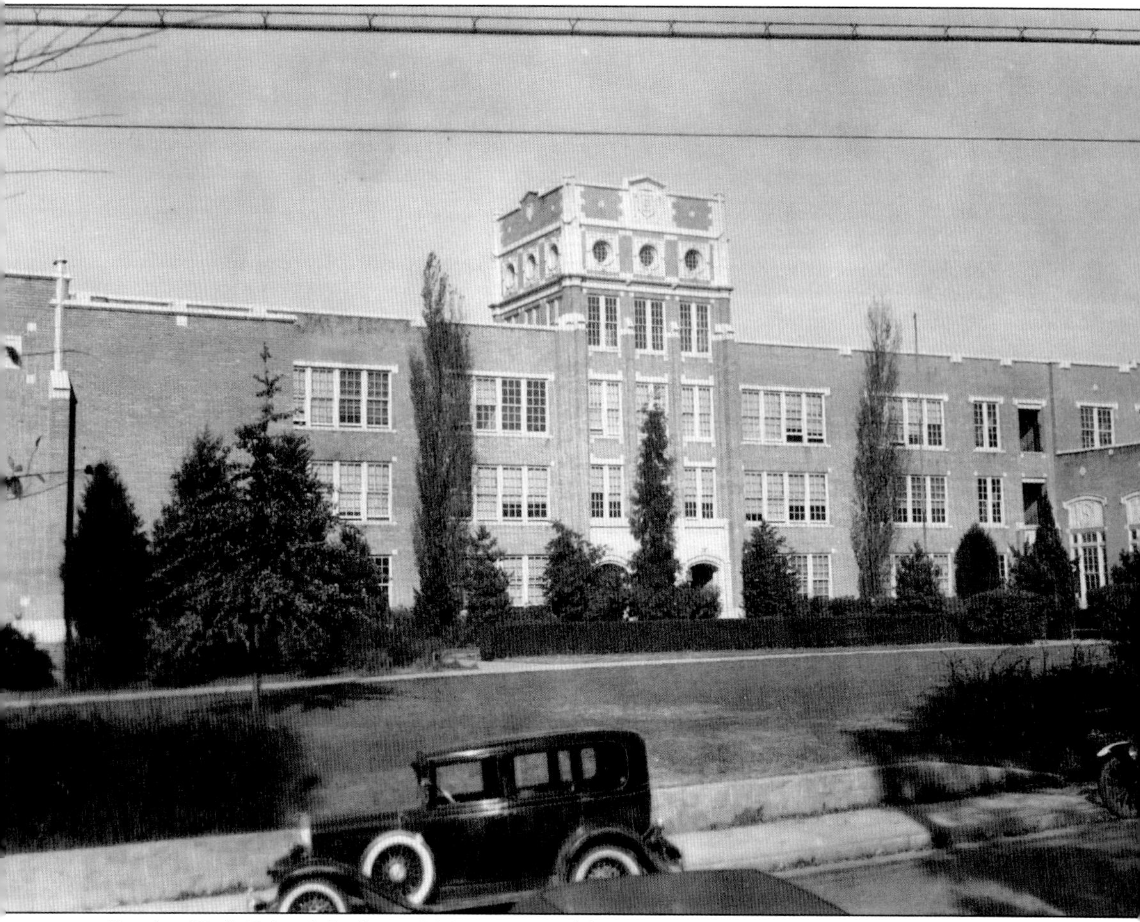

Boyden High School, built in 1926, was named for Mayor Archibald Henderson Boyden, who also served on the school board for 32 years. The school was designed by C. Gadsen Sayre and built by L.S. Bradshaw. Boyden was later merged with J.C. Price High School to form Salisbury High School. (Courtesy Edith M. Clark History Room of the Rowan Public Library.)

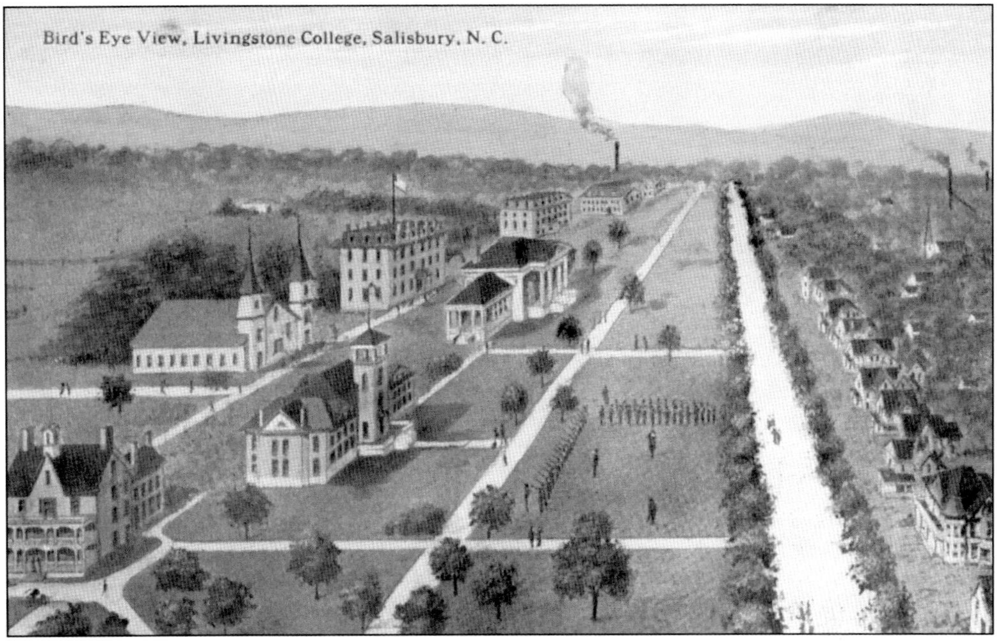

Livingstone College, originally known as Zion Wesley College, opened in October 1882 on 38 acres of land purchased from James Madison Gray. Rev. Joseph Charles Price became the first president. The school, affiliated with the African Methodist Episcopal Zion church, became one of the leading black colleges in the South. The name was officially changed to Livingstone in 1887, named for the famous explorer of Africa, Dr. David Livingstone. (Courtesy Rowan Museum Collection.)

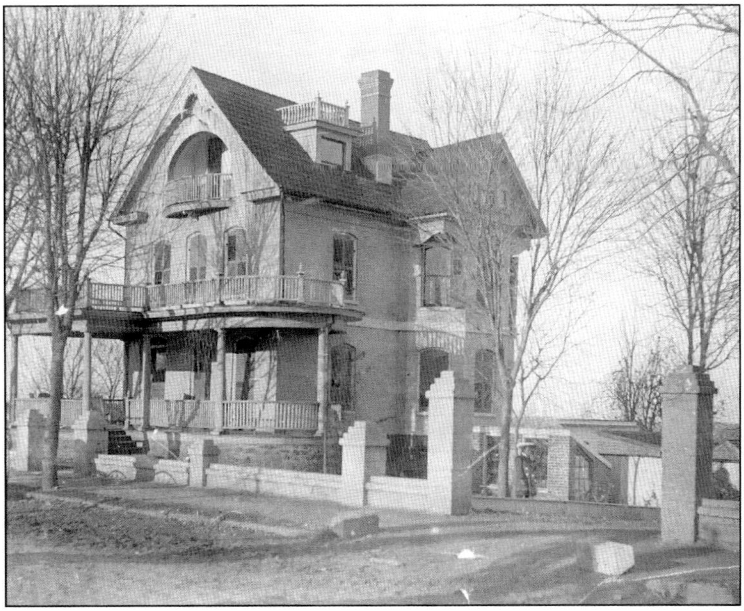

Shown here is the home of William Henry Goler, second president of Livingstone College. During the years of his tenure (1893–1917), the college added the Carnegie Library, Hood Theological Seminary, and Goler Hall, a women's dormitory. (Courtesy Rowan Museum Collection.)

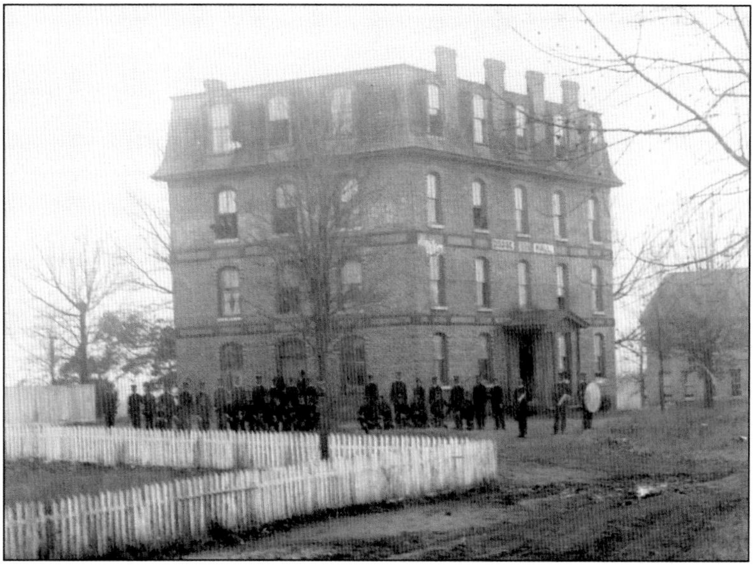

Dodge Hall, constructed as a men's dormitory in 1886, had some classrooms on the first floor. The building was named for William Earl Dodge, a dry-goods merchant from New York. This photograph was taken by Buerbaum in 1904. (Courtesy Rowan Museum Collection.)

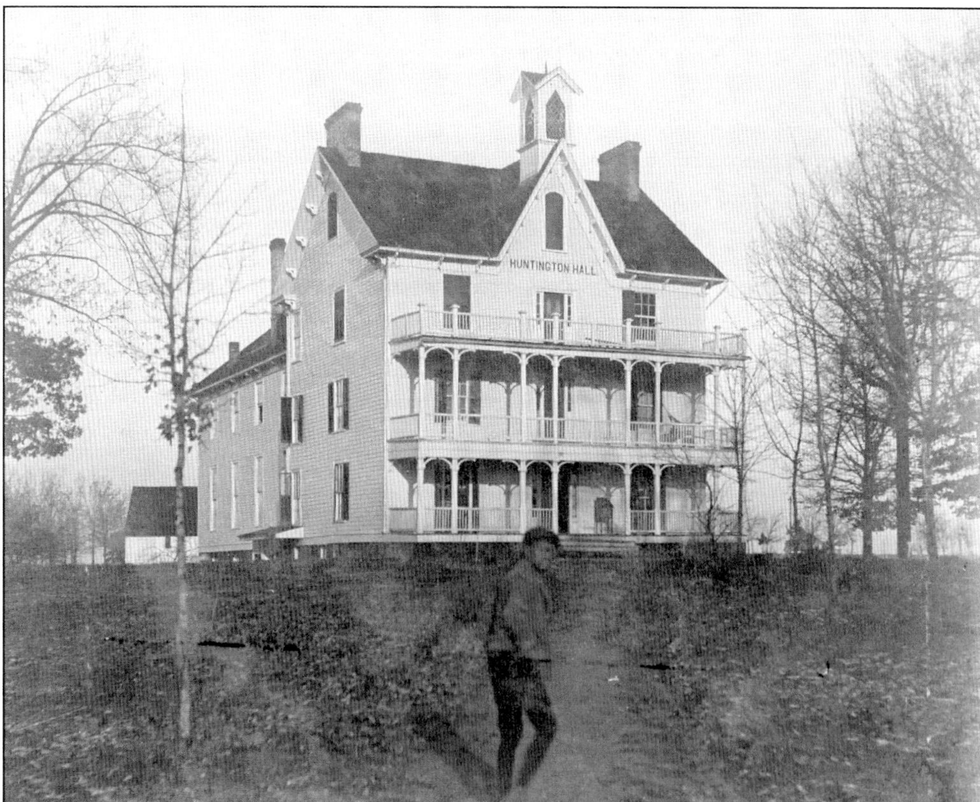

Huntington Hall was named for Collis P. Huntington, a California philanthropist and railroad magnet. The building, originally J.M. Gray's farmhouse, was extensively modified, funded in part by Huntington. This became one of the first dormitories for the new college in the 1880s. (Courtesy Rowan Museum Collection.)

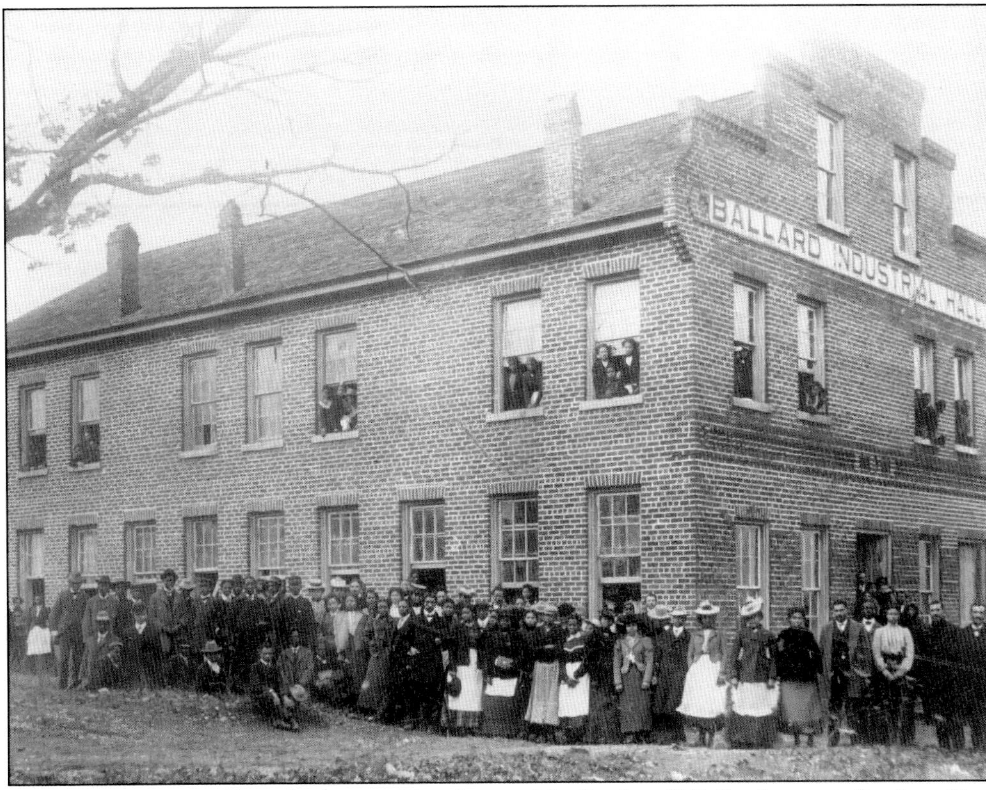

Ballard Industrial Hall was built in 1887 and named for Stephen F. Ballard, a capitalist from New York. Here, students pose for a photograph during a break from classes in 1903. (Courtesy Rowan Museum Collection.)

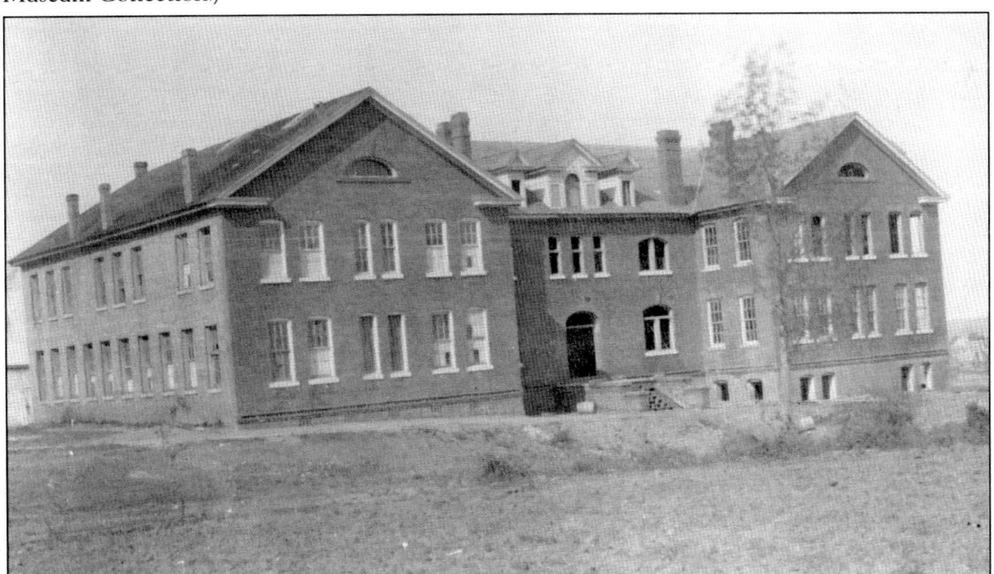

Ballard Industrial Hall is shown here in the early 1910s after its rebuilding. This is one of the few buildings from the early 20th century still in use at Livingstone. (Courtesy Rowan Museum Collection.)

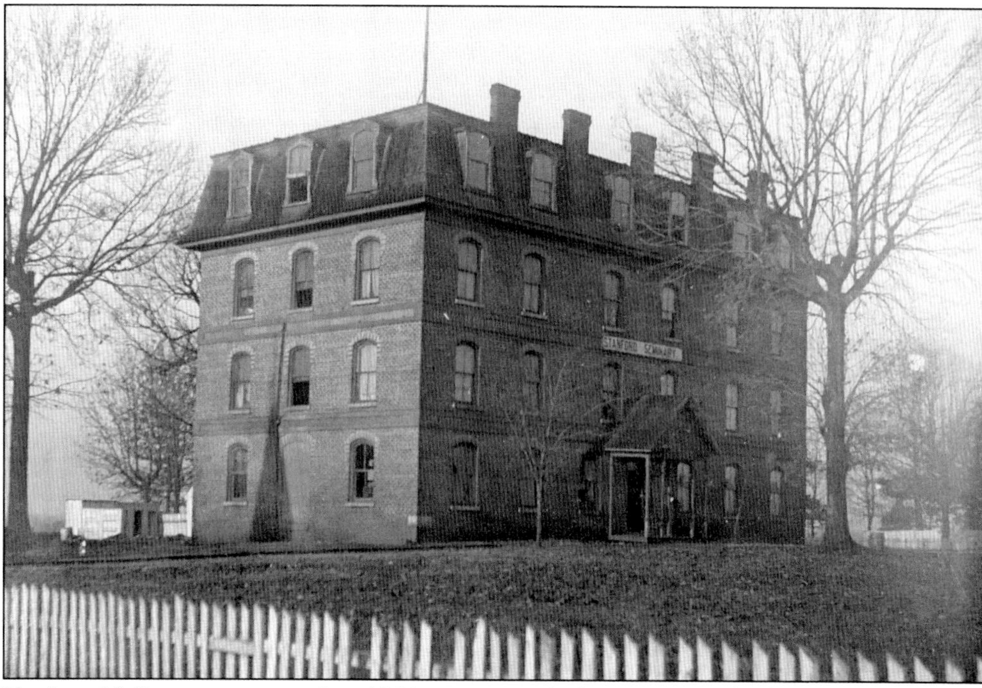

Hopkins Hall was constructed in 1886 as a women's dormitory. It also housed the Stanford Seminary. The building was similar in appearance to Dodge Hall, constructed in the same year. This photograph was taken on December 15, 1904. (Courtesy Rowan Museum Collection.)

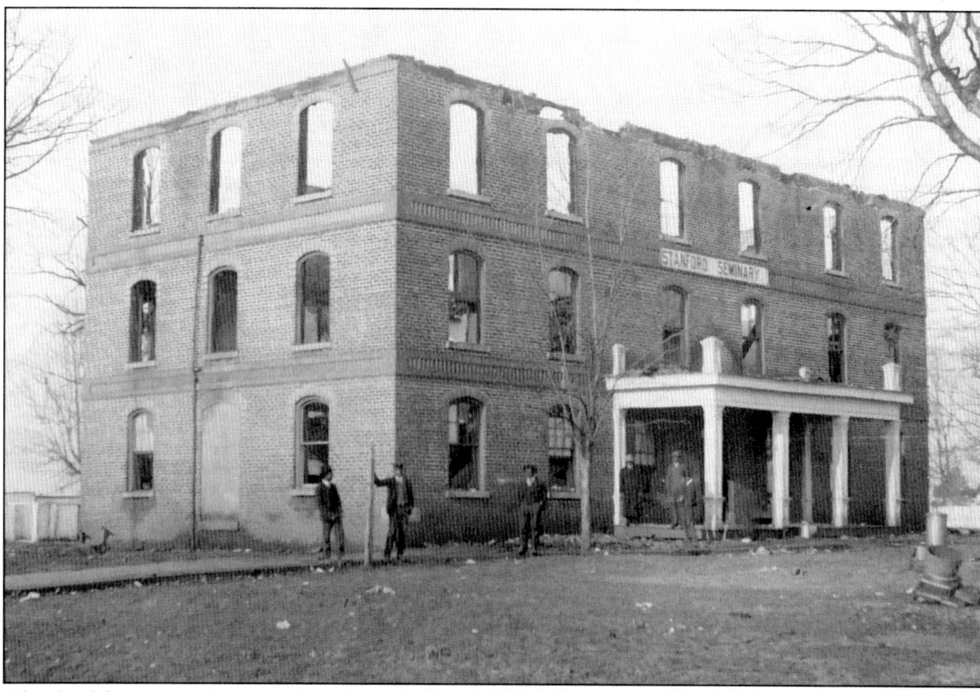

The building was destroyed by fire in April 1906, leaving only the exterior walls. A new seminary building was constructed, but it did not use the Stanford name. (Courtesy Rowan Museum Collection.)

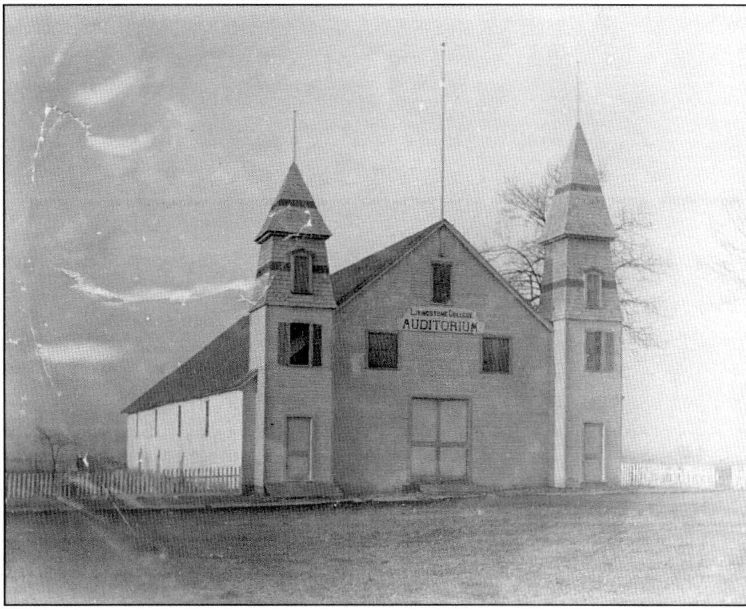

The auditorium/chapel was constructed in 1902 close to the center of the Livingstone College campus. This photograph was taken on December 15, 1904, four months before the disastrous cyclone. (Courtesy Rowan Museum Collection.)

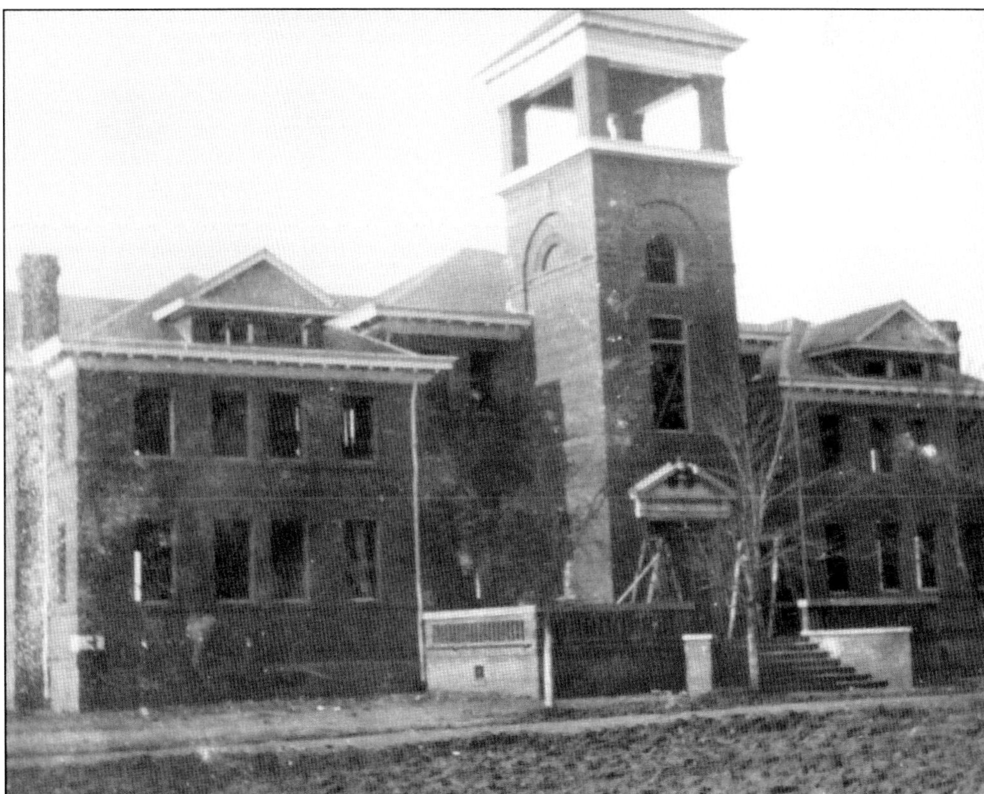

This April 1907 photograph shows Hood Theological Seminary under construction. Completed and opened in 1910, the building was named for Bishop James Walker Hood, an early proponent of Livingstone College. Today, this seminary operates out of the original Holiday Inn hotel off of I-85. (Courtesy Rowan Museum Collection.)

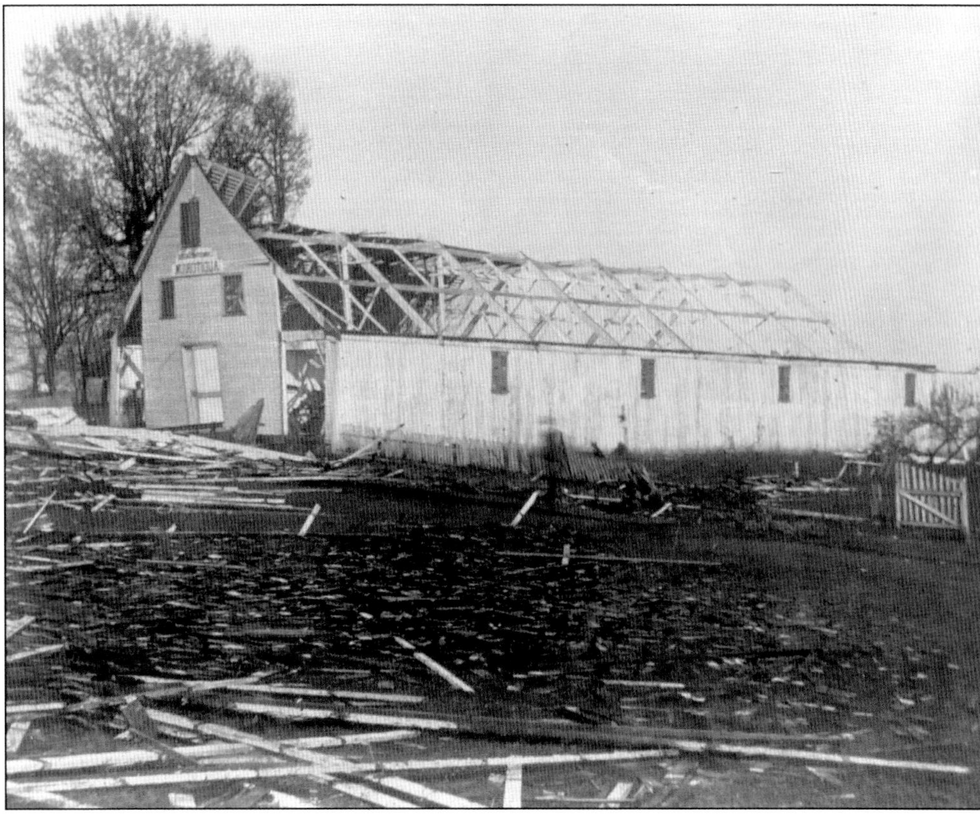

On April 5, 1905, a tornado, or cyclone as it was called, struck the campus of Livingstone College, damaging several buildings. The auditorium, shown here, appeared to take a direct hit, the cyclone ripping apart the wooden structure. Along with the roof peeling off, the two tall steeples were reduced to splinters. (Courtesy Rowan Museum Collection.).

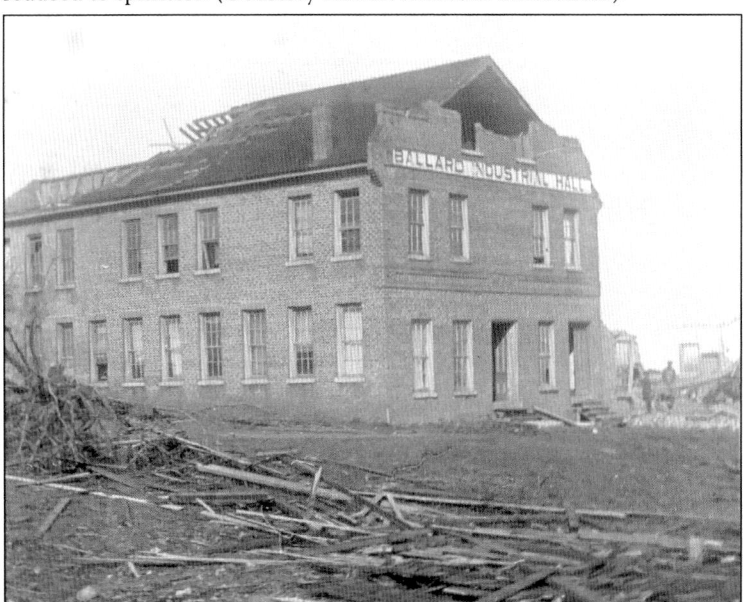

Ballard Industrial Hall took a direct hit from the storm. Most of the structure, including a 1900 addition, was heavily damaged. (Courtesy Rowan Museum Collection.)

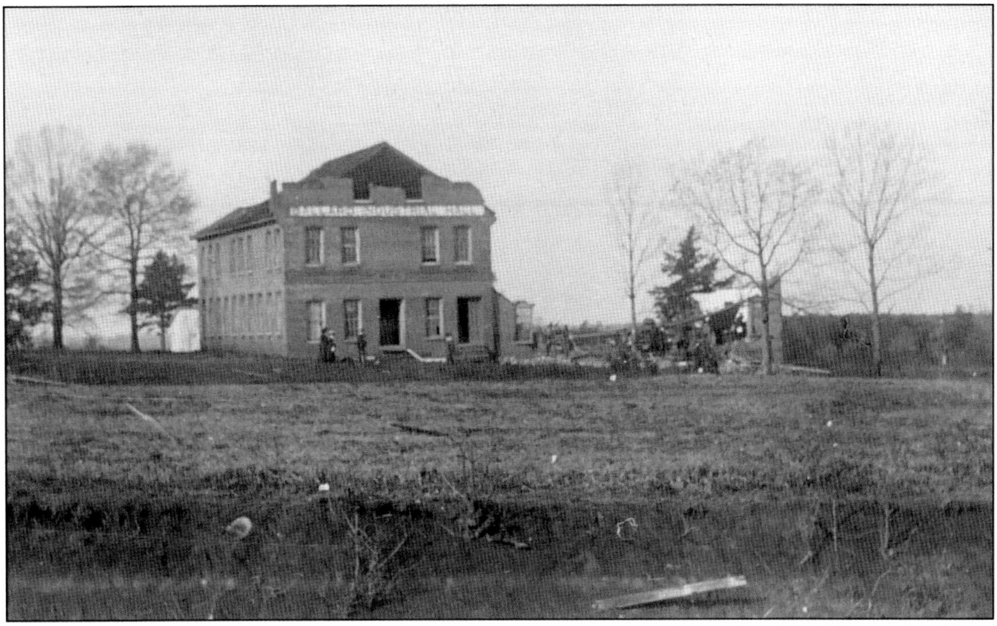

These two photographs show the extent of damage to Ballard Industrial Hall. The 1900 building addition was completely destroyed, and debris was sent at least 500 feet onto nearby structures. The main building was later rebuilt and is still used as a classroom at Livingstone. (Both, courtesy Rowan Museum Collection.)

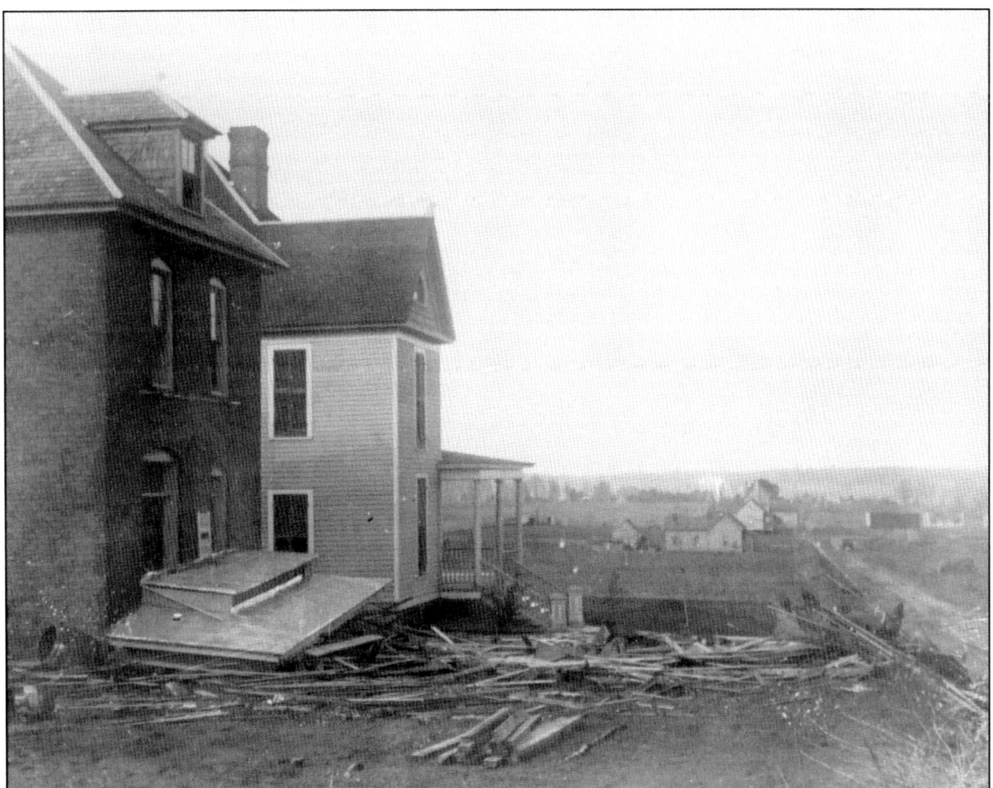

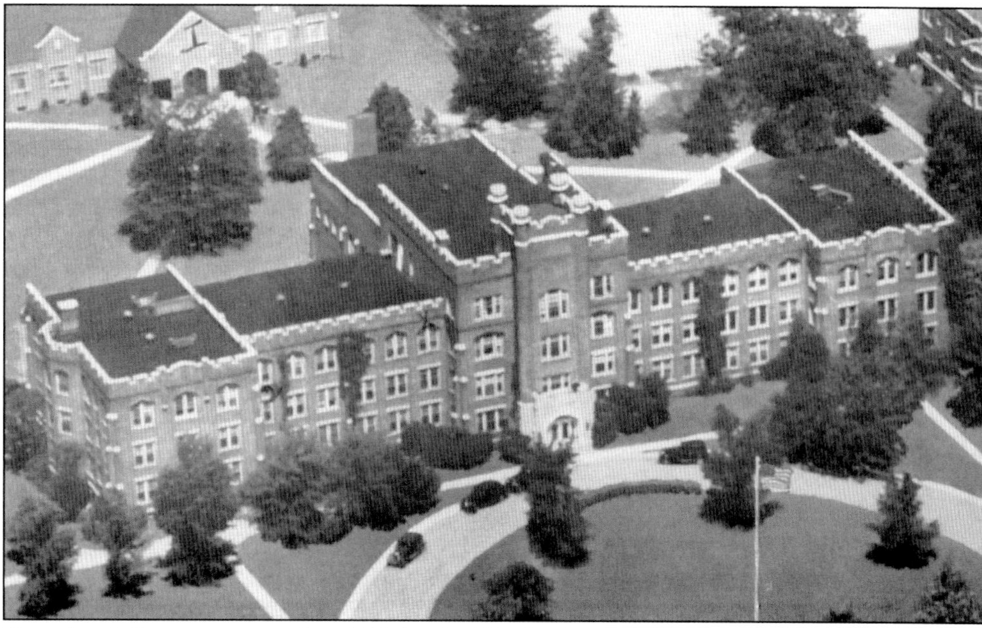

Catawba College was created in 1851 by the North Carolina Classis of the Reformed Church in Newton, North Carolina. The college, named for its county of origin, became one of the few coeducational facilities when it started admitting women in 1890. The campus moved to Salisbury in 1925, taking over the property of the Salisbury Normal and Industrial Institute. (Courtesy Rowan Museum Collection.)

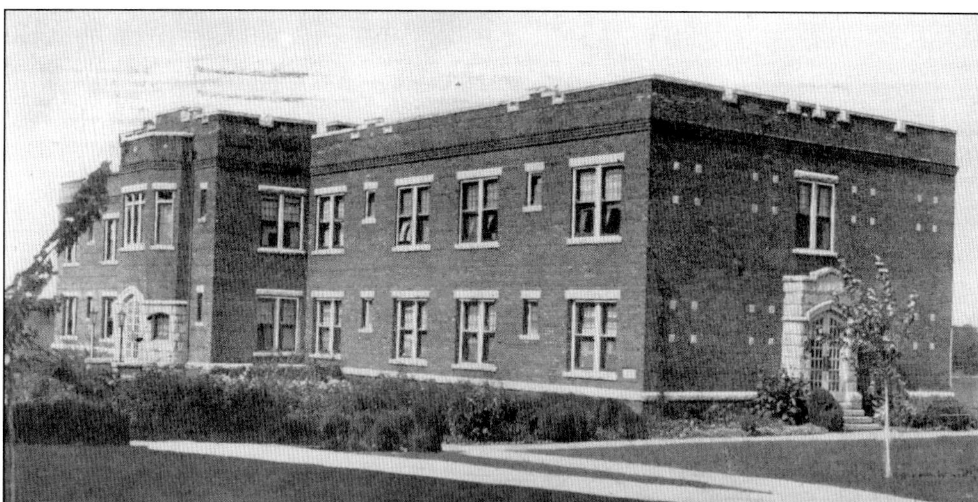

Zartman Hall, Girls' Dormitory, Catawba College, Salisbury, N. C.

Originally built as a girls' dormitory, today this hall is reserved for upperclassmen and known as the Zeda Peeler Barger and Elizabeth Conrad Zartman Hall. Erected in 1926, this is the oldest remaining dormitory building on campus. (Courtesy Rowan Museum Collection.)

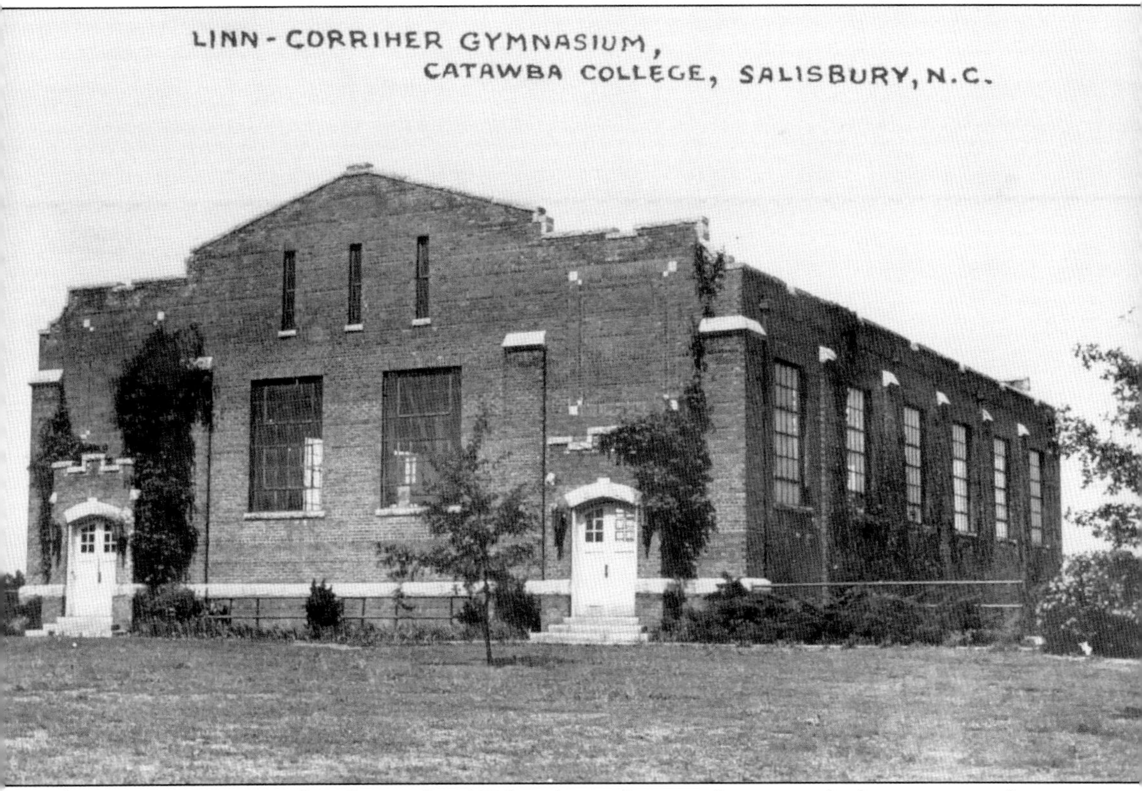

This gymnasium opened in September 1926 with ample space for sports, locker rooms, and a small dormitory for visiting teams. The total cost for the building was $35,000. It was replaced by the Enoch A. Goodman Gymnasium and Julius W. Abernathy Physical Education Center on September 26, 1970. (Courtesy Rowan Museum Collection.)

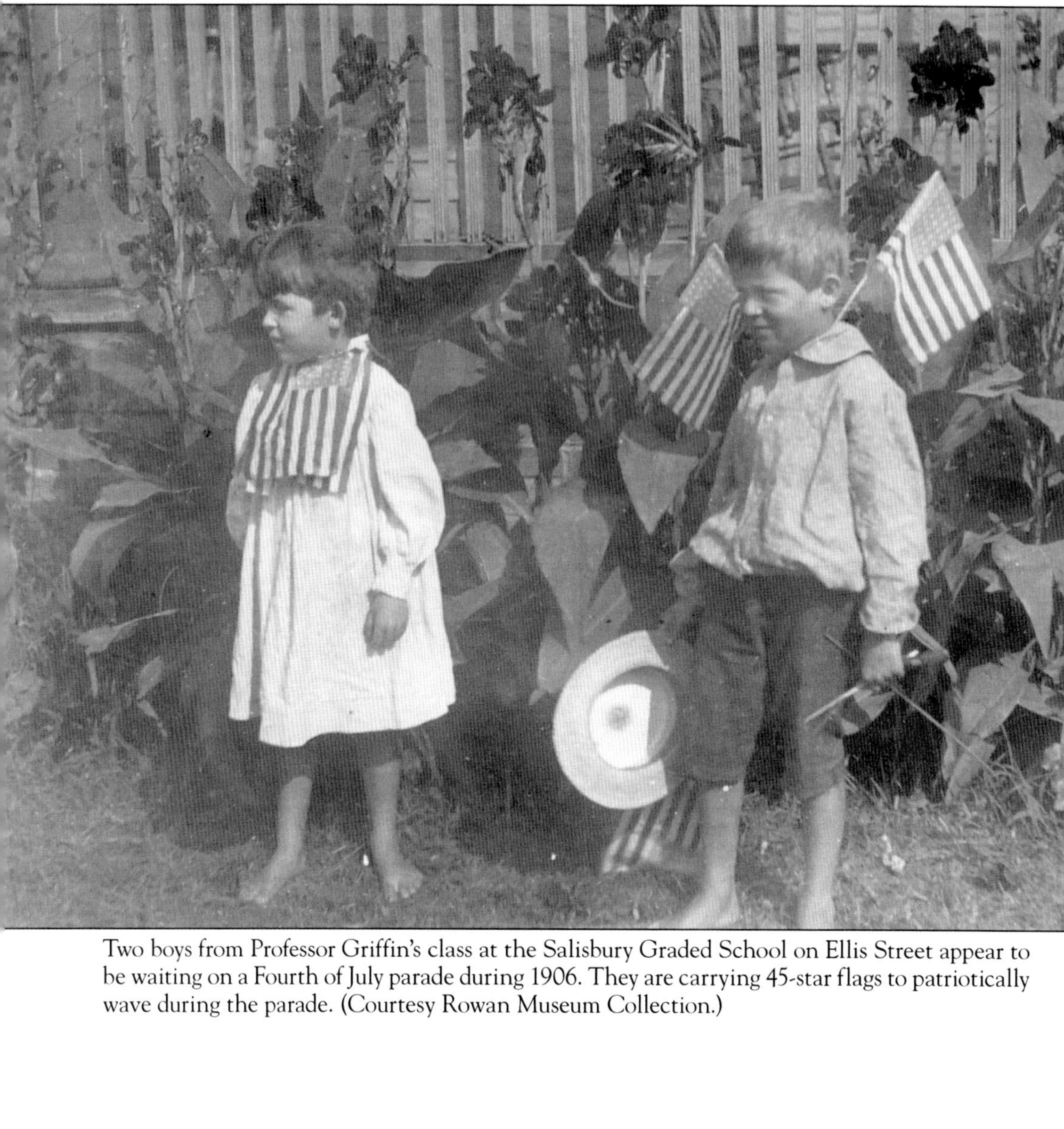

Two boys from Professor Griffin's class at the Salisbury Graded School on Ellis Street appear to be waiting on a Fourth of July parade during 1906. They are carrying 45-star flags to patriotically wave during the parade. (Courtesy Rowan Museum Collection.)

Four

BUSINESSES

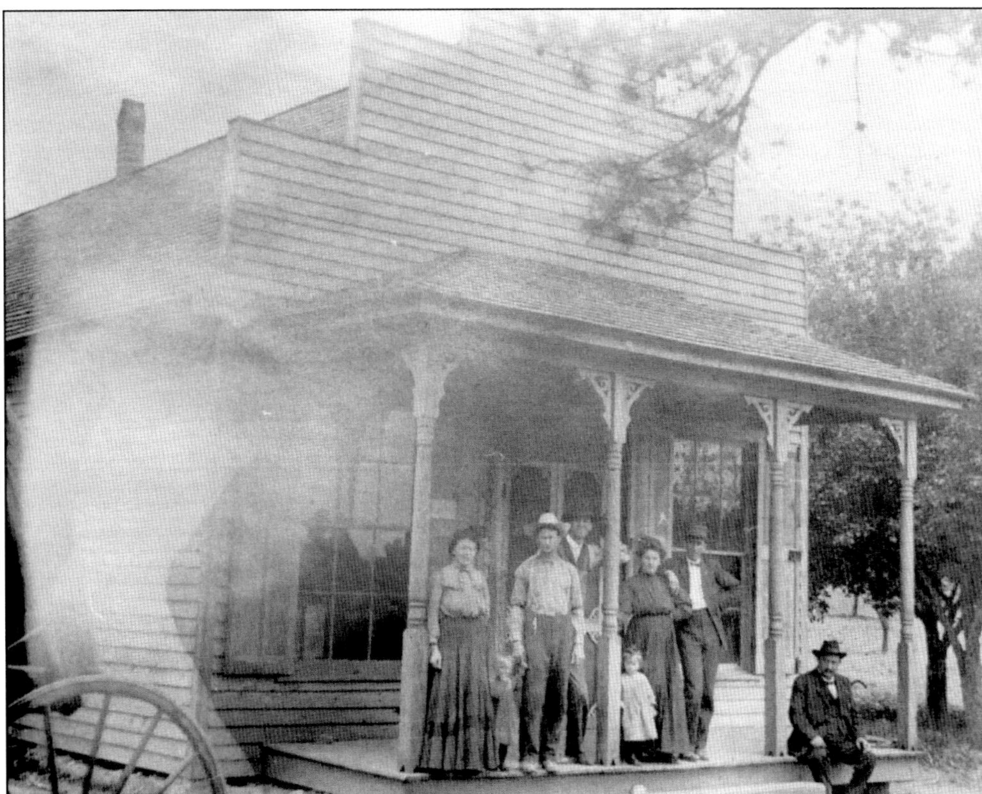

Eller's Store, located on Bringle Ferry Road, was eight and a half miles from Salisbury. The only person positively identified here is D.L. Eagle, third from the left. This photograph was taken on April 27, 1909. (Courtesy Rowan Museum Collection.)

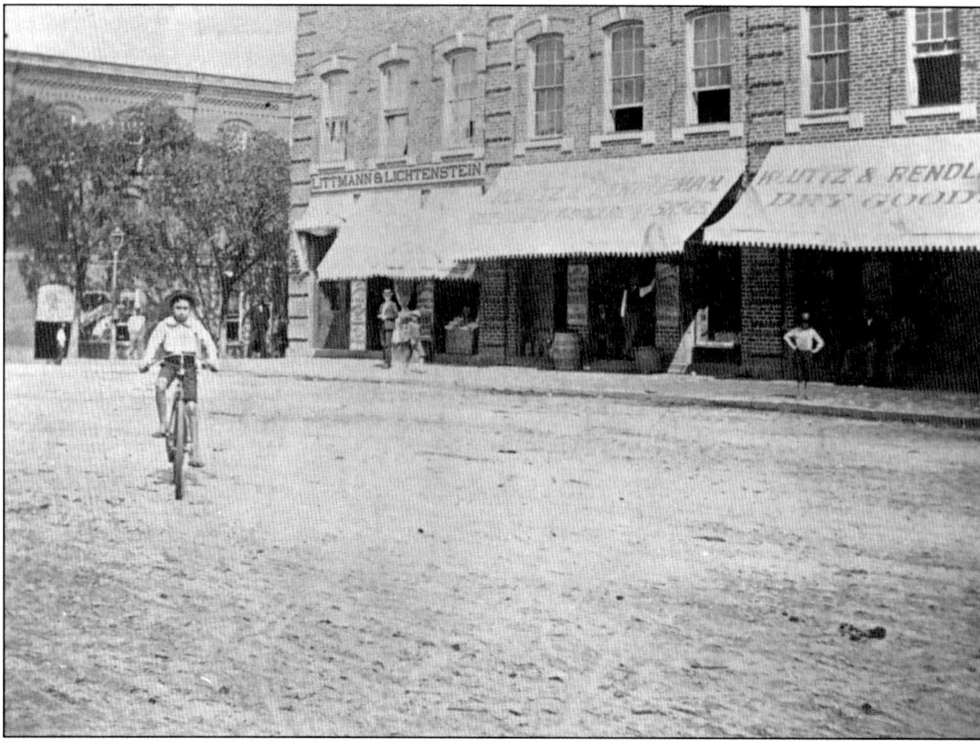

This block of identical buildings, numbers 101–105 on South Main Street, was constructed in 1873. Both Littmann & Lichtenstein and Kluttz & Rendleman dealt in dry goods—textiles, ready-to-wear clothes, sundries, and other consumer items. (Courtesy Rowan Museum Collection.)

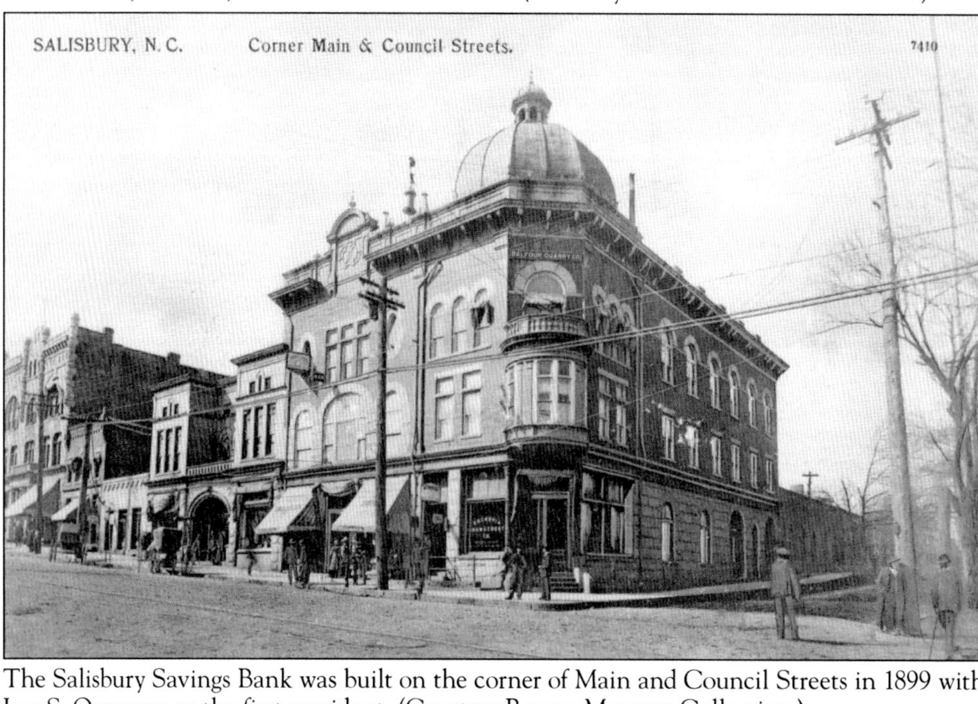

The Salisbury Savings Bank was built on the corner of Main and Council Streets in 1899 with Lee S. Overman as the first president. (Courtesy Rowan Museum Collection.)

M.S. Brown Dealer's Clothing store was located in Murphy's Granite Row. It sold boots, shoes, hats, and furnishings, among other items. The mannequin posing with the gentlemen demonstrates the latest 1890s ready-to-wear suits. (Courtesy Rowan Museum Collection.)

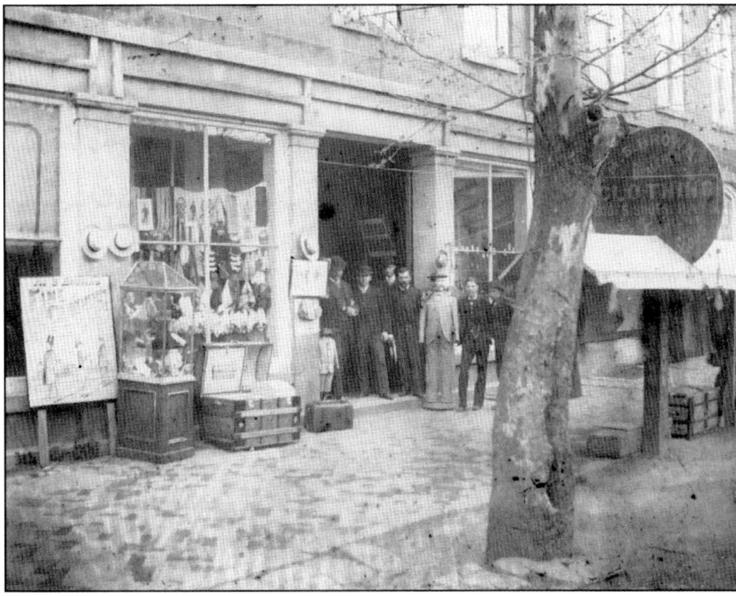

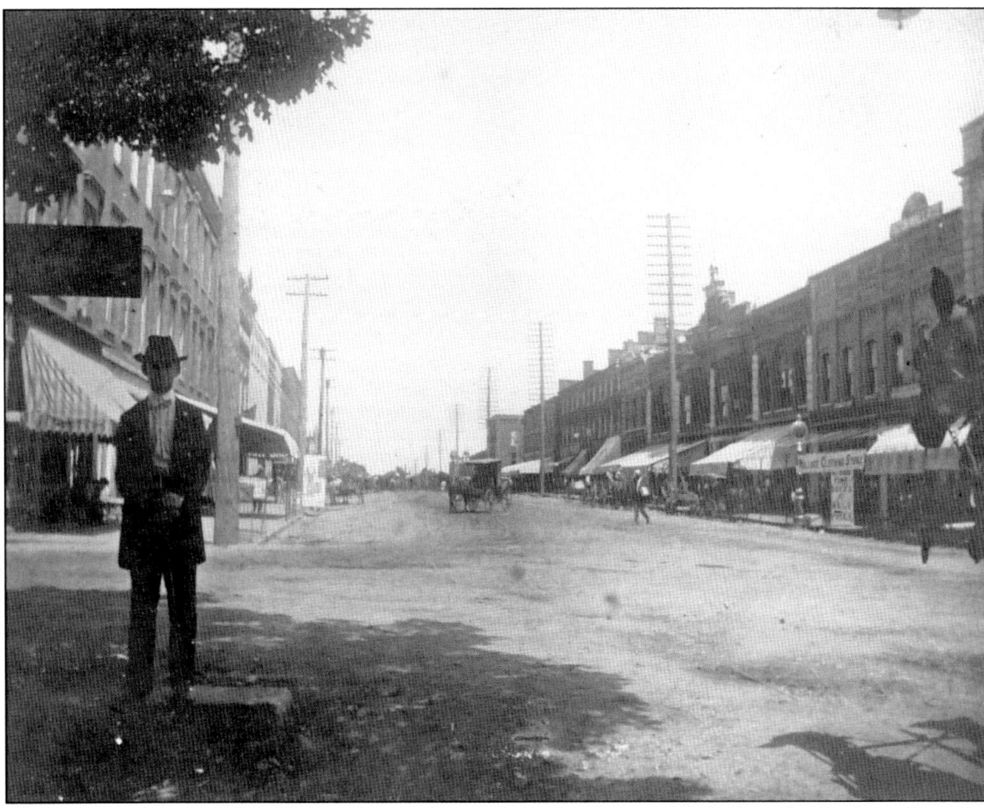

This 1890s photograph of Main Street shows the many awnings used to shade the sidewalks. The store sign on the right is advertising a half-price suit sale at the V. Wallace Clothing Store. Salisbury had developed a large retail infrastructure by this time with all types of goods available from around the globe. (Courtesy Rowan Museum Collection.)

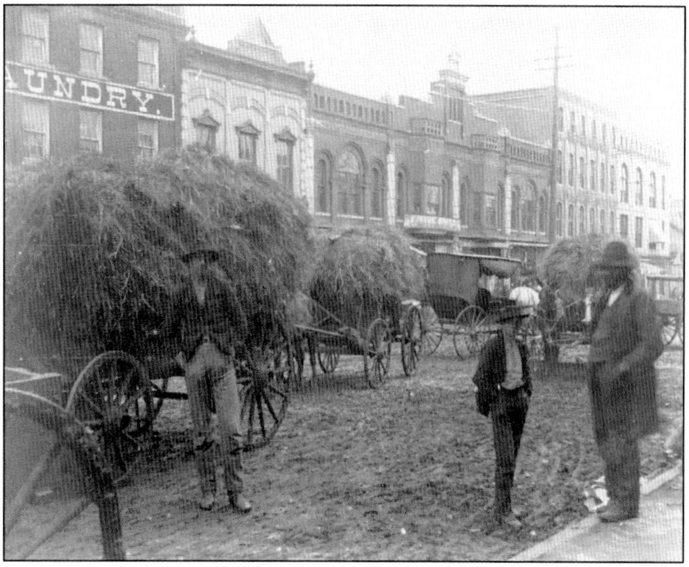

Wagons filled with hay for sale line Main Street in this April 6, 1905, photograph. Most of this hay would have been purchased by dry-goods stores to be resold as feed for horses and cattle. (Courtesy Rowan Museum Collection.)

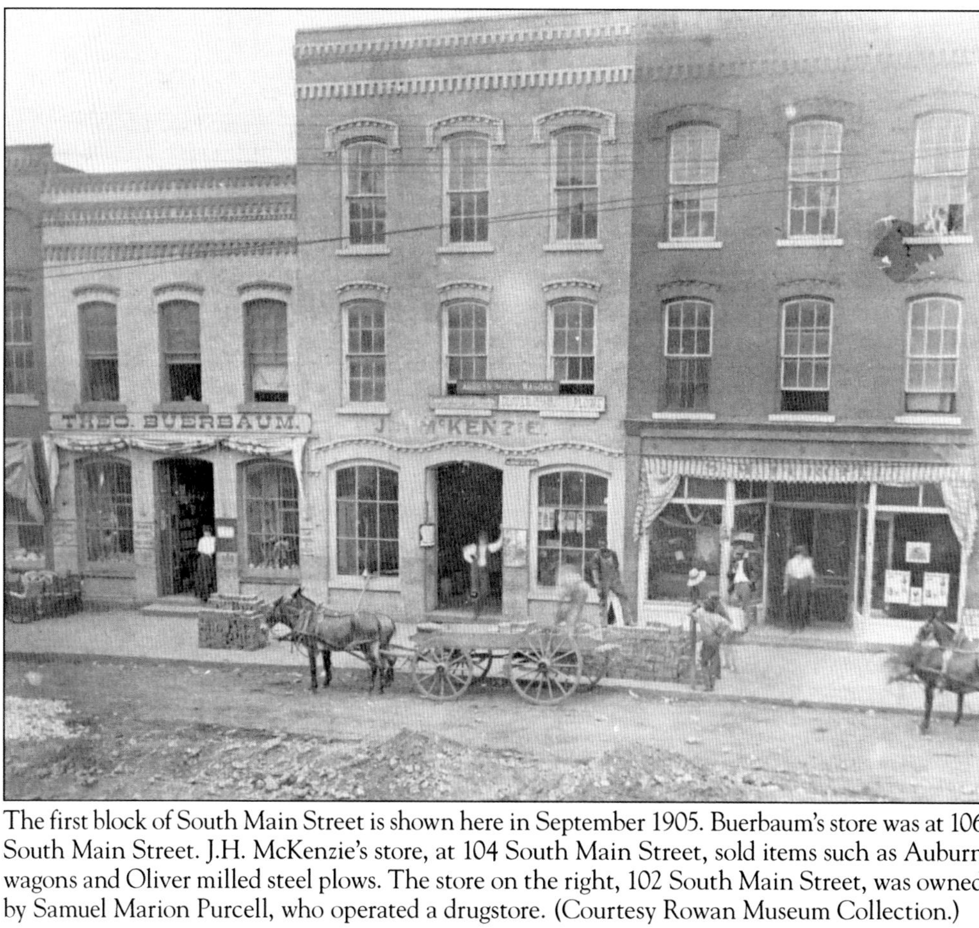

The first block of South Main Street is shown here in September 1905. Buerbaum's store was at 106 South Main Street. J.H. McKenzie's store, at 104 South Main Street, sold items such as Auburn wagons and Oliver milled steel plows. The store on the right, 102 South Main Street, was owned by Samuel Marion Purcell, who operated a drugstore. (Courtesy Rowan Museum Collection.)

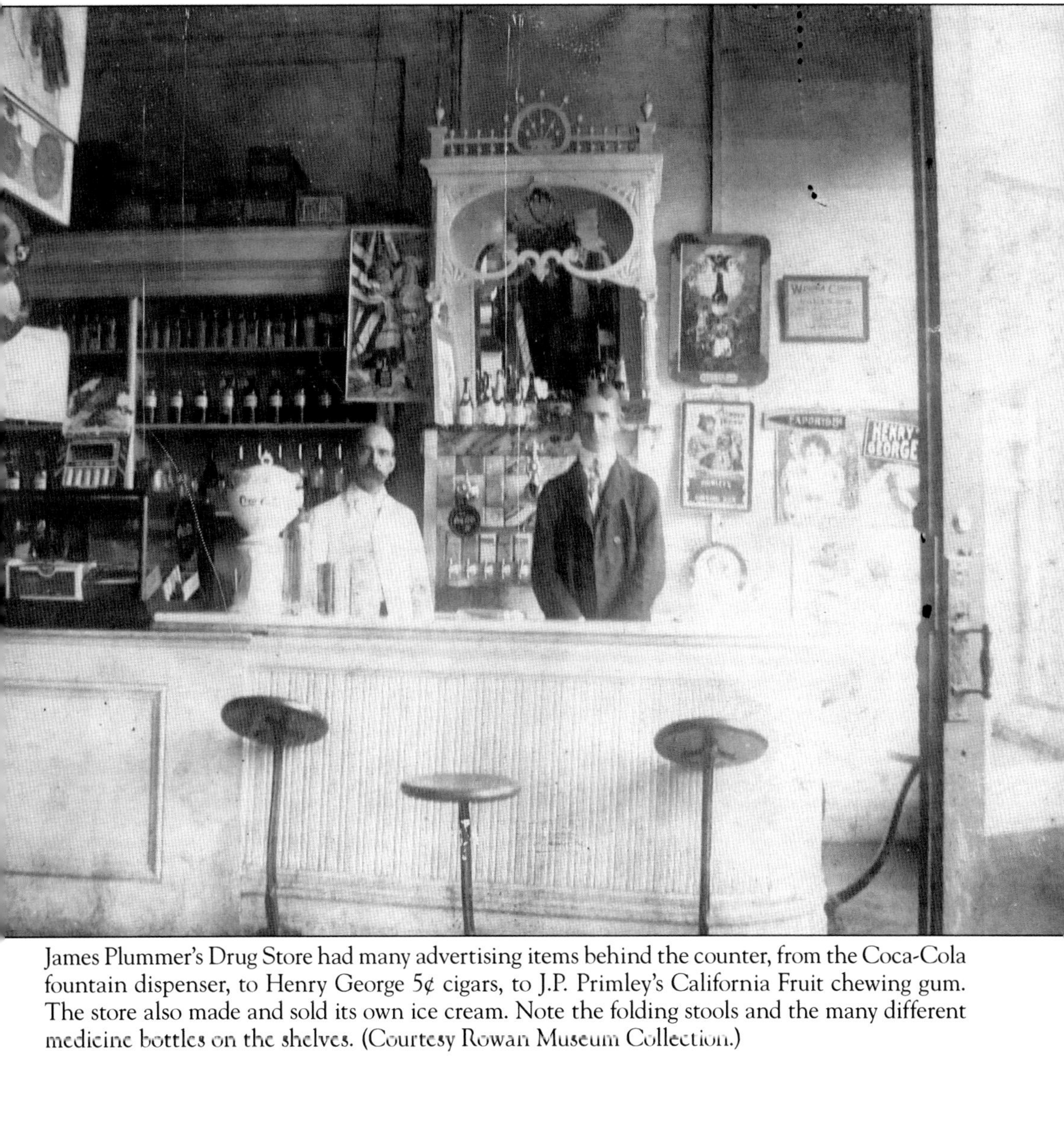

James Plummer's Drug Store had many advertising items behind the counter, from the Coca-Cola fountain dispenser, to Henry George 5¢ cigars, to J.P. Primley's California Fruit chewing gum. The store also made and sold its own ice cream. Note the folding stools and the many different medicine bottles on the shelves. (Courtesy Rowan Museum Collection.)

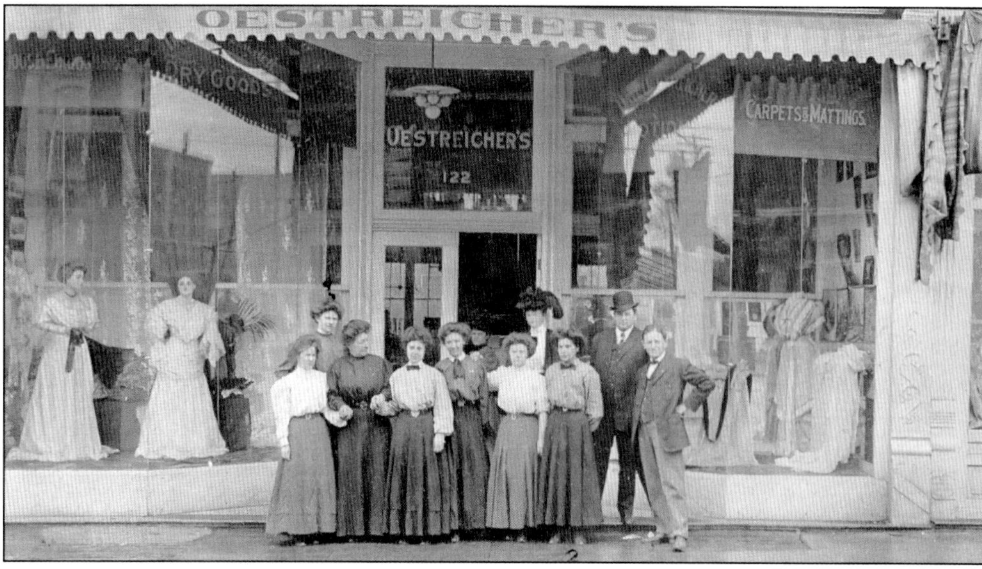

Oestreicher's (pronounced "Ay-strickers") was a general store that carried items such as wedding dresses, dry goods, carpets, matting, and home furnishings. The store was operated by Dave Oestreicher and his wife, Rachel, at 122 South Main Street. This store remained a Salisbury landmark through the 1960s. (Courtesy Edith M. Clark History Room of the Rowan Public Library.)

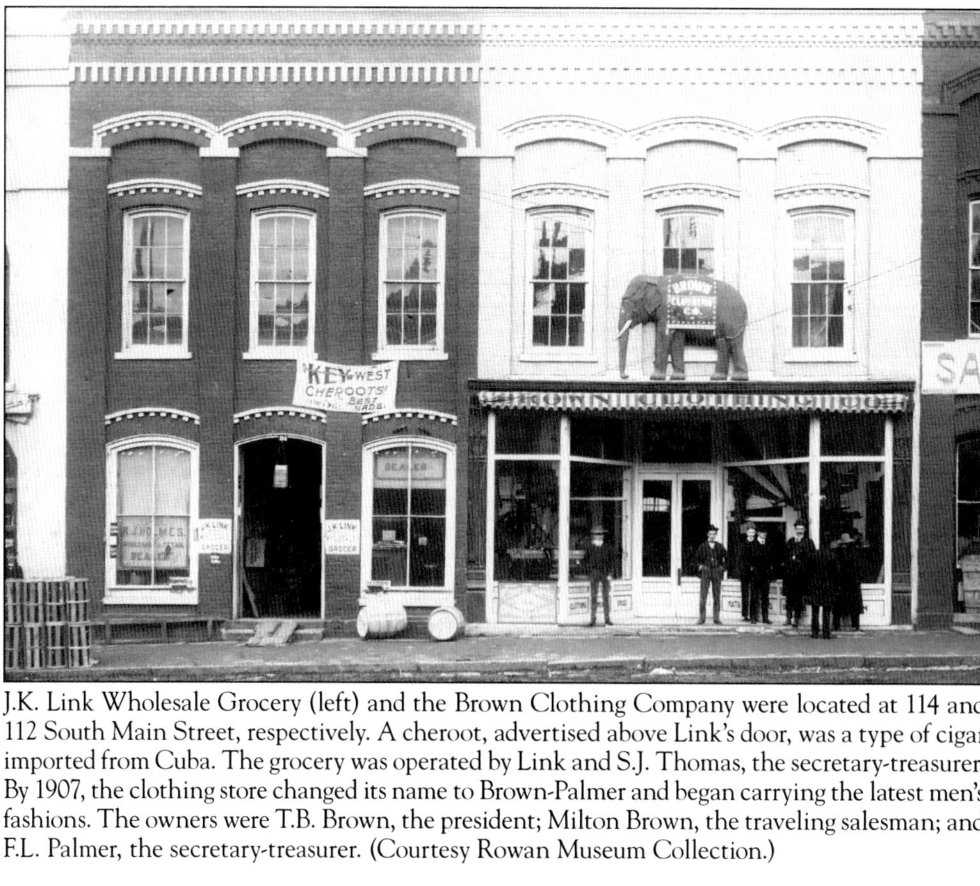

J.K. Link Wholesale Grocery (left) and the Brown Clothing Company were located at 114 and 112 South Main Street, respectively. A cheroot, advertised above Link's door, was a type of cigar imported from Cuba. The grocery was operated by Link and S.J. Thomas, the secretary-treasurer. By 1907, the clothing store changed its name to Brown-Palmer and began carrying the latest men's fashions. The owners were T.B. Brown, the president; Milton Brown, the traveling salesman; and F.L. Palmer, the secretary-treasurer. (Courtesy Rowan Museum Collection.)

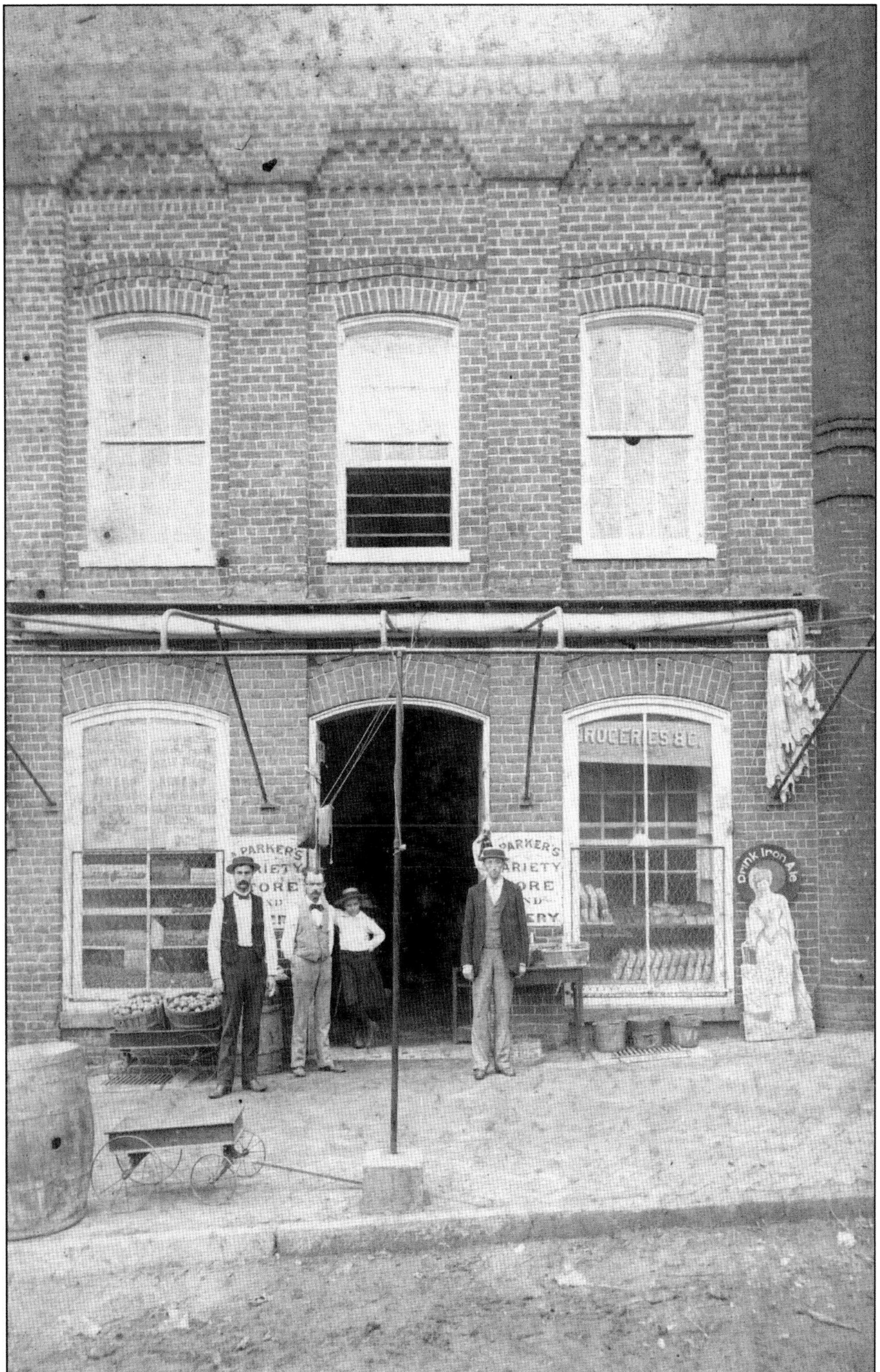

The Parker Variety Store and Grocery, located at 103 North Main Street, was operated by Alex Parker. When extended, the awning would have covered the entire sidewalk, as is evident from the framework. The faint lettering across the top of the facade reads, "A. Parker's Grocery." (Courtesy Edith M. Clark History Room of the Rowan Public Library.)

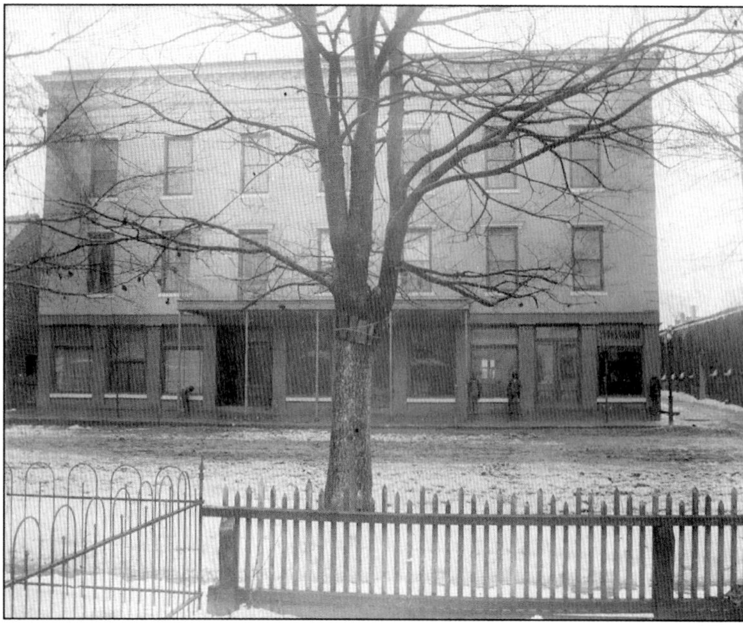

This photograph offers an original view of the Central Hotel, located in the 200 block of South Main. Nathaniel Boyden began construction on the building in 1855, and it opened for business in 1859. For many years, it was known as the Boyden House before being renamed the Central Hotel. (Courtesy Rowan Museum Collection.)

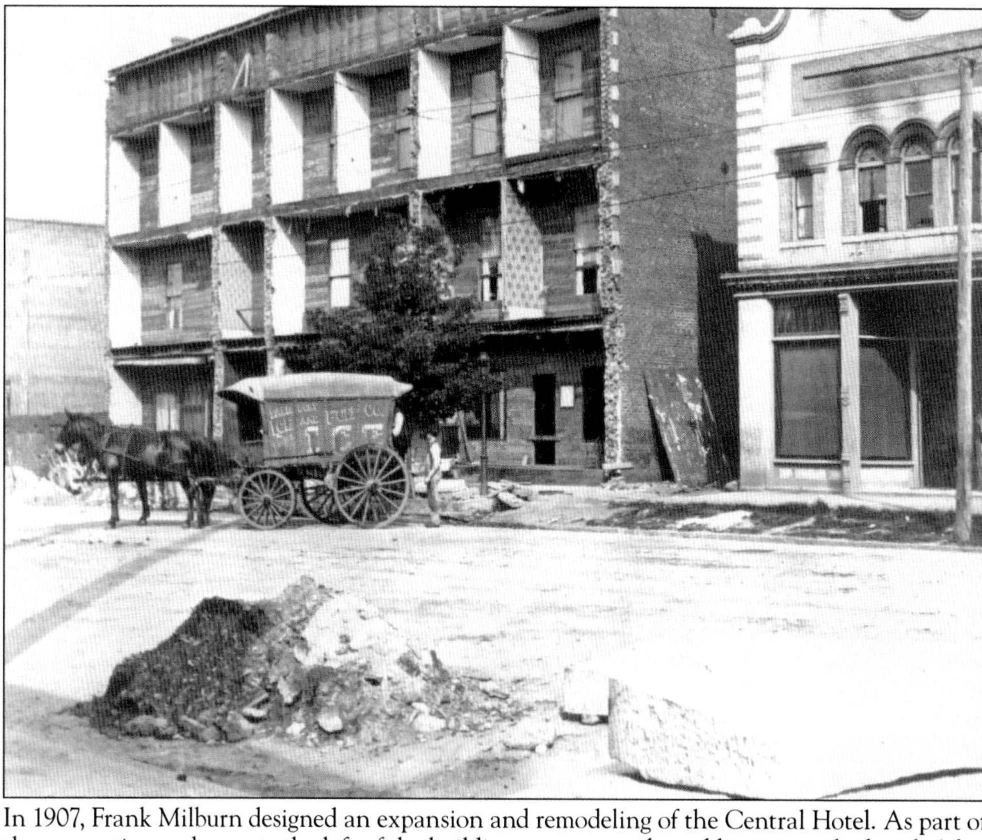

In 1907, Frank Milburn designed an expansion and remodeling of the Central Hotel. As part of the renovations, a house to the left of the building was removed to add rooms to the hotel. After reopening, it was named the Empire Hotel. The wagon was operated by the Salisbury Ice and Fuel Company. (Courtesy Rowan Museum Collection.)

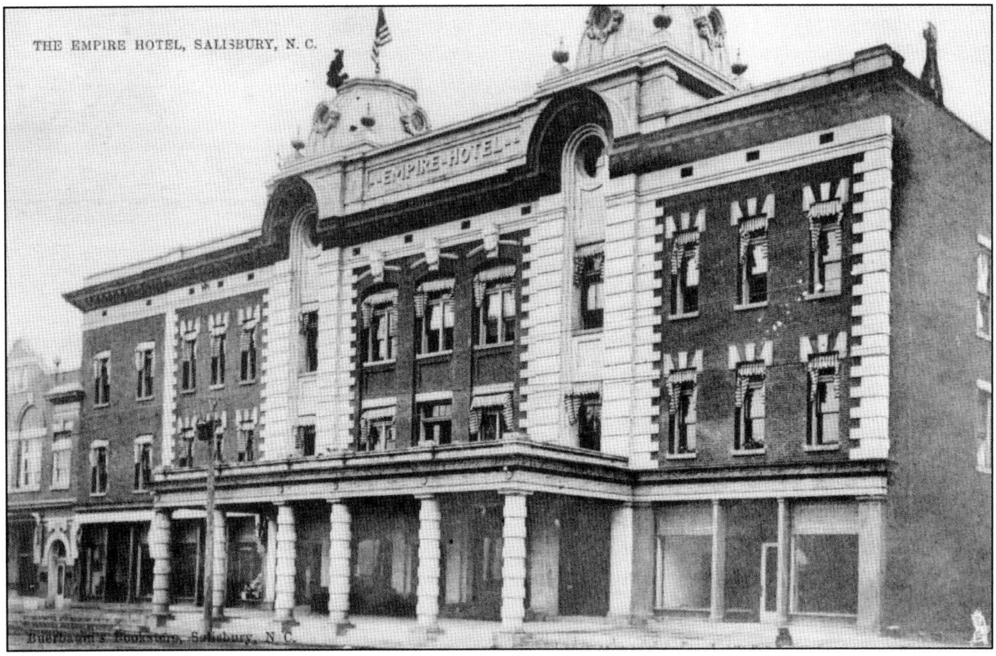

The Empire Hotel is pictured here after its renovation. It was located across from the Meroney Theater, and a tunnel was built under the road for the benefit of the actors. The hotel was operated by O.W. Spencer and Laura B. Crouch in the 1910s. (Courtesy Rowan Museum Collection.)

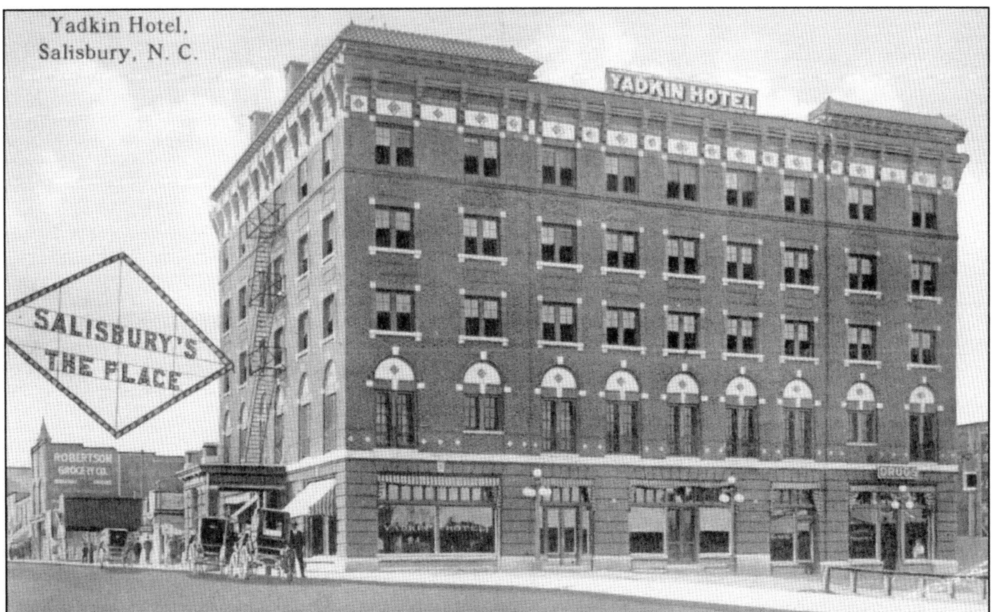

The Yadkin Hotel was for many years a mainstay for weary travelers coming through Salisbury. The large sign on the left may have convinced travelers to pause and stay a day or two, eager to know why Salisbury was so special. W.C. Pettie operated the hotel when it opened in 1912. Today, this building is known as the Yadkin House Apartments and has recently undergone a renovation. (Courtesy Rowan Museum Collection.)

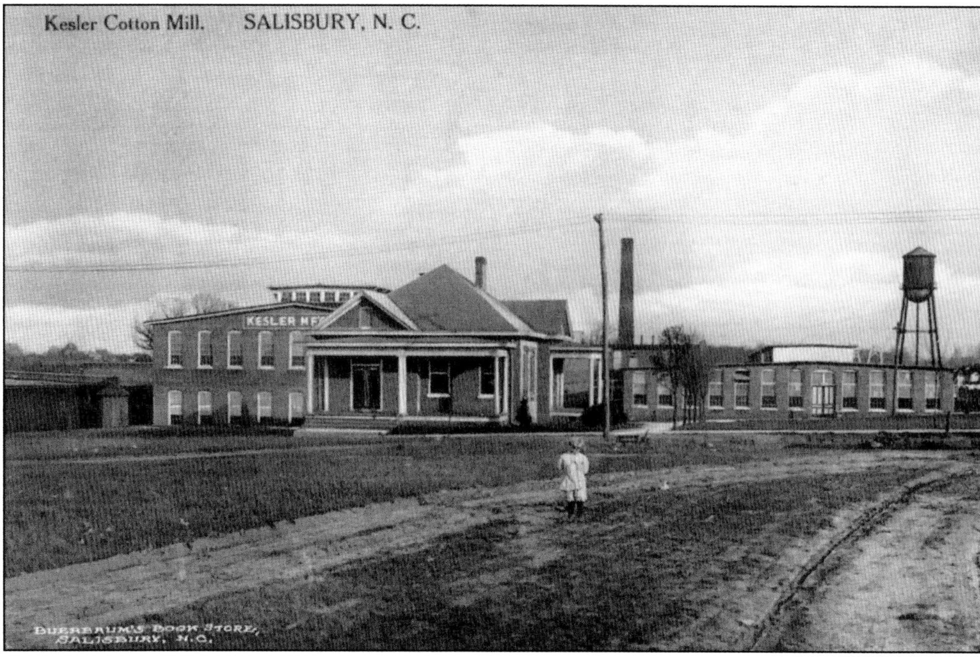

The Kesler Cotton Mill, also known as Kesler Manufacturing, was built in 1895 in a location near Park Avenue and Boundary Street. In the 1910s, James W. Cannon was president, son Charles A. Cannon was vice president, and C.E. Stephenson was secretary-treasurer. The facility later became Cannon Mills Plant No. 7 and operated until 2000. (Courtesy Rowan Museum Collection.)

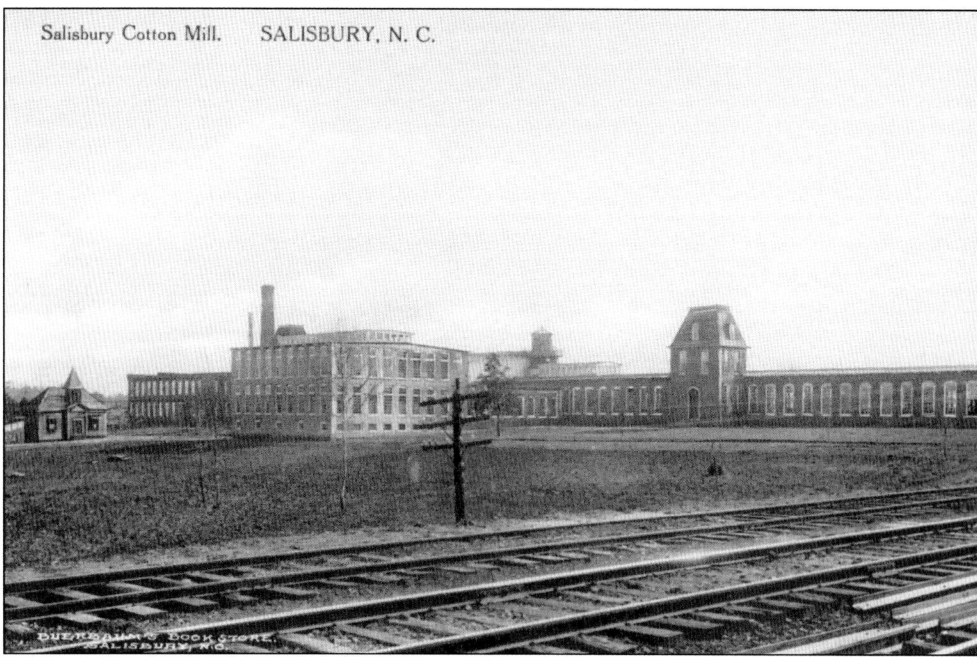

The Salisbury Cotton Mill was built in 1888 at 705 South Railroad Avenue. Within just 10 years of operation, it became one of the largest mills in the state. Cone Mills purchased the facility in 1920 and eventually converted production from chamois and flannel to denim and chambray. The mill closed in 1999. (Courtesy Rowan Museum Collection.)

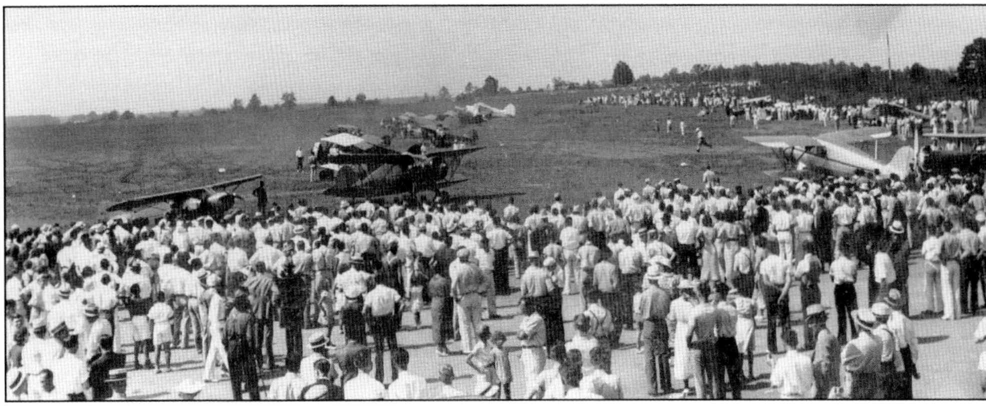

The Salisbury Municipal Airport was dedicated on November 11, 1930, and commemorated by the Salisbury Chamber of Commerce. From that point forward, air shows became a common sight, bringing in stunt pilots and the latest aircraft. These two photographs were taken at a Salisbury air show on August 15, 1937. Hundreds of spectators lined the field to get a clear view of the action. (Both, courtesy Edith M. Clark History Room of the Rowan Public Library.)

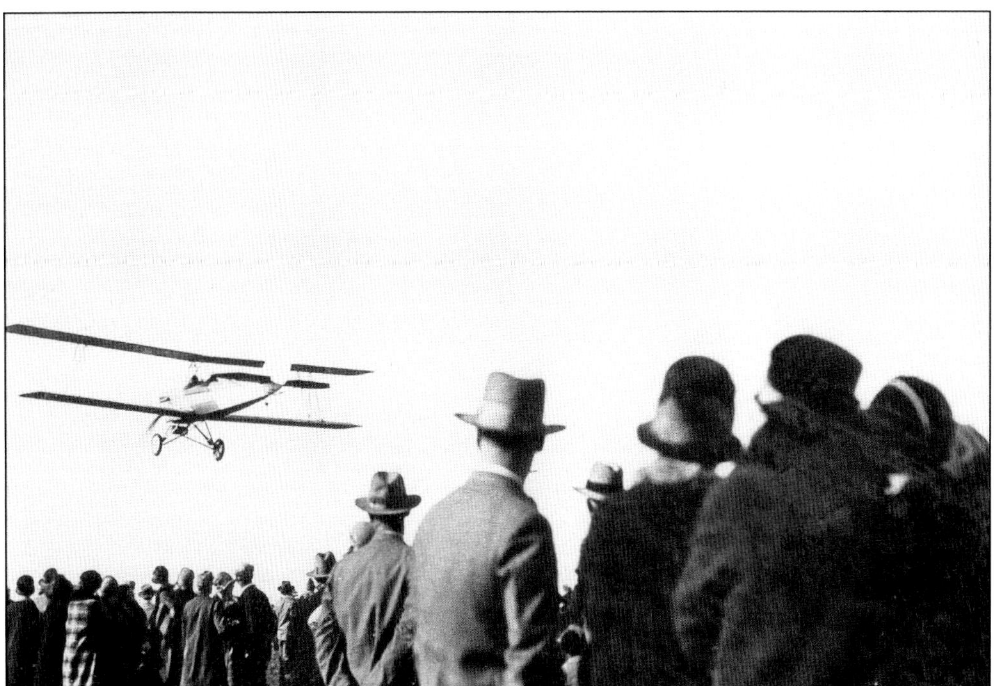

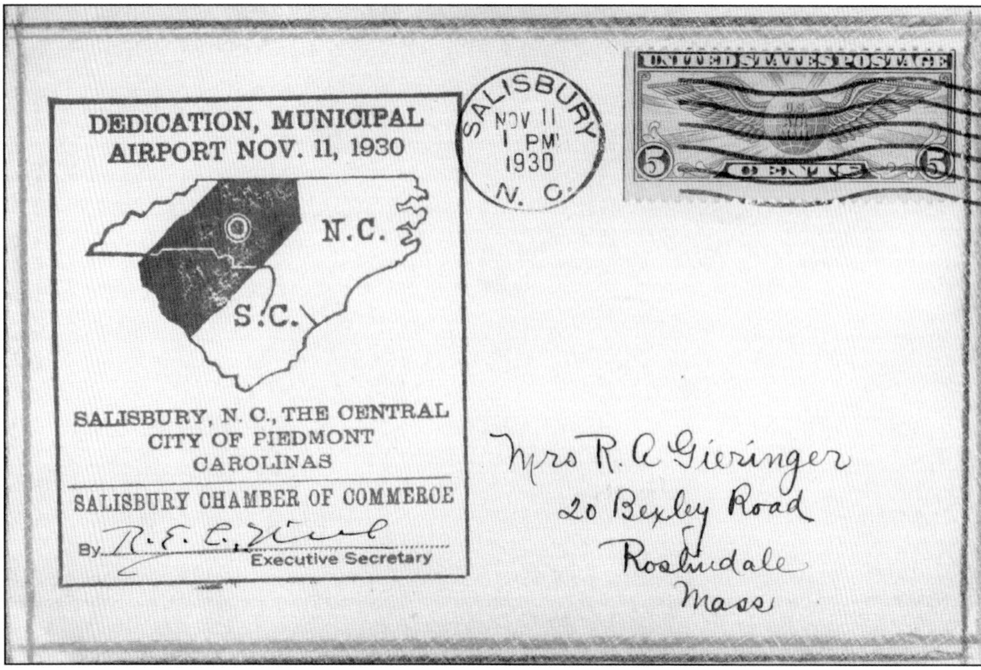

This is a commemorative postal cover for the Salisbury Municipal Airport dedication on November 11, 1930. (Courtesy Larry K. Neal Jr. collection.)

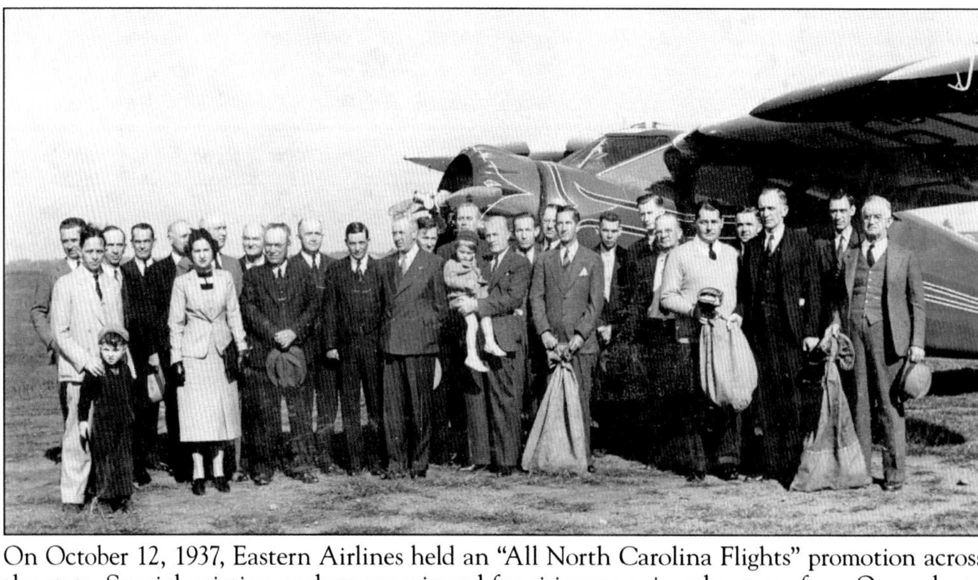

On October 12, 1937, Eastern Airlines held an "All North Carolina Flights" promotion across the state. Special aviation cachets were issued for cities spanning the state, from Ocracoke to Asheville. Salisbury was included in the promotion, and representatives of the city and the airport pose with mailbags ready to be flown to Charlotte, each postmarked from Salisbury, to be carried on Eastern flights. (Courtesy Edith M. Clark History Room of the Rowan Public Library.)

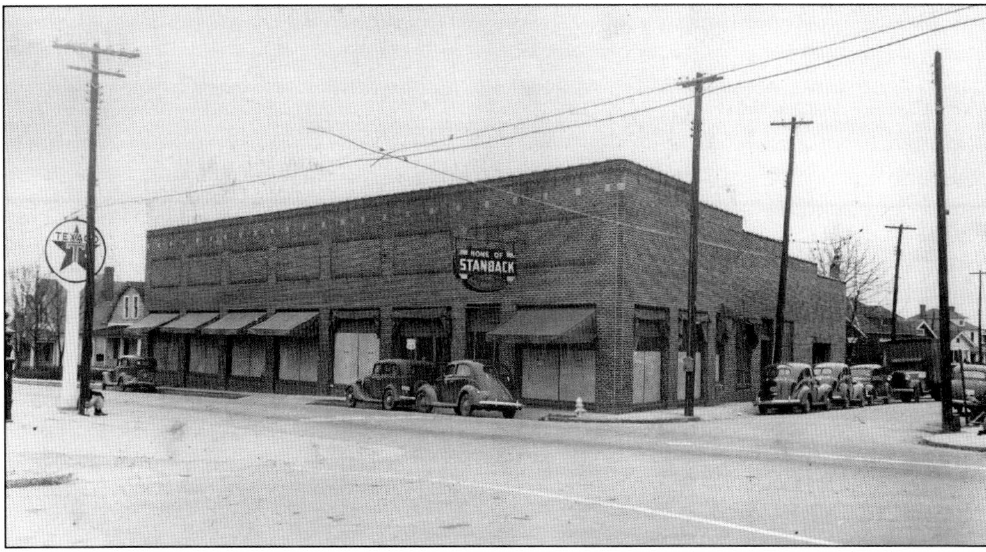

Stanback Headache Powder was invented in the early 1900s by Thomas M. Stanback. In 1911, he moved the company to Spencer, North Carolina, the home of Spencer Shops. The company continued to thrive and constructed a new headquarters and plant building in 1937 at the corner of Main Street and Klumac Road. In 1998, Stanback was purchased by The Block Drug Company, and all production eventually ceased in Salisbury. (Courtesy Edith M. Clark History Room of the Rowan Public Library.)

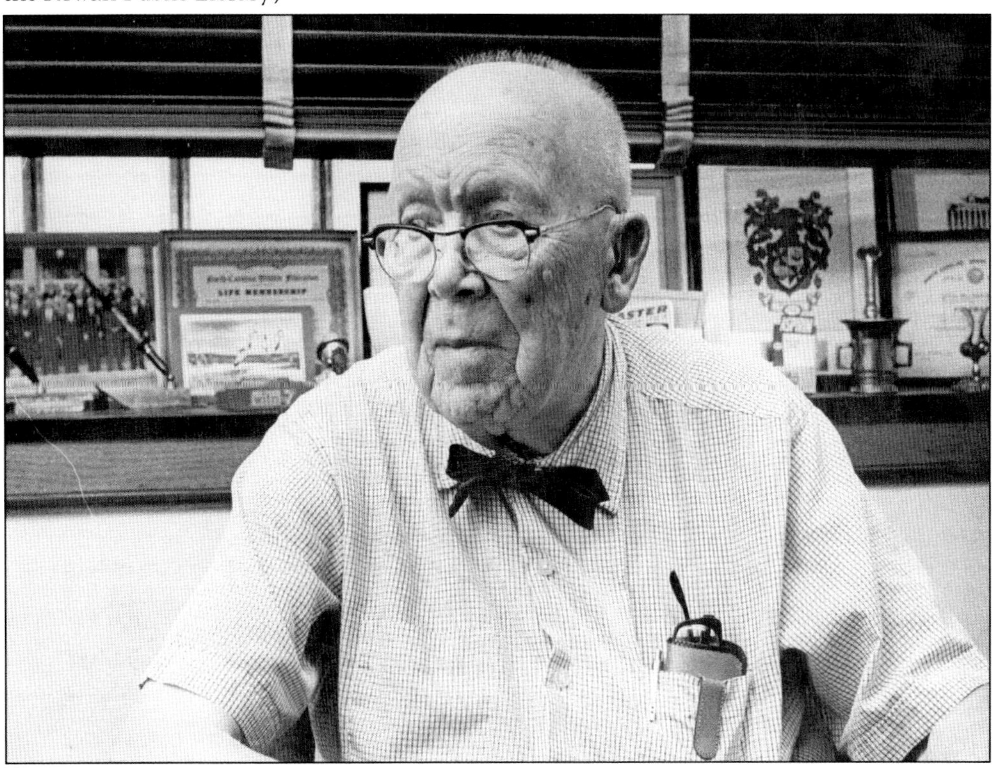
Thomas Stanback is shown here in his later years, when he was still active in the operation of the company. (Courtesy Edith M. Clark History Room of the Rowan Public Library.)

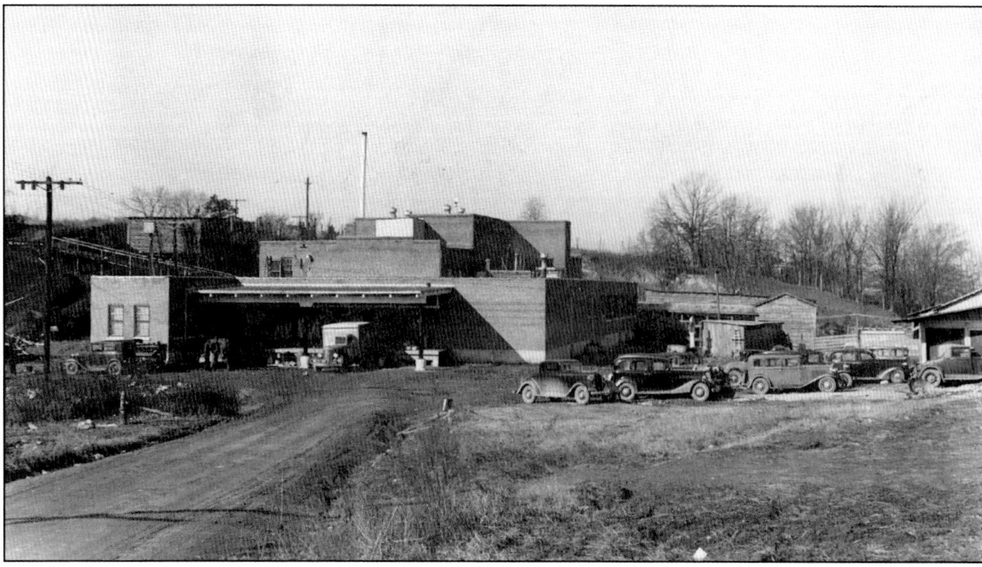

The White Packing Company was located at the end of West Liberty Street. During the 1940s, the officers were as follows: Wesley M. Elliott, president; Benjamin B. White, first vice president; W. Marvin Snyder, second vice president; and Annie L.W. Cress, secretary-treasurer. The company primarily dressed and packed various types of meat products. (Courtesy Edith M. Clark History Room of the Rowan Public Library.)

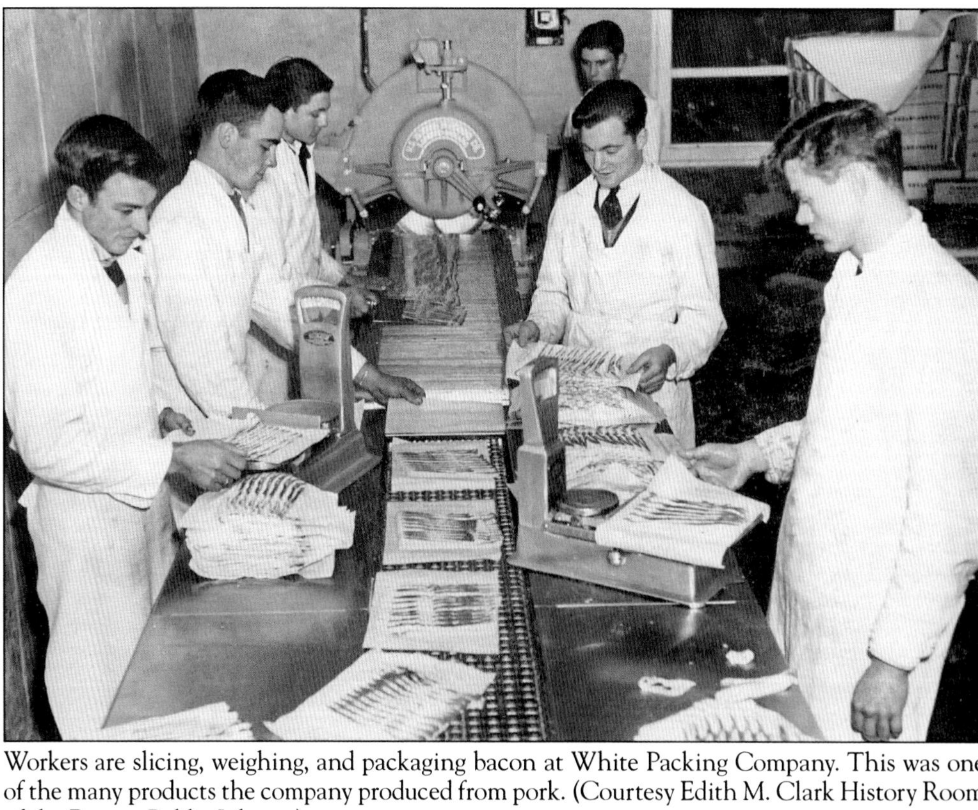

Workers are slicing, weighing, and packaging bacon at White Packing Company. This was one of the many products the company produced from pork. (Courtesy Edith M. Clark History Room of the Rowan Public Library.)

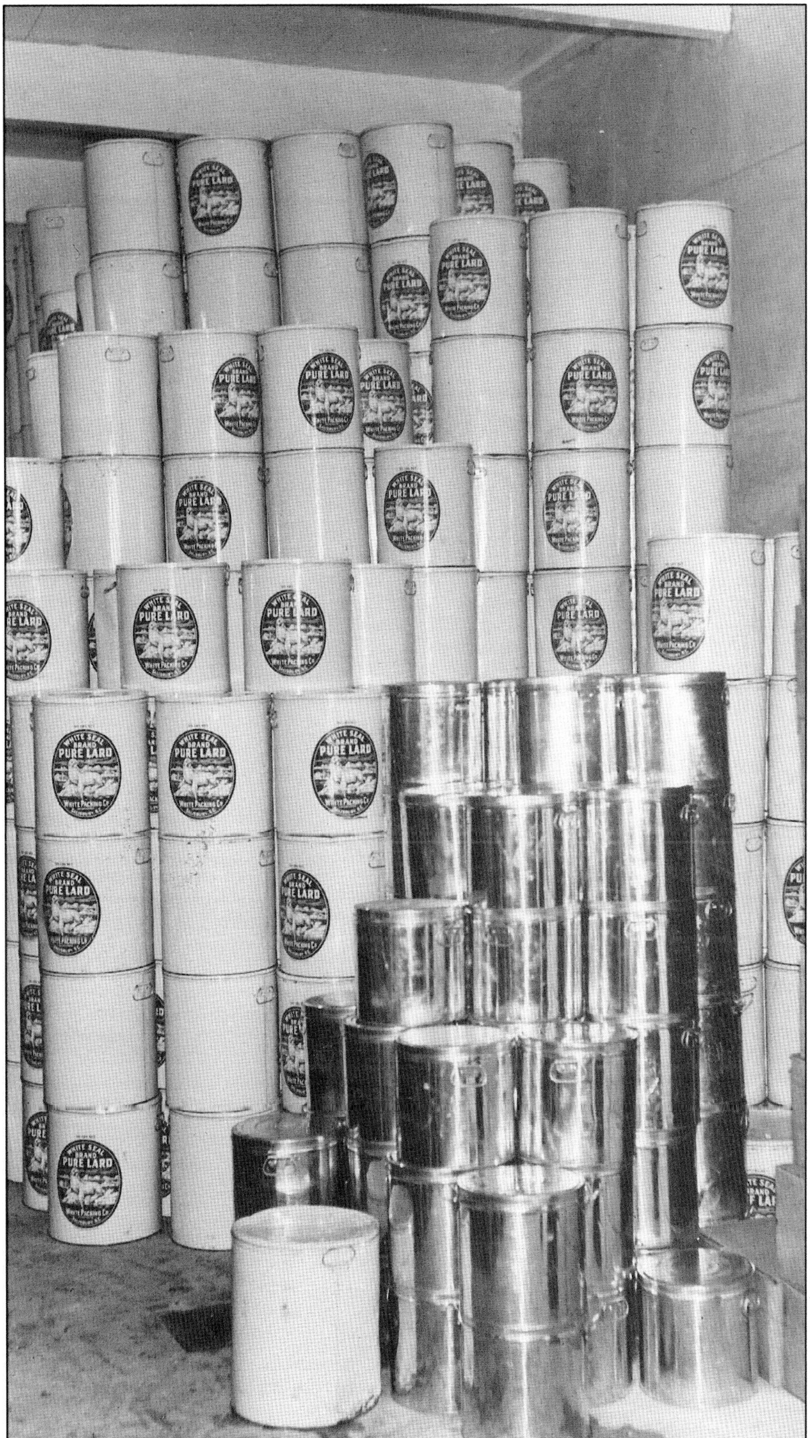

Cans of pure lard are packaged and ready for sale. These bulk-sized containers would be sold to restaurants or schools for cooking. Lard was made by processing the fat from a hog. (Courtesy Edith M. Clark History Room of the Rowan Public Library.)

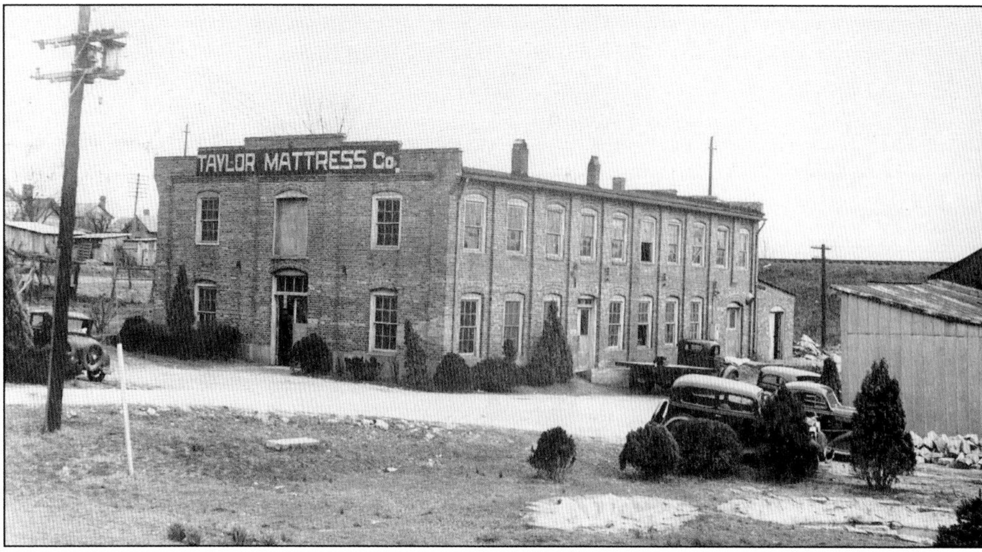

Taylor Mattress Company was started in 1905 and is still in the business of constructing and selling mattresses. The original building was razed several years ago, but the company is still based out of the original location at 1036 South Main Street. J.D. Heilig was both the general manager and secretary-treasurer when the plant began operation. (Courtesy Edith M. Clark History Room of the Rowan Public Library.)

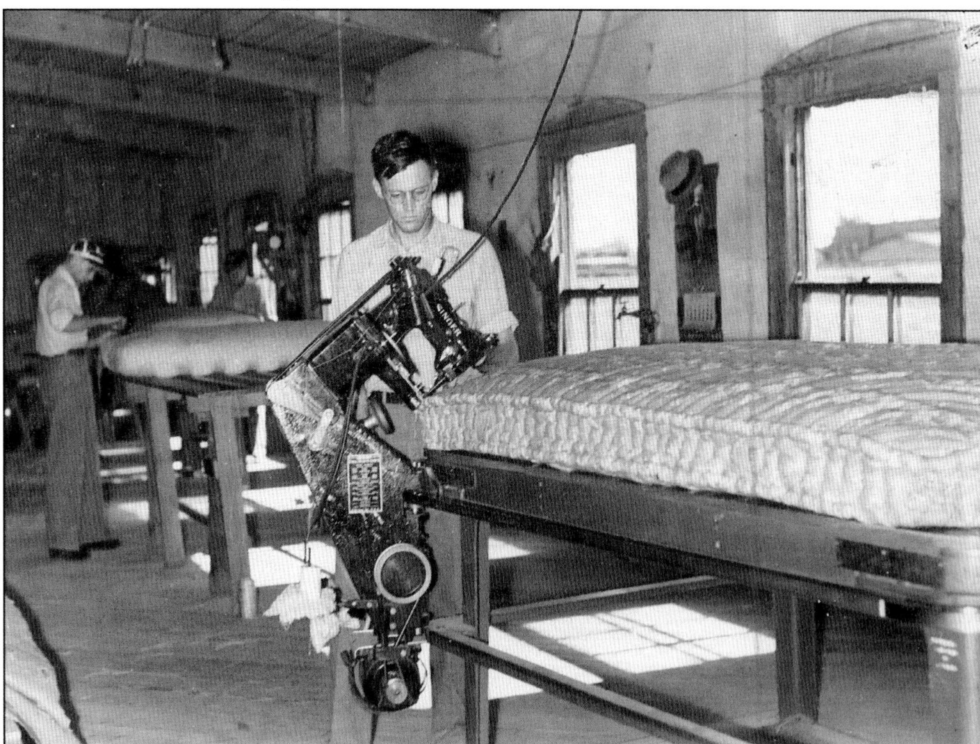

Workers use automated machines, like the one shown here, to sew the outer cover onto the mattress. One of the company's well-known mattresses was the "Royal Sleeper," developed in the early years of production. (Courtesy Edith M. Clark History Room of the Rowan Public Library.)

Salisbury is home to a well-known, bright red cherry-flavored soft drink. Cheerwine was first produced in 1917 by the Mint Cola Bottling Company. L.D. Peeler wanted a unique soft drink to sell, and he worked with cherries to create the special flavor. It was an immediate success, as evident by this delivery truck loaded with cases of the drink. A distinctive bottle was designed just for this soda. (Courtesy Edith M. Clark History Room of the Rowan Public Library.)

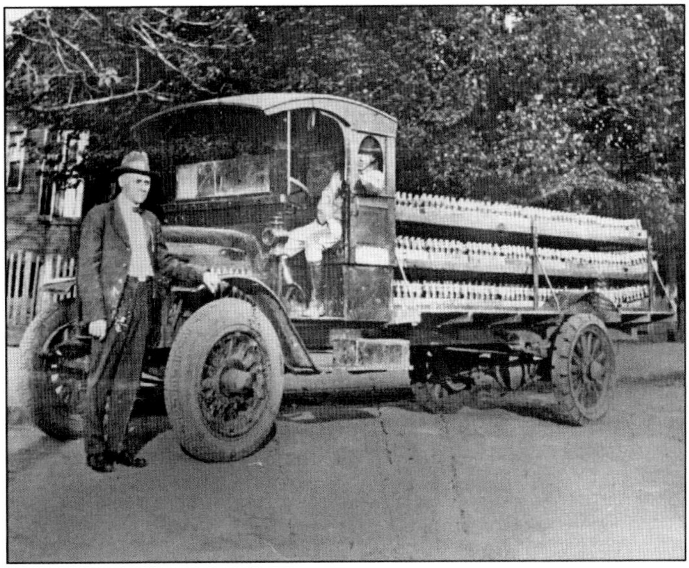

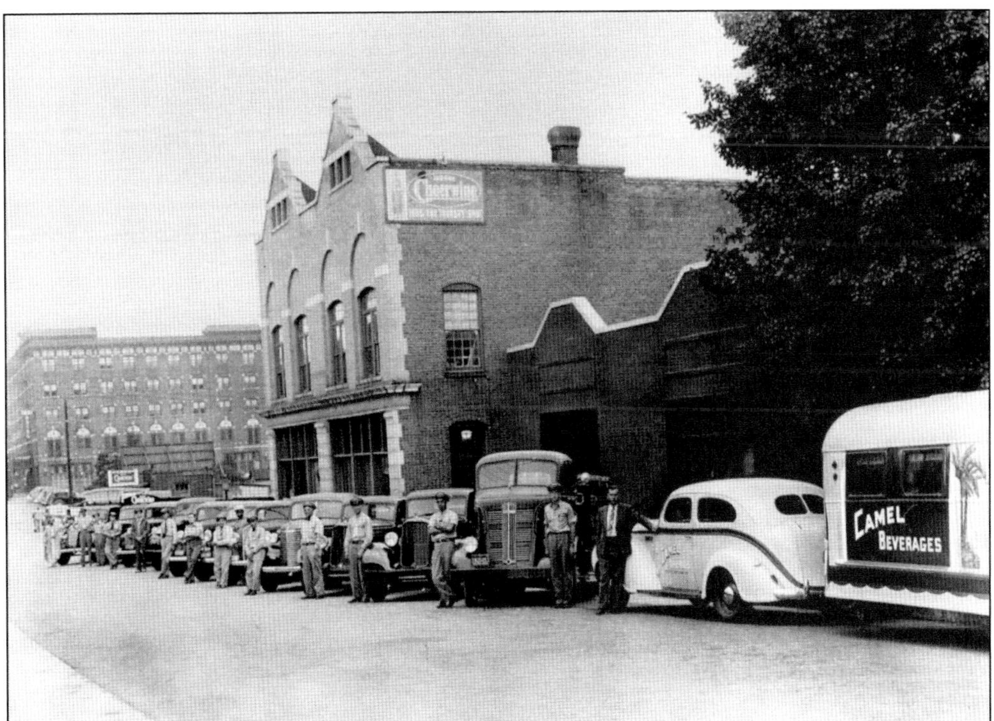

Cheerwine was headquartered on Council Street, just across the tracks from the Yadkin Hotel. By the 1930s, Camel Soda had been added to the company's product line. Cheerwine remained at this location until 1967, when it moved to its present location on Jake Alexander Boulevard. (Courtesy Edith M. Clark History Room of the Rowan Public Library.)

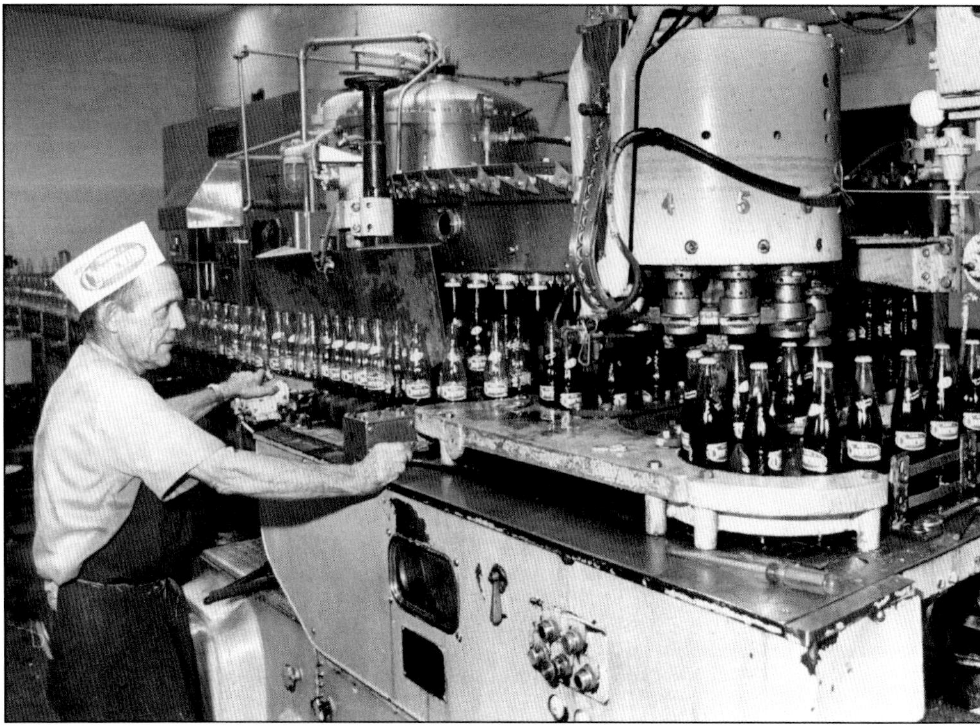

In this photograph, bottles of Cheerwine are filled and capped as they work their way along the conveyor line. For many years, the only way to obtain a Cheerwine was to visit or live near Rowan County. Today, Cheerwine has distribution across the East Coast and can be purchased in California. (Courtesy Edith M. Clark History Room of the Rowan Public Library.)

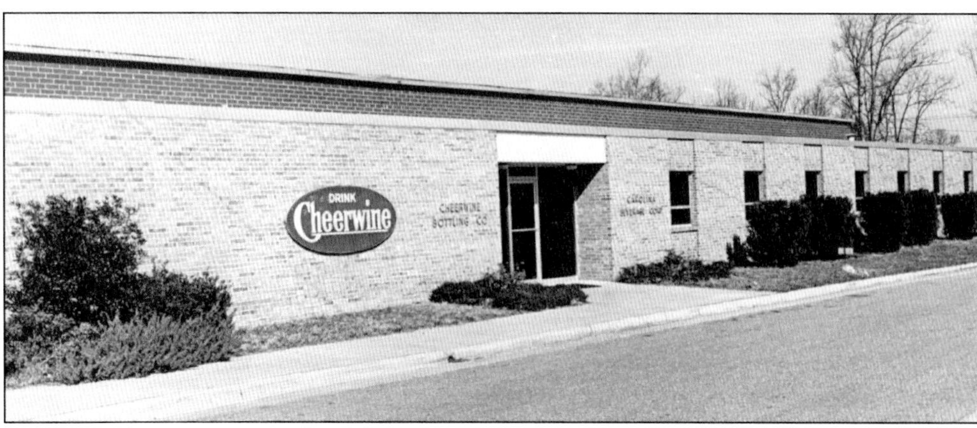

The current offices of the Cheerwine Bottling Company are located off Jake Alexander Boulevard near Rowan Cabarrus Community College. Besides Cheerwine, Carolina Beverage Corporation also carries Blue Mist bottled water and Cool Moon. (Courtesy Edith M. Clark History Room of the Rowan Public Library.)

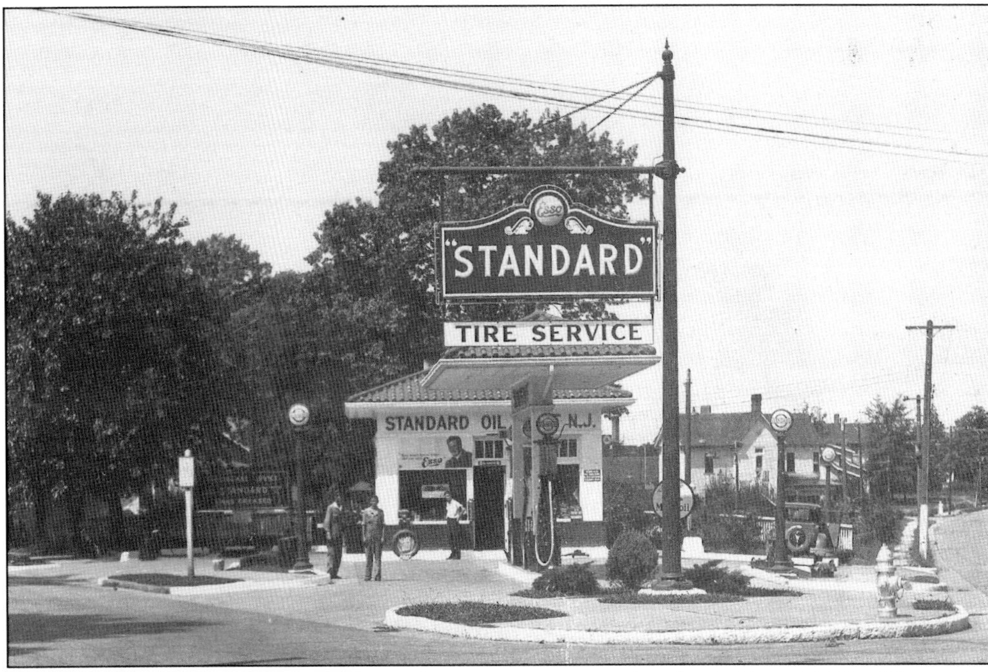

Pictured here is the Buck Rogers Service Station as it appeared in the 1920s and 1930s. The station was located at the corner of South Fulton Street and Lincolnton Roads. This was a distributor for the Standard Oil Company of New Jersey and later became an Exxon station. (Courtesy Edith M. Clark History Room of the Rowan Public Library.)

The Gulf Point Service Station was located at the corner of South Main Street and Fulton Street, where Curt and Gerry's ice cream shop is today. Operators listed in the 1950s included Lloyd J. Parker, Fred W. Leazer, and Preston W. Lesley. (Courtesy Edith M. Clark History Room of the Rowan Public Library.)

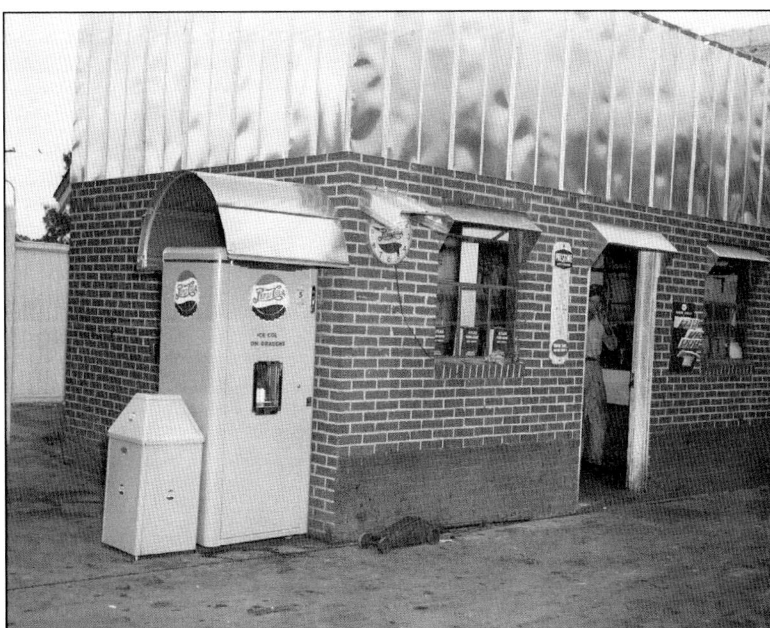

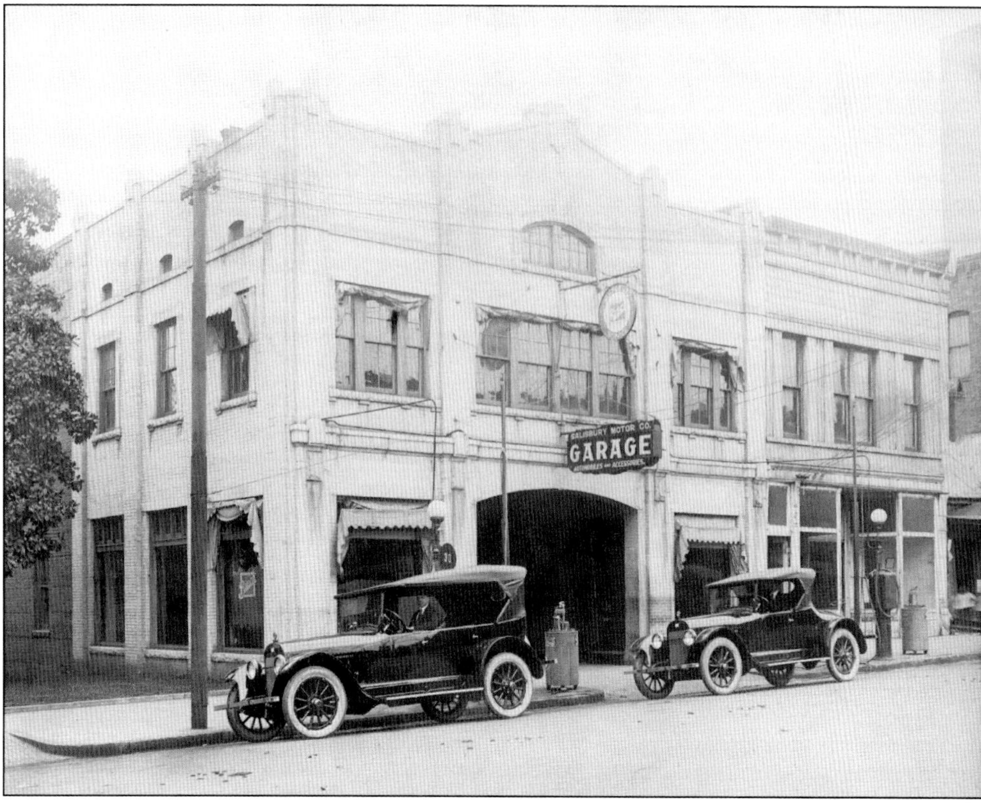

The Salisbury Motor Company, which opened in 1919 in the 100 block on West Innes Street, advertised the latest Buick automobiles for sale. This 1922 photograph shows two new Buicks, one a touring car and the other a coupe. Gas was available for 30¢ a gallon right off the curb. The company built a showroom and service center at the corner of West Innes and Craig Streets in 1946. Based on the design of the new building, General Motors wanted to display cars on the roof, and a reinforced ramp was constructed for that purpose. Though this dealership is still in business, it lost its Buick franchise in 2009. (Courtesy Salisbury Motor Company.)

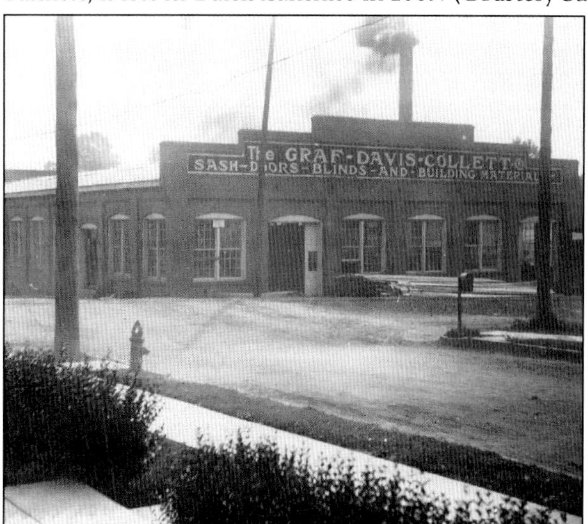

The Graf-Davis-Collett Company was located at the corner of North Long and Lafayette Streets. Albert H. Graf was the president, Arthur E. Davis was the treasurer, and Noah W. Collett was the vice president. Their phone number in 1917 was just 93. By the 1940s, the name had been changed to the Rowan Lumber & Supply Company, and the firm was located at 600 North Long Street. Arthur Davis had become president, Albert Graf vice president, and Dan Nicholas treasurer. (Courtesy Edith M. Clark History Room of the Rowan Public Library.)

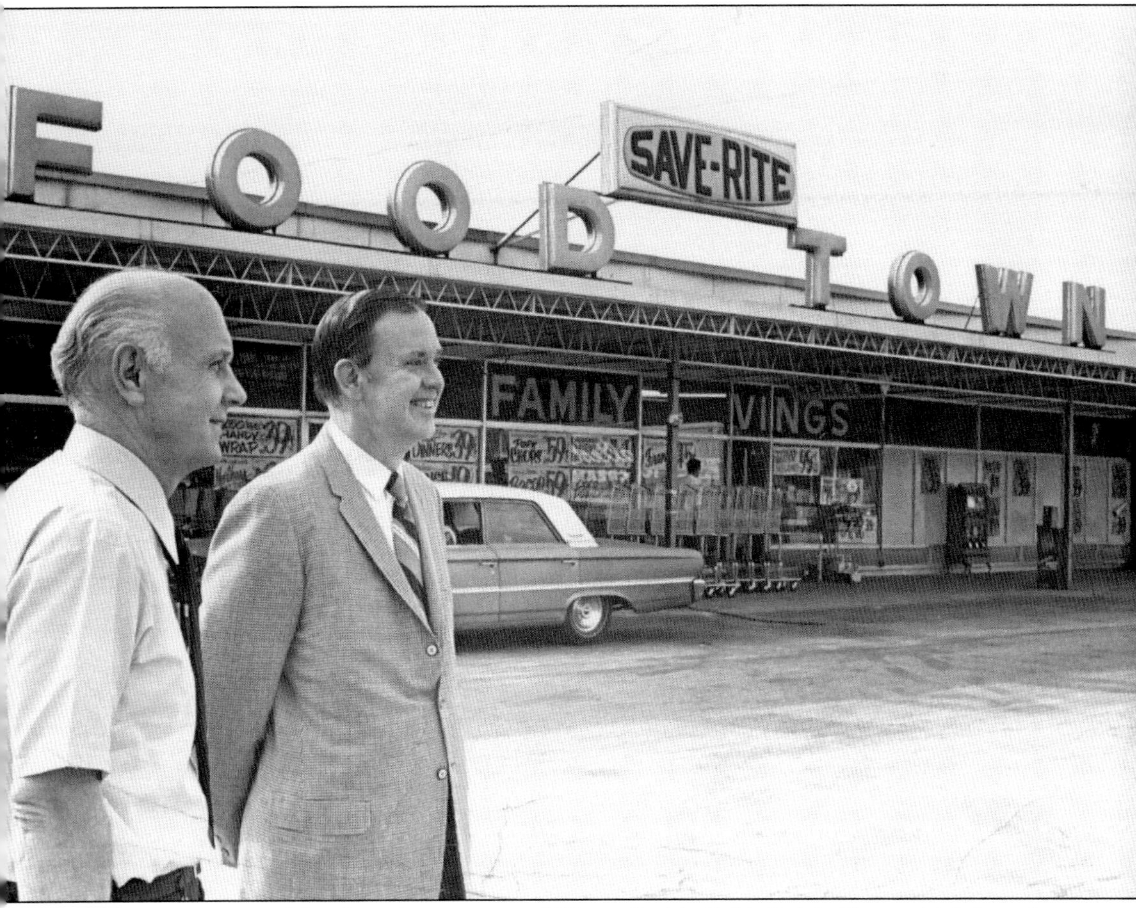

Food Town was started by three businessmen, Wilson Smith (left), Ralph Ketner (right), and Brown Ketner (not pictured), in 1957. The company has always been headquartered in Salisbury and is located today off Jake Alexander Boulevard. The company was sold to the Belgian firm Delhaize in 1983, which changed the name to Food Lion. Today, this grocery chain is located in 11 states, from Delaware to Virginia. (Courtesy Edith M. Clark History Room of the Rowan Public Library.)

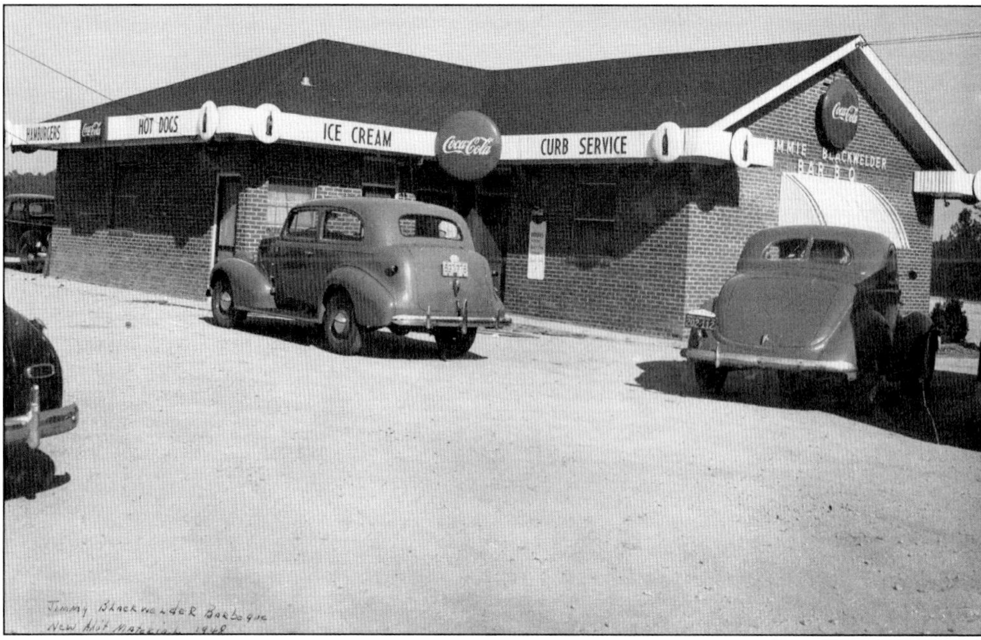

Jimmie Blackwelder Bar-B-Q was located on West Innes Street, near the intersection with Statesville Boulevard. It also had a restaurant at 314 Depot Street. Blackwelder became famous for selling barbeque from food trucks, and restaurants were established between Charlotte and Raleigh. Today, this site is home to Hendrix Barbeque, which carries on this Salisbury tradition. (Both, courtesy Edith M. Clark History Room of the Rowan Public Library.)

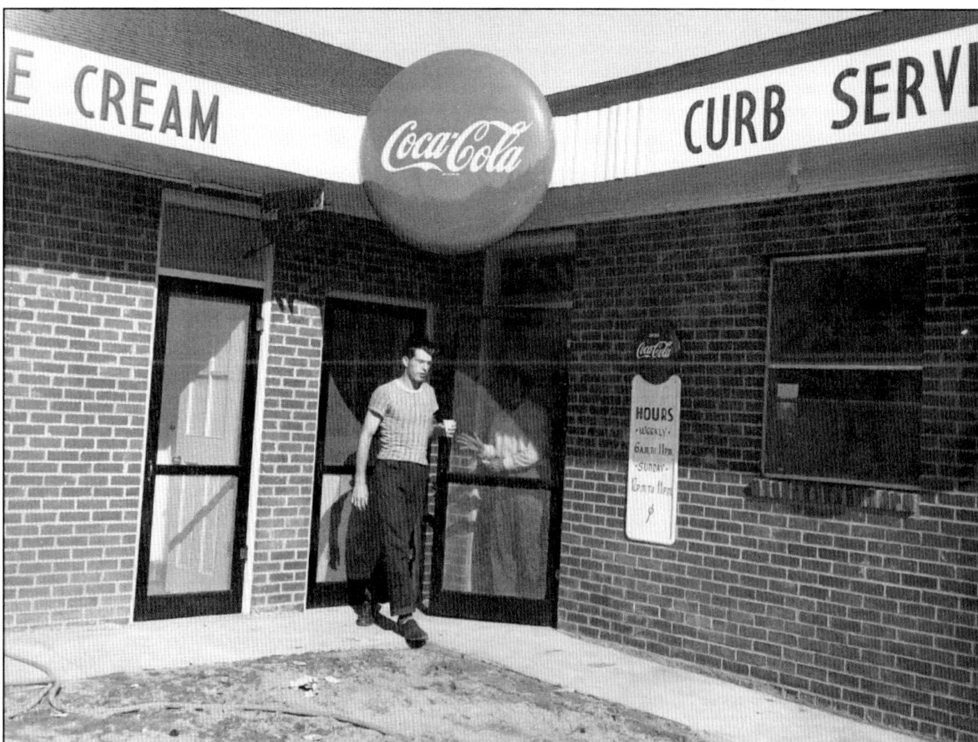

Five

CHURCHES

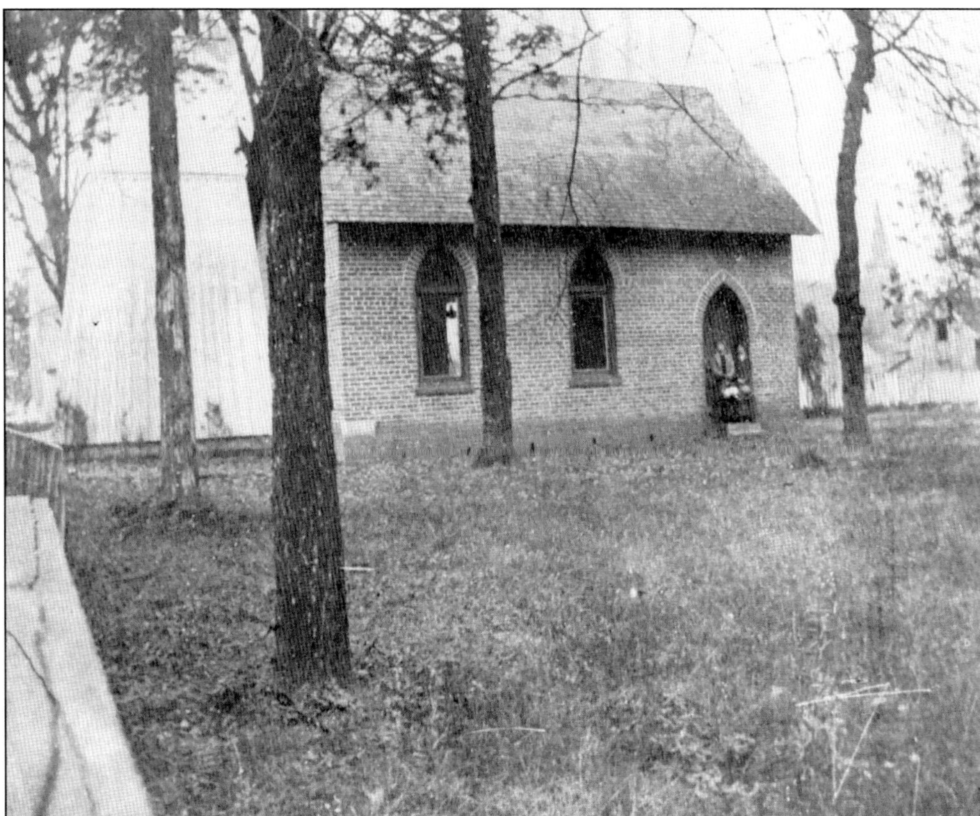

The chapter house and bell tower of St. Luke's Episcopal Church are seen here in 1902. The bell was moved into the current bell tower in 1945. (Courtesy Rowan Museum Collection.)

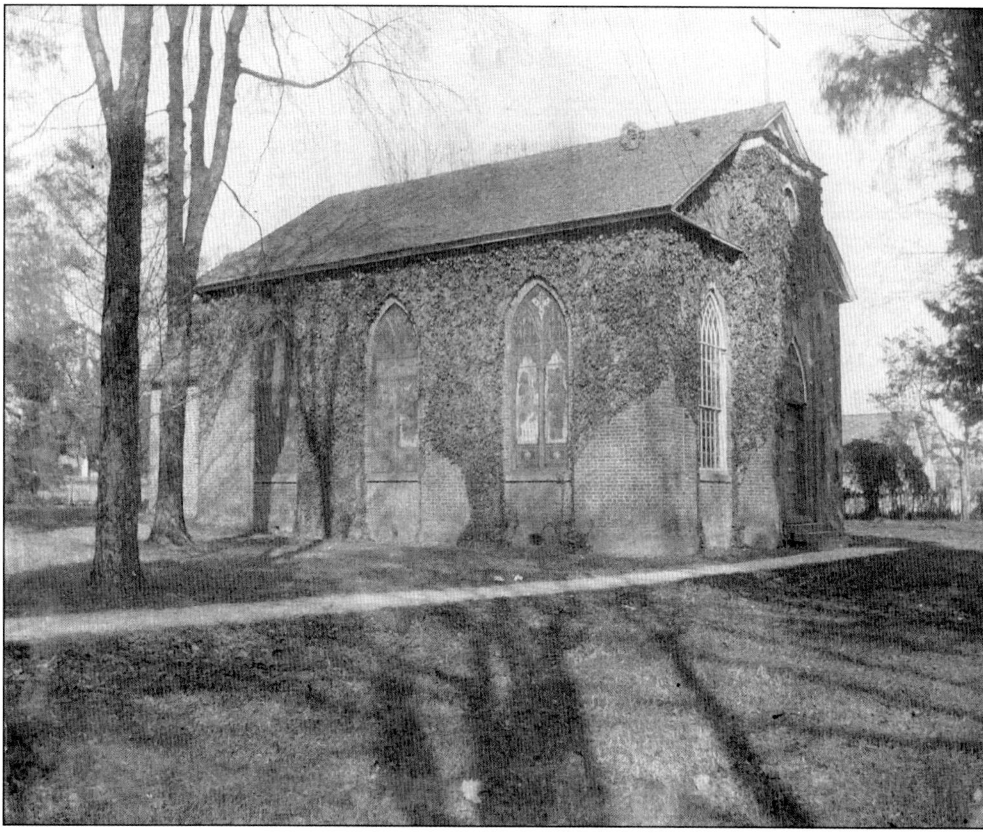

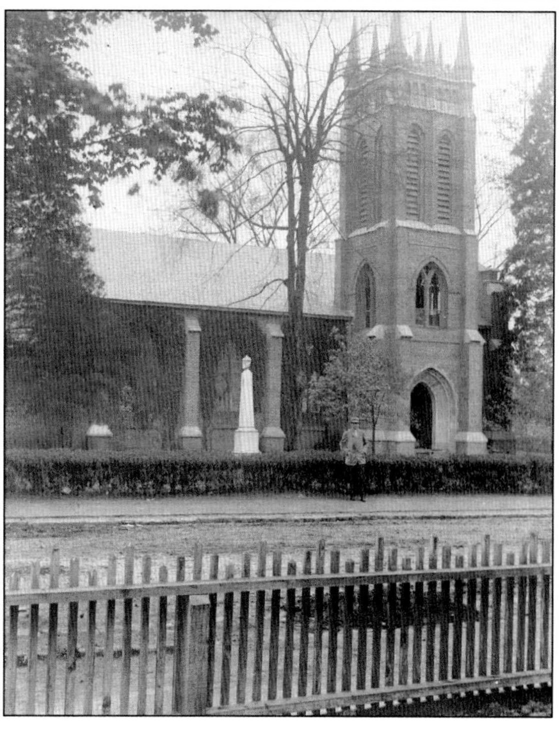

St. Luke's Episcopal Church was started in 1753, the same year Rowan County was formed. The first permanent building was constructed in 1828 on West Council Street by John Berry of Hillsborough. St. Luke's became the first church in Rowan County to purchase and use an organ. (Courtesy Rowan Museum Collection.)

The bell tower and baptistery were added to the original structure in 1909. Other additions include, in 1895, a building for the King's Daughters, now used as a chapel. A parish house was added by 1938 and enlarged by the end of the 20th century. (Courtesy Rowan Museum Collection.)

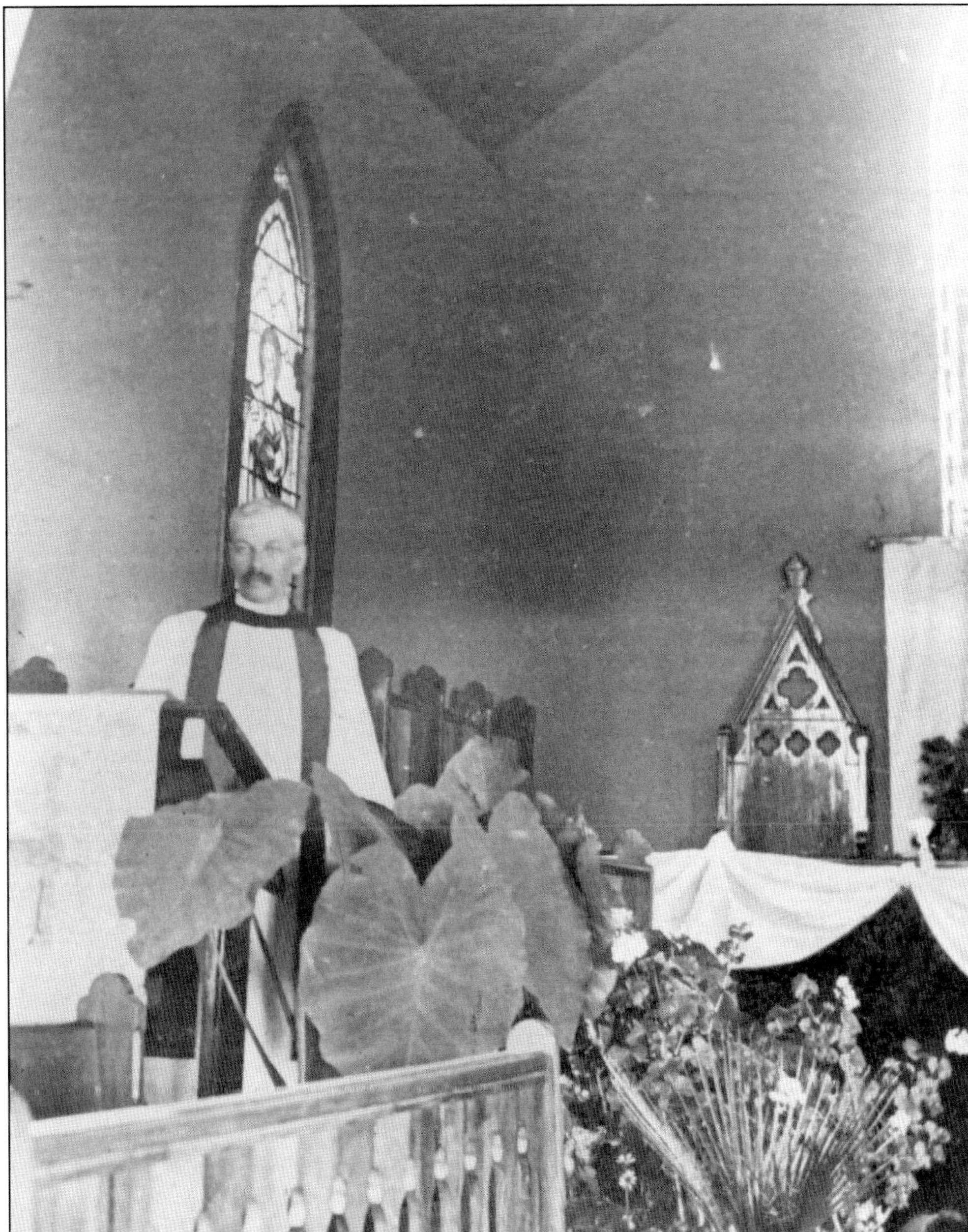

This interior view shows Rev. Francis J. Murdoch of St. Luke's during a General Convention of the Daughters of the King in 1894. When Buerbaum was taking this and other similar photographs, he was experimenting with gaslights to illuminate the building. (Courtesy Rowan Museum Collection.)

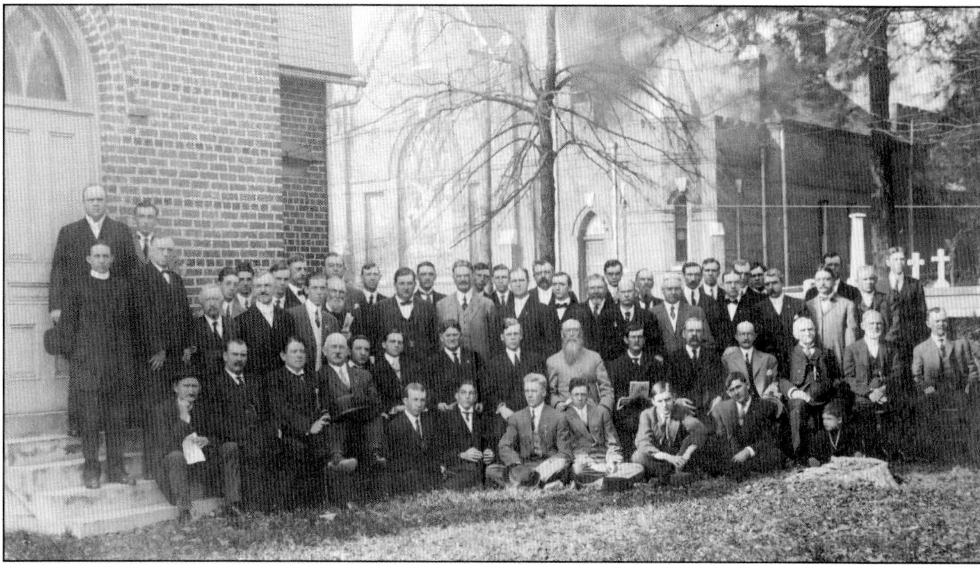

The men of St. Luke's Episcopal pose for a photograph in the early 1900s. Some of the stained glass for which this church is known can be seen in the background. (Courtesy Rowan Museum Collection.)

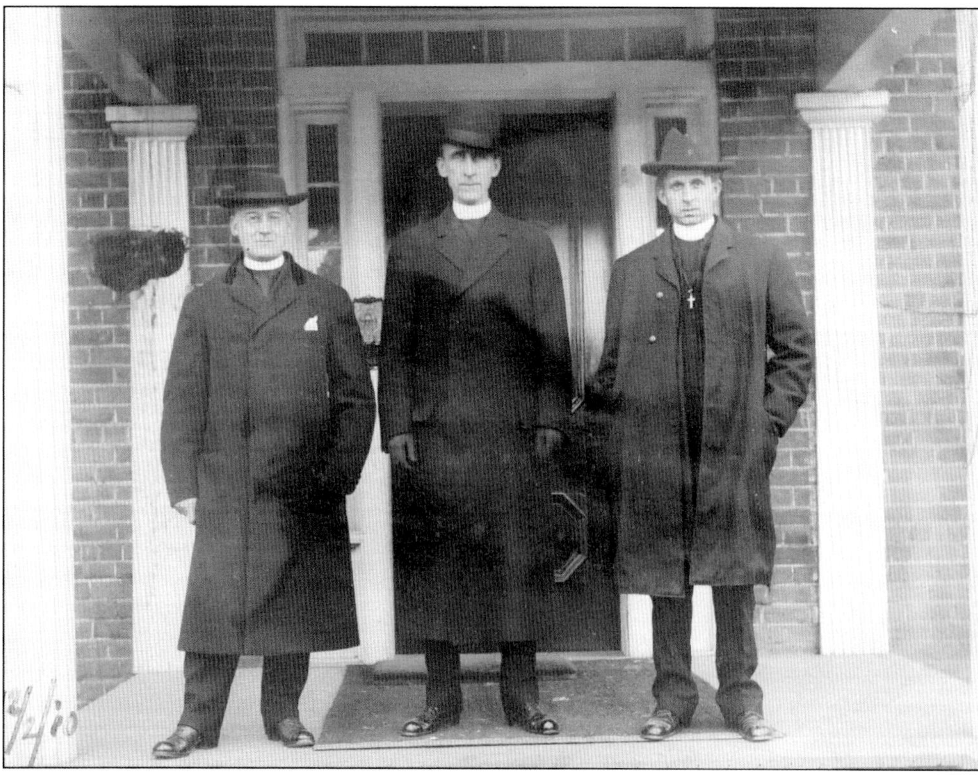

St. Luke's purchased a building across from the church in 1872 to serve as the rectory, which it used in that capacity until 1961. These three dapper men of the church pose on the front steps on December 2, 1910, on a cold late fall day. Reverend Cheatham (right) had succeeded Reverend Murdoch by this time. (Courtesy Rowan Museum Collection.)

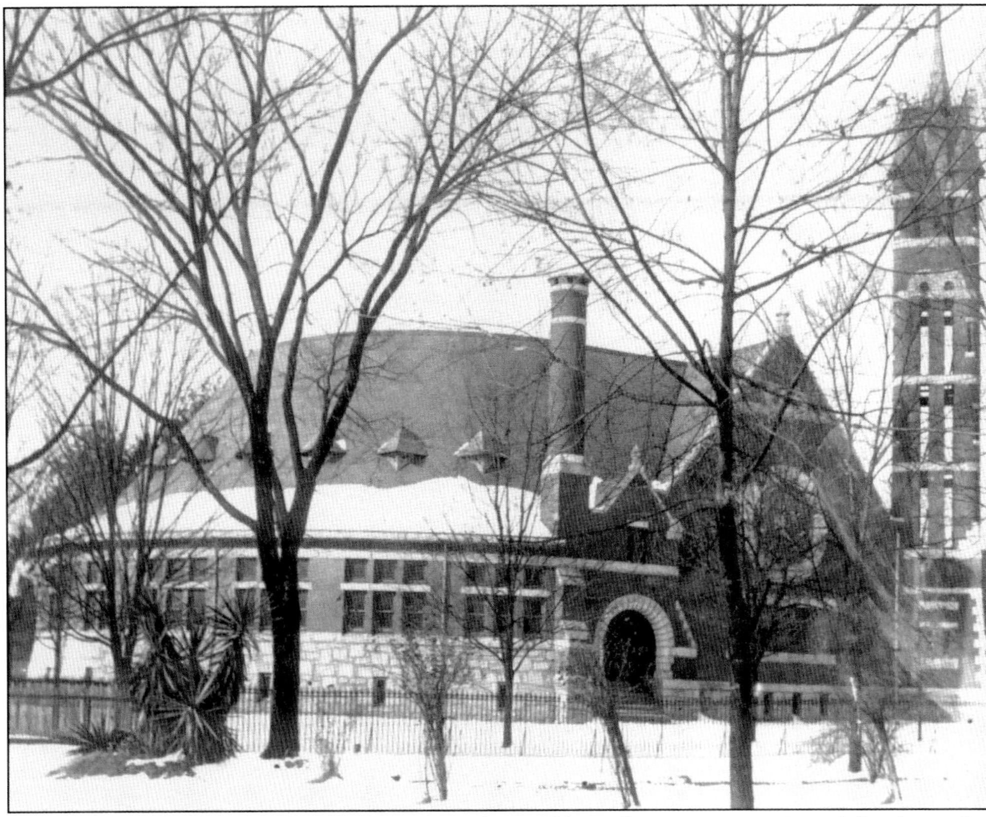

The second church structure was constructed in 1892 on the same ground used for the earlier building. The architect, Charles W. Bolton of Philadelphia, incorporated the Romanesque style of the period. This building was torn down in 1971, but the bell tower remains as a local landmark for the church and the citizens of Salisbury. (Courtesy Rowan Museum Collection.)

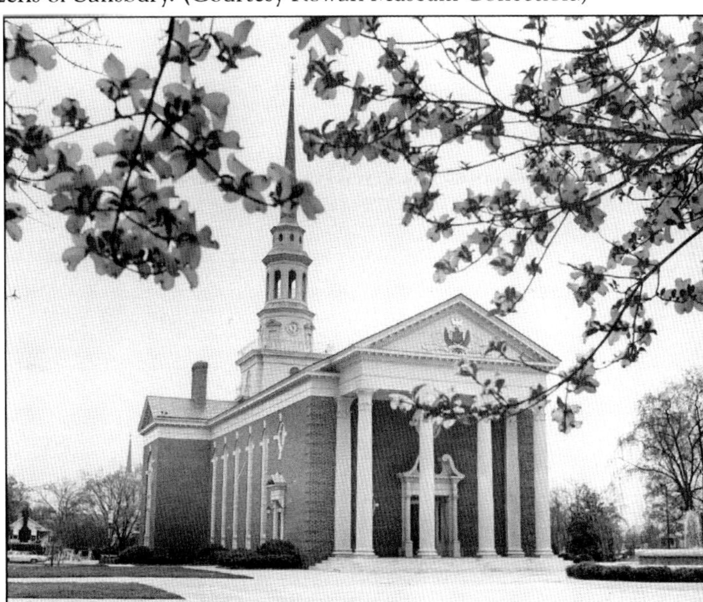

First Presbyterian Church, located at the corner of Innes and Jackson Streets, constructed its first church building in 1826 with the Reverend Jonathan Otis Freeman as pastor. This shows the third church building, designed by architect John Erwin Ramsay. The first service was held in this building on April 6, 1969. (Courtesy Edith M. Clark History Room of the Rowan Public Library.)

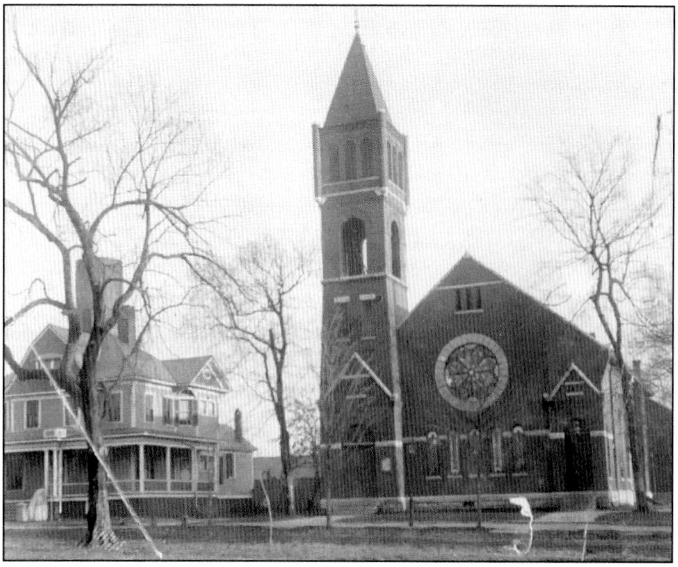

The First Methodist Church was formed in Salisbury in the 1780s, but a permanent church building was not started until 1857. A.B. Herndon designed this Romanesque building. The parsonage, shown beside the church, was built at the same time. The church was eventually replaced with a newer building in 1920. The parsonage was razed in 1958 to allow for construction of the present church, located on Church Street. (Courtesy Rowan Museum Collection.)

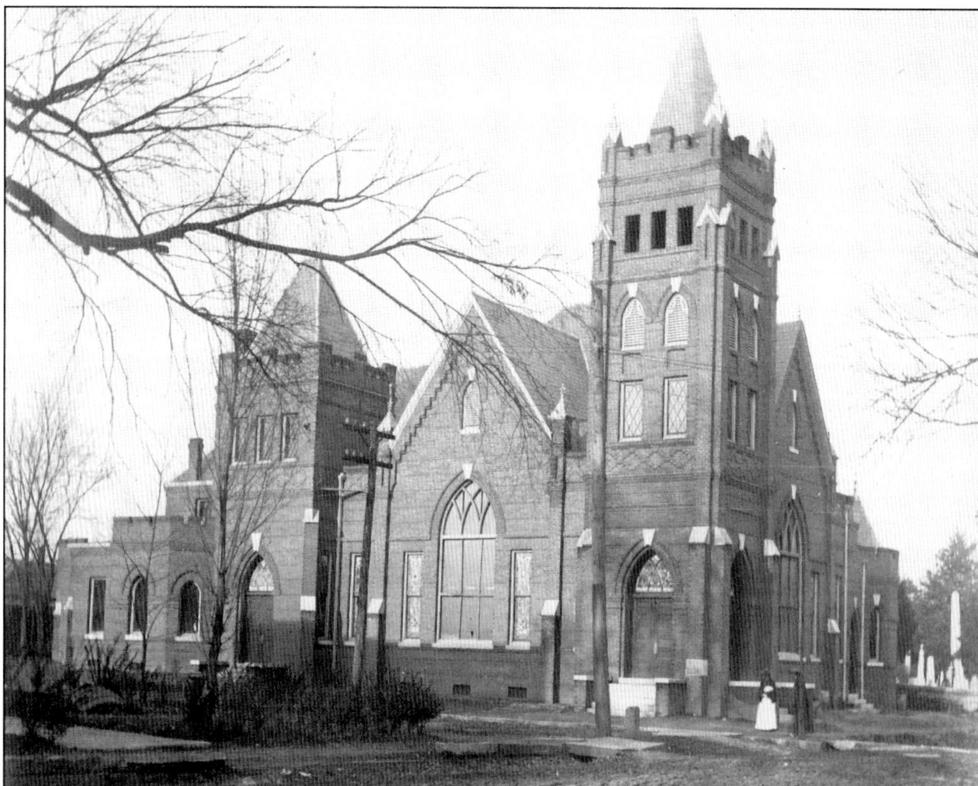

First Baptist Church was organized in 1849 with less than 20 members. The second church building, shown here, was constructed in 1903 at North Church and West Council Streets. As the congregation grew, this building was replaced in 1952 with a new structure at 223 North Fulton Street. (Courtesy Rowan Museum Collection.)

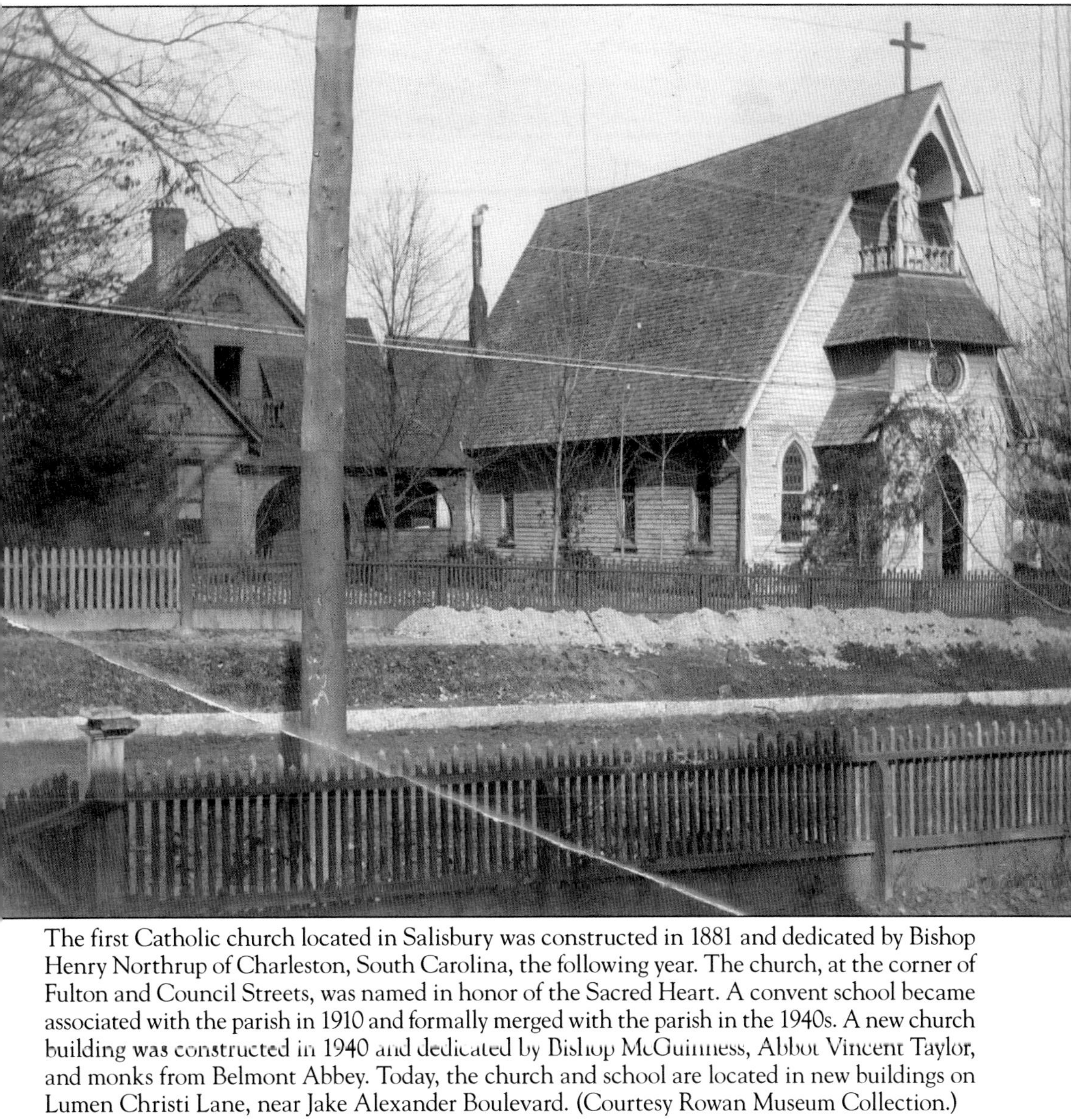

The first Catholic church located in Salisbury was constructed in 1881 and dedicated by Bishop Henry Northrup of Charleston, South Carolina, the following year. The church, at the corner of Fulton and Council Streets, was named in honor of the Sacred Heart. A convent school became associated with the parish in 1910 and formally merged with the parish in the 1940s. A new church building was constructed in 1940 and dedicated by Bishop McGuinness, Abbot Vincent Taylor, and monks from Belmont Abbey. Today, the church and school are located in new buildings on Lumen Christi Lane, near Jake Alexander Boulevard. (Courtesy Rowan Museum Collection.)

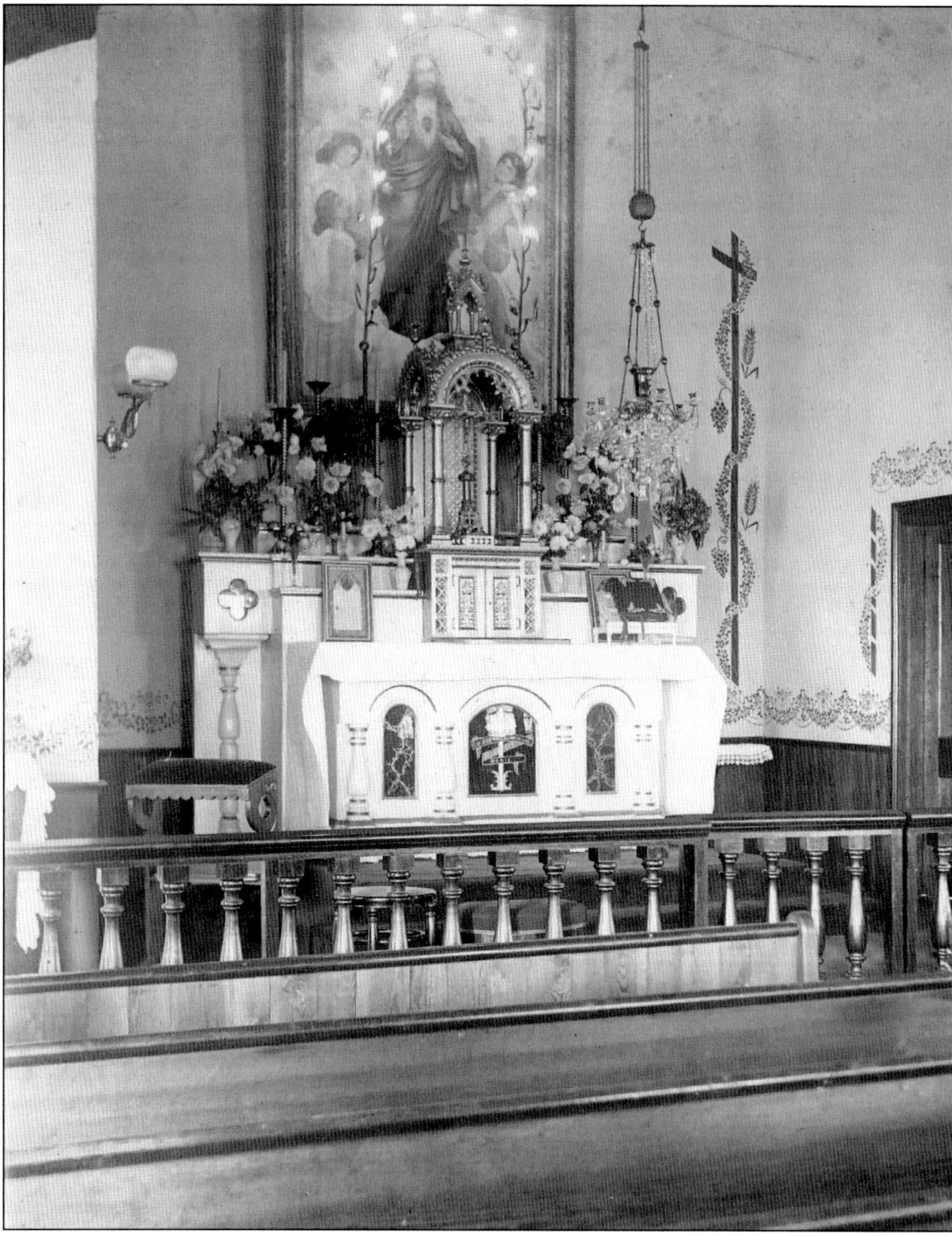

This photograph from the early 1900s shows the interior of Sacred Heart Church, including its altar. (Courtesy Rowan Museum Collection.)

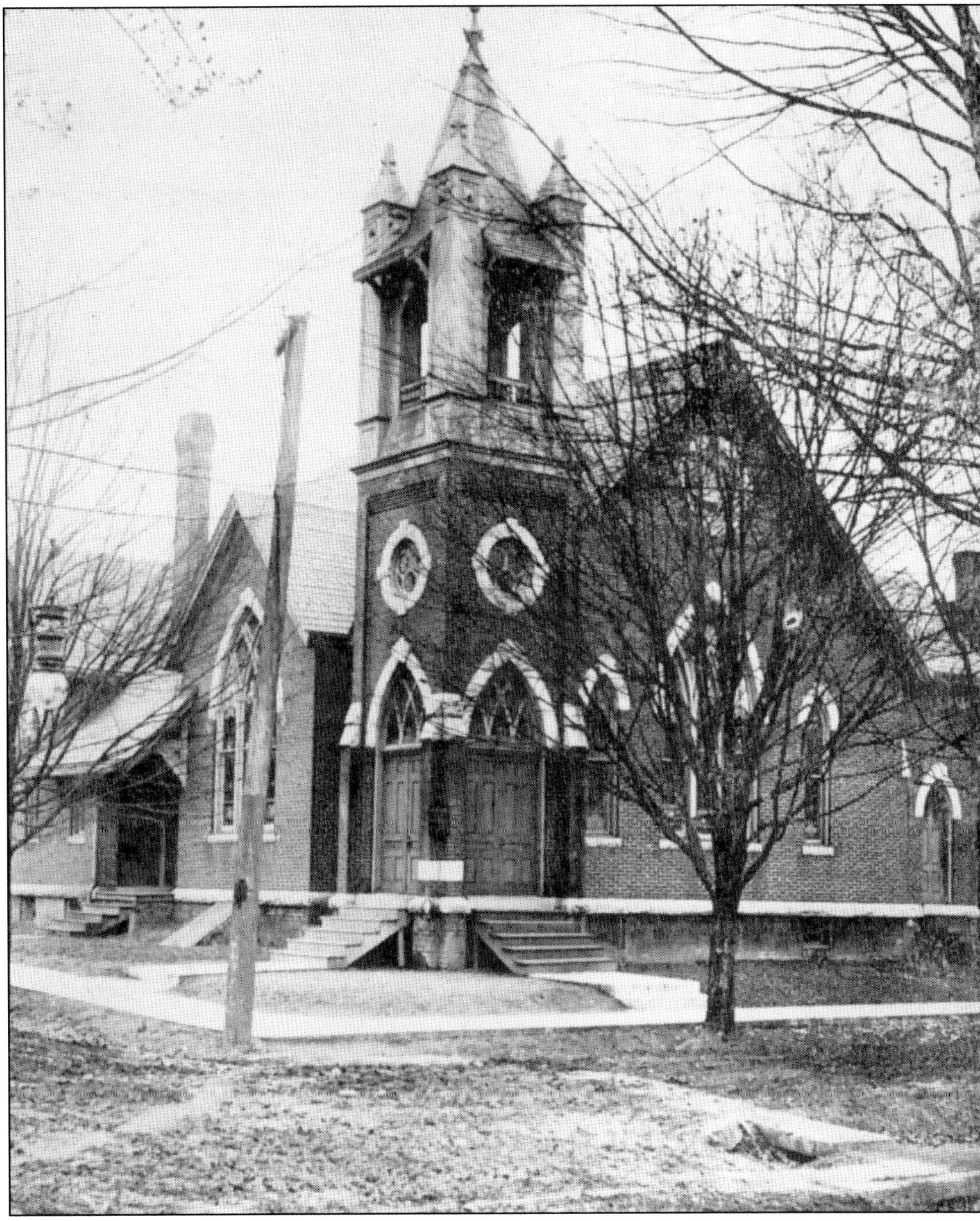

Faith Reformed Church was constructed in 1897 at the corner of South Church and Horah Streets. The church changed its name to First Reformed Church in 1919 and again in 1934 to the First Evangelical and Reformed Church of Salisbury. The last service was performed on September 16, 1954. Today, this building is home to La Cava Restaurant, specializing in Italian cuisine. (Courtesy Rowan Museum Collection.)

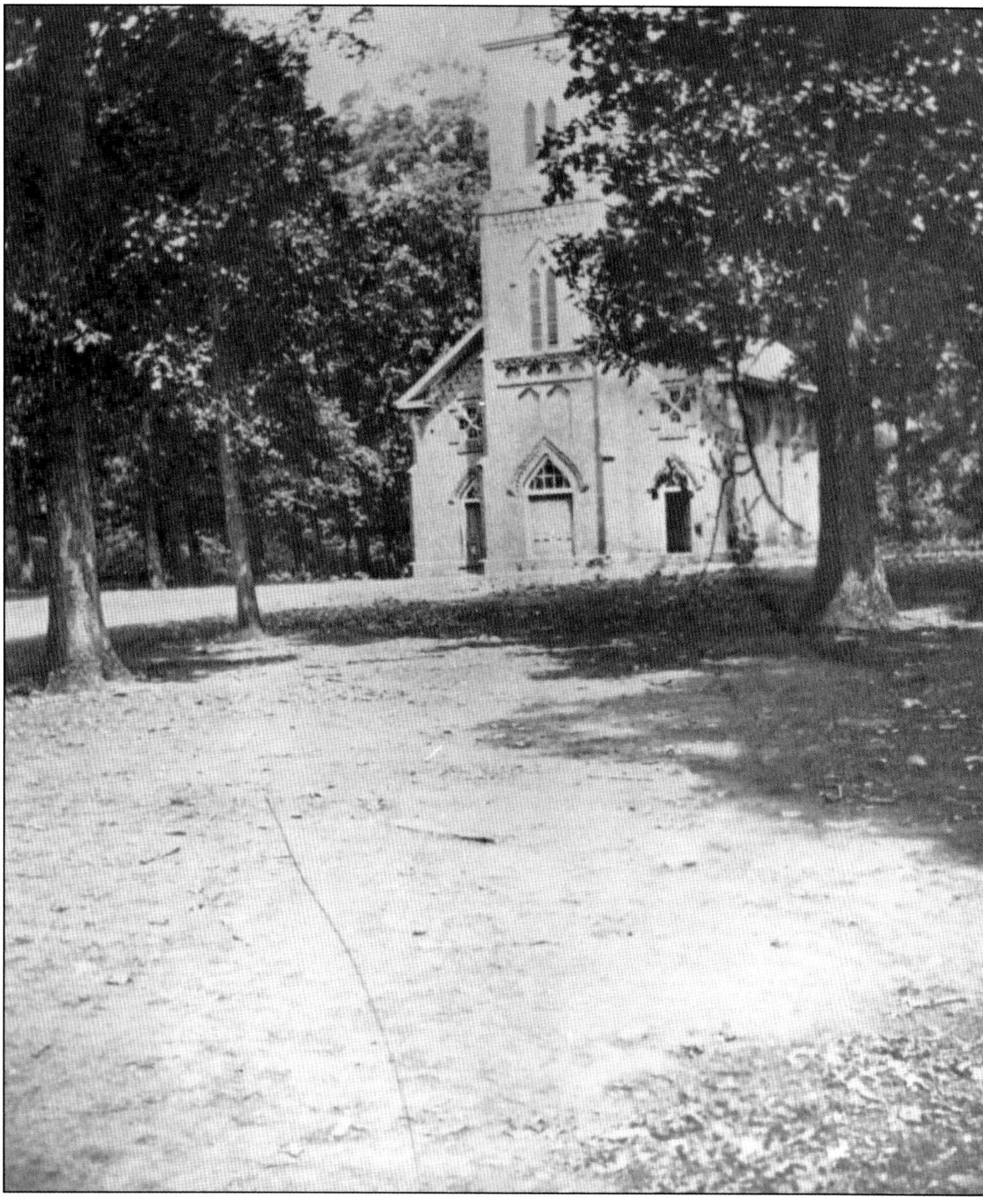

Thyatira Presbyterian Church, located off Highway 150, may be the oldest Presbyterian church west of the Yadkin River. The church received land to construct a building in 1753, and Cathey's Meeting House was eventually constructed. The fourth and last church building, shown here, was constructed in 1860. Today, this structure is still used in conjunction with newer buildings nearby. (Courtesy Rowan Museum Collection.)

Six

Images of Modern Salisbury

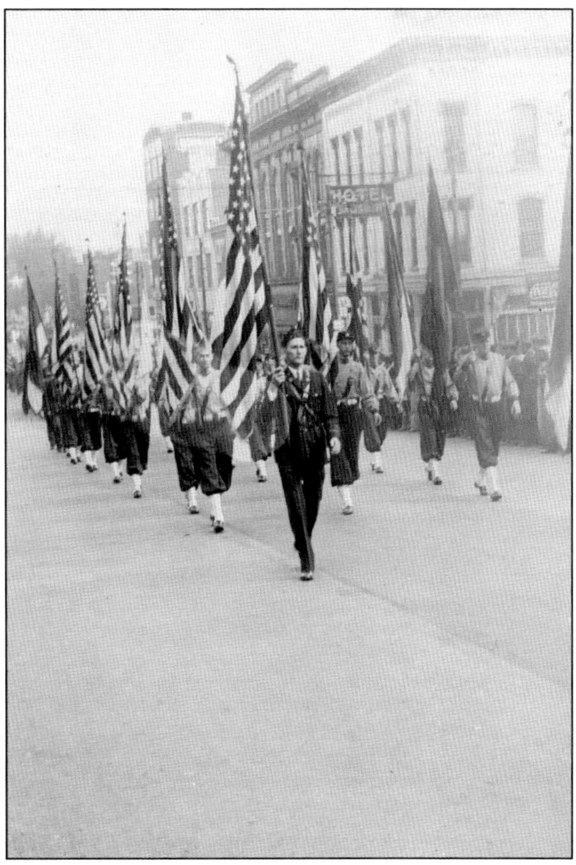

Participants in this early-1940s American Legion Parade march down Main Street in front of the Hotel Salisbury. (Courtesy Edith M. Clark History Room at the Rowan Public Library.)

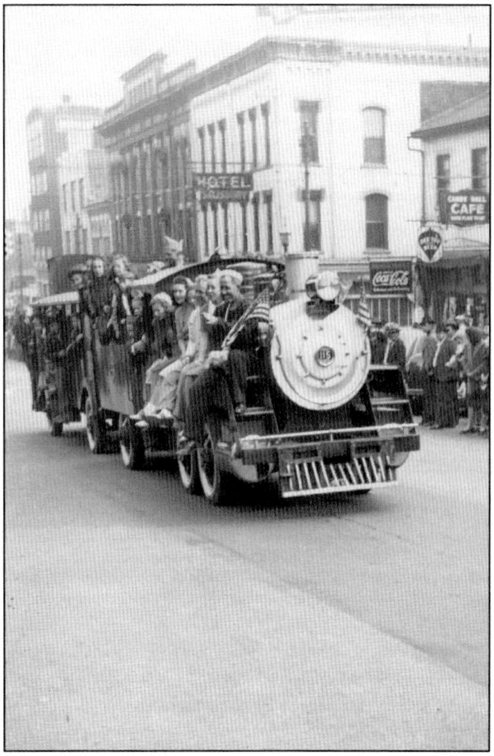

This is a special "40 & 8" train created by Southern Railway's Spencer Shops in the late 1930s and early 1940s for the Rowan County Voiture Society. (Courtesy Edith M. Clark History Room of the Rowan Public Library.)

This is a side view of the "40 & 8" train during a 1942 parade. This train is still in use today by the society, but it sports a different paint scheme. (Courtesy Edith M. Clark History Room of the Rowan Public Library.)

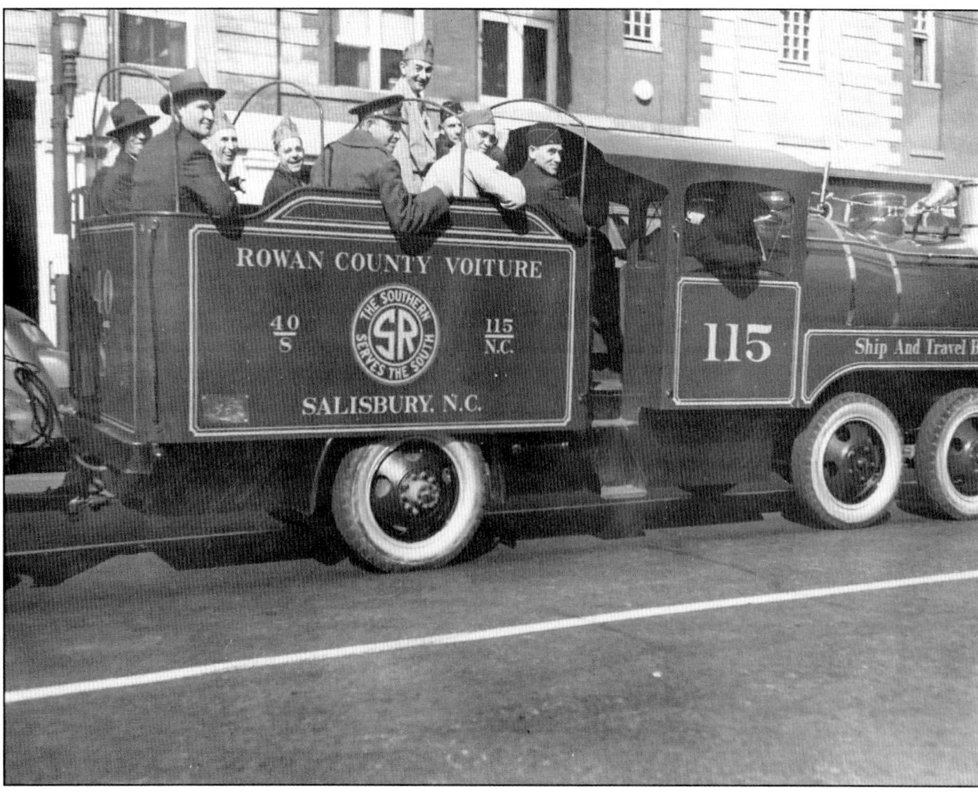

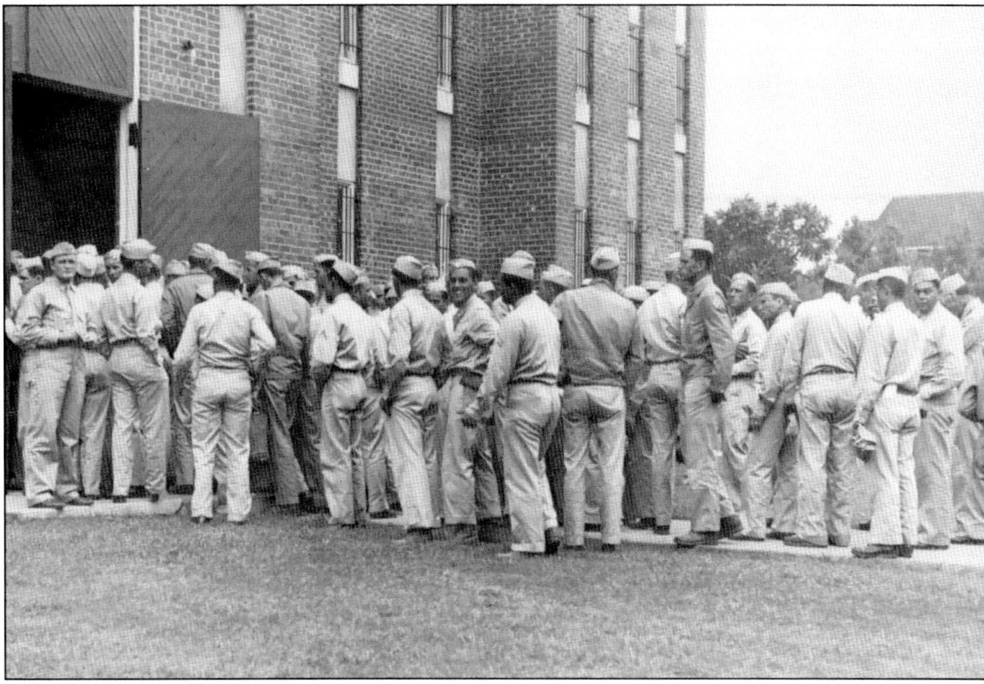

North Carolina National Guard troops mobilize at the Salisbury Armory on December 8, 1941, one day after the attack on Pearl Harbor. The armory was located where City Park is today, at 1000 North Jackson Street. (Both, courtesy Edith M. Clark History Room of the Rowan Public Library.)

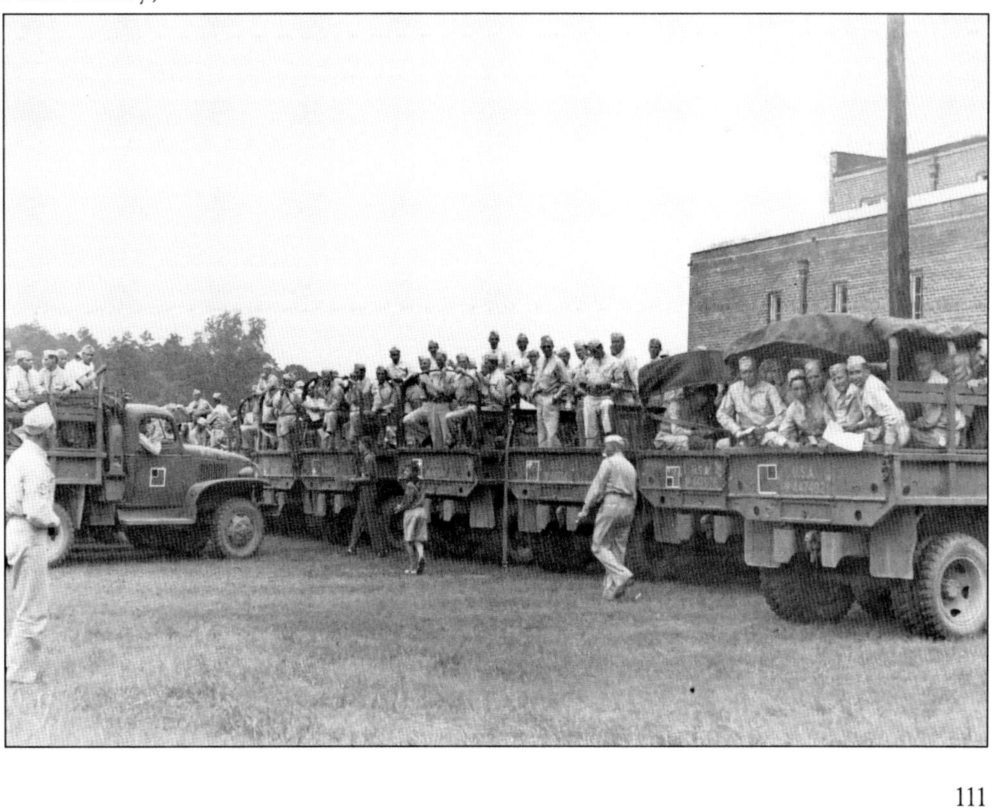

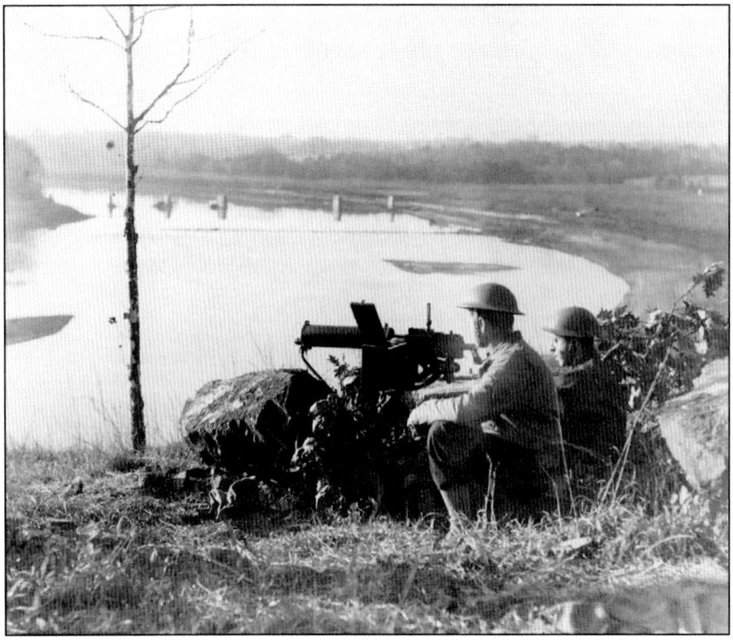

North Carolina National Guard troops protect the Yadkin River with a .30-caliber water-cooled machine gun. These troops were dispersed throughout Rowan County to protect vital roads, businesses, and waterways. (Courtesy Edith M. Clark History Room of the Rowan Public Library.)

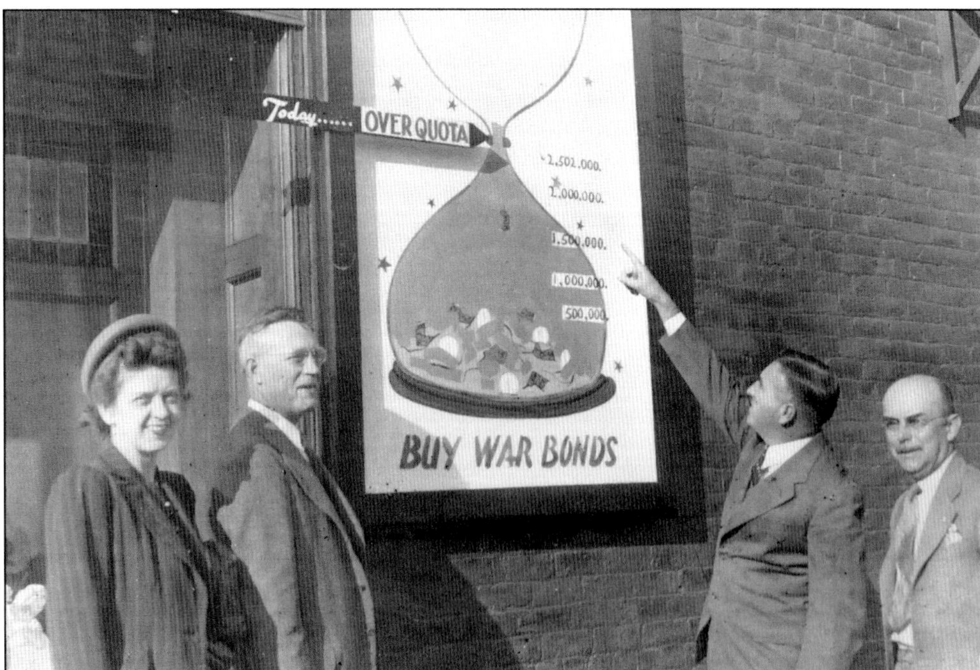

War bond sales became very popular during World War II. The sales raised money for needed supplies related to the war effort. (Courtesy Edith M. Clark History Room of the Rowan Public Library.)

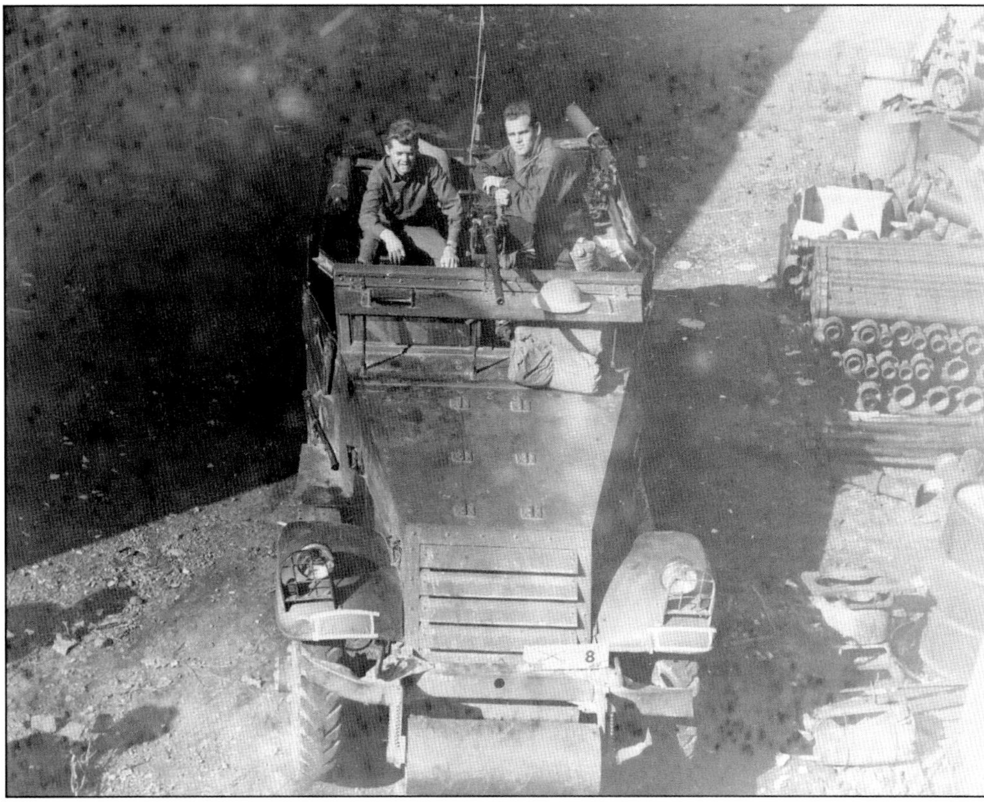

During the fall of 1941, the US Army conducted the Carolina Maneuvers in the Piedmont of North Carolina and upstate South Carolina. Though no direct action took place around Salisbury, the National Guard from Salisbury may have taken part in the exercise. Equipment was brought in by rail and unloaded in various cities along the route. These photographs show a halftrack (above), used for antiaircraft artillery, and an early war tank (below) in action. (Both, courtesy Edith M. Clark History Room of the Rowan Public Library.)

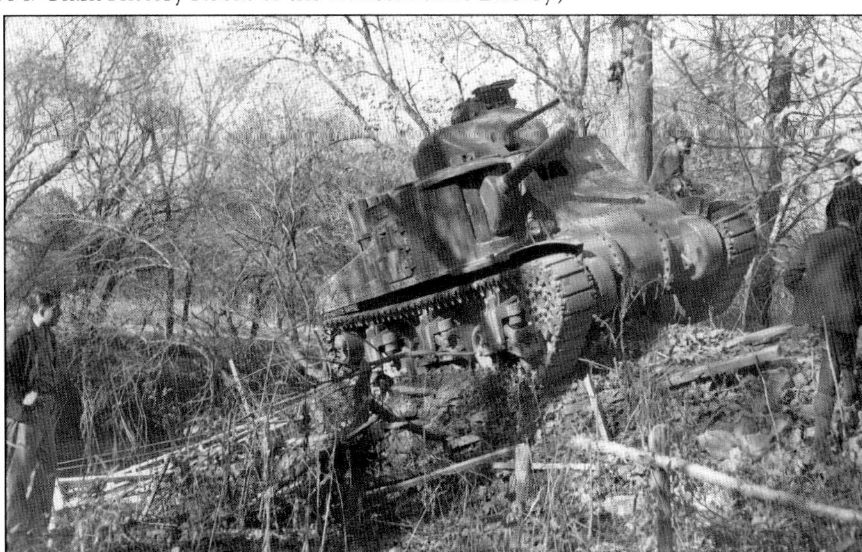

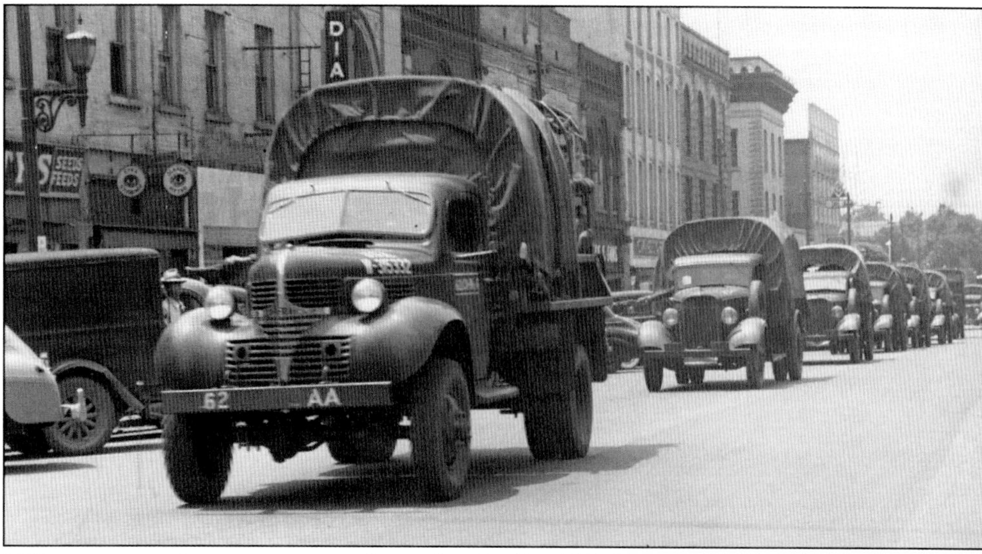

Military parades became commonplace after the Pearl Harbor attack. The parades showed the might of the American military and featured trucks, tanks, and other vehicles. (Courtesy Edith M. Clark History Room of the Rowan Public Library.)

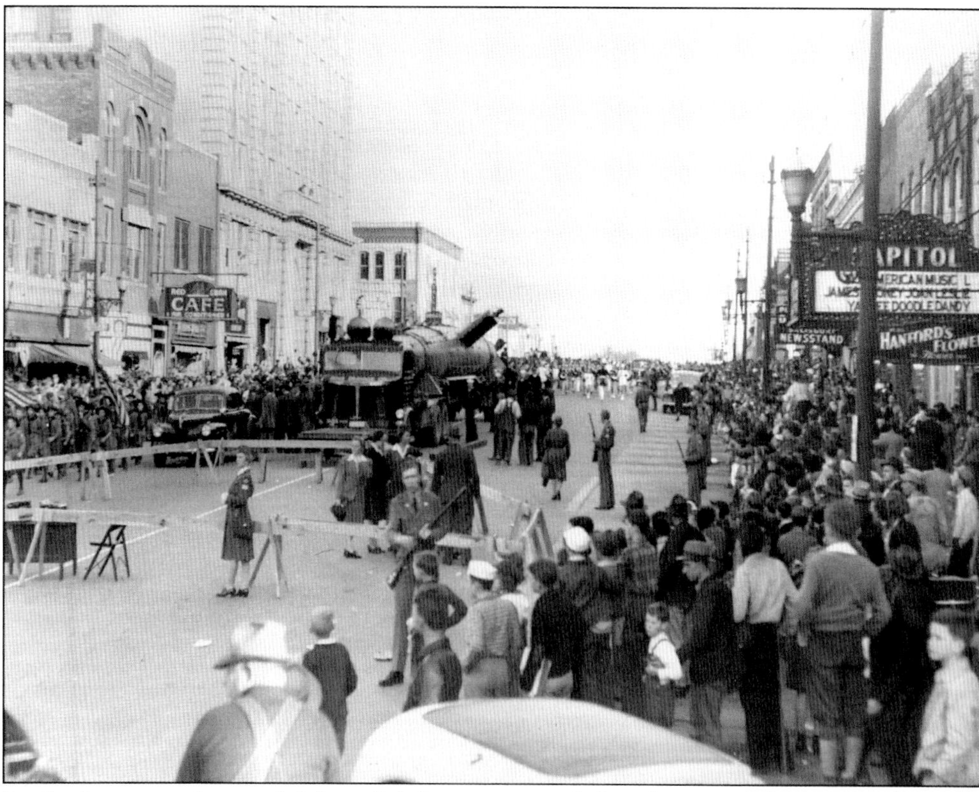

Spoils of war were also paraded down Salisbury streets, including this captured Japanese submarine. These parades were also designed to aid war bond drives, which were used to offset the cost of the war. When people saw the military winning the war, they were more likely to continue purchasing these bonds. (Courtesy Edith M. Clark History Room of the Rowan Public Library.)

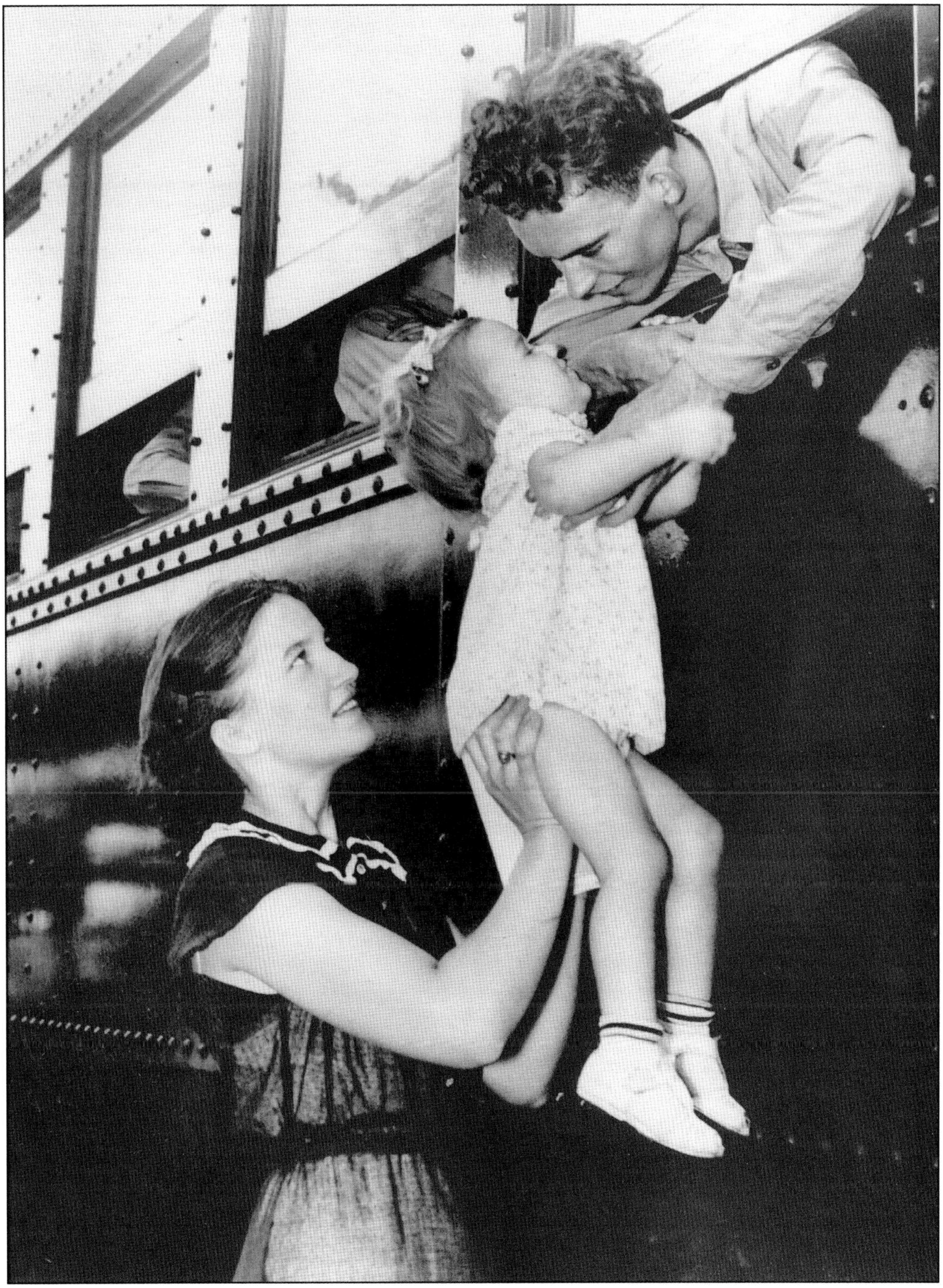

As soldiers were shipped off to war, many residents of Salisbury gave their last good-byes at the train station. This woman holds up her little girl for one last hug and kiss with her dad before the whistle blew. (Courtesy Edith M. Clark History Room of the Rowan Public Library.)

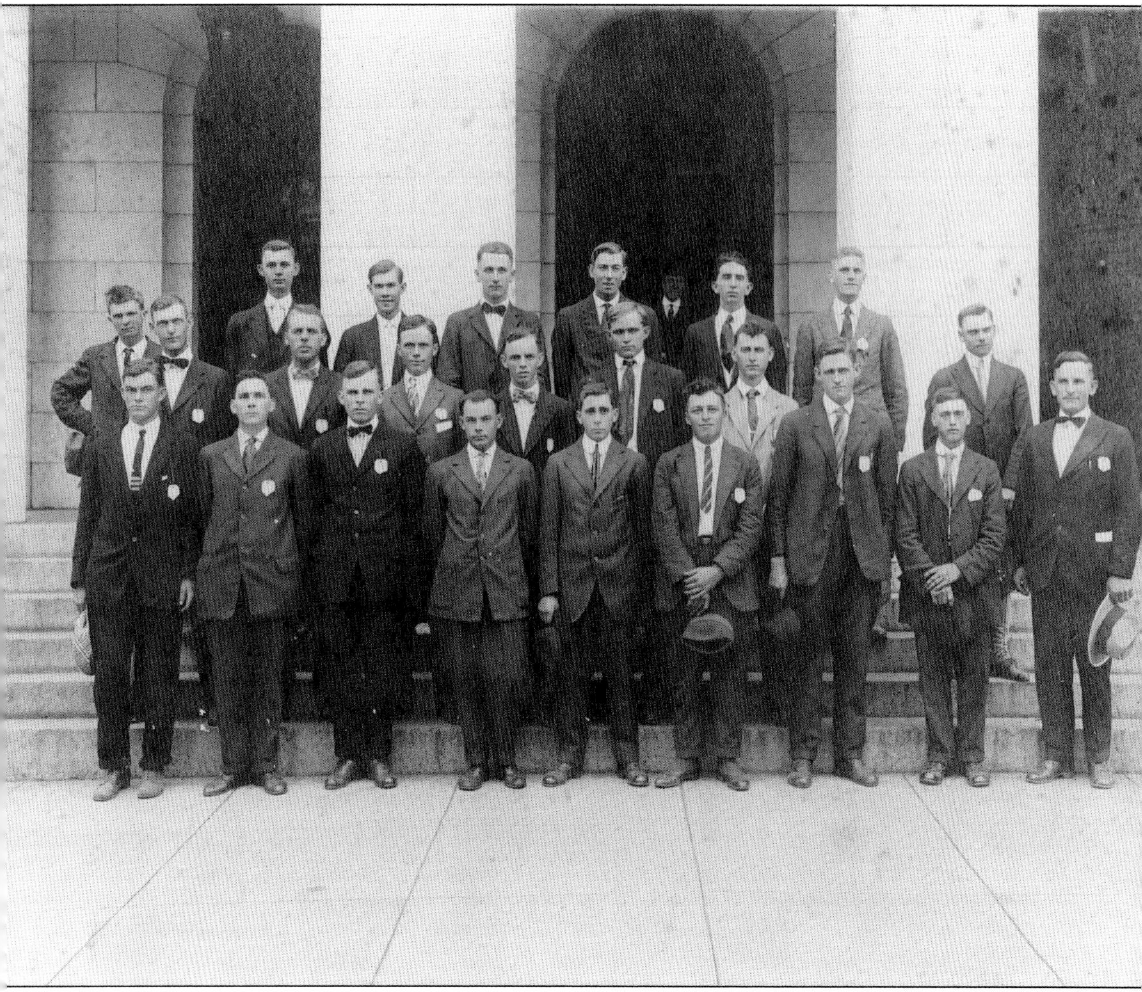

Salisbury has a proud military tradition dating to the Civil War. The town has supplied men and material for national causes. Just as men signed up at America's entrance into World War II, these men volunteered to fight in France during the First World War. (Courtesy Edith M. Clark History Room of the Rowan Public Library.)

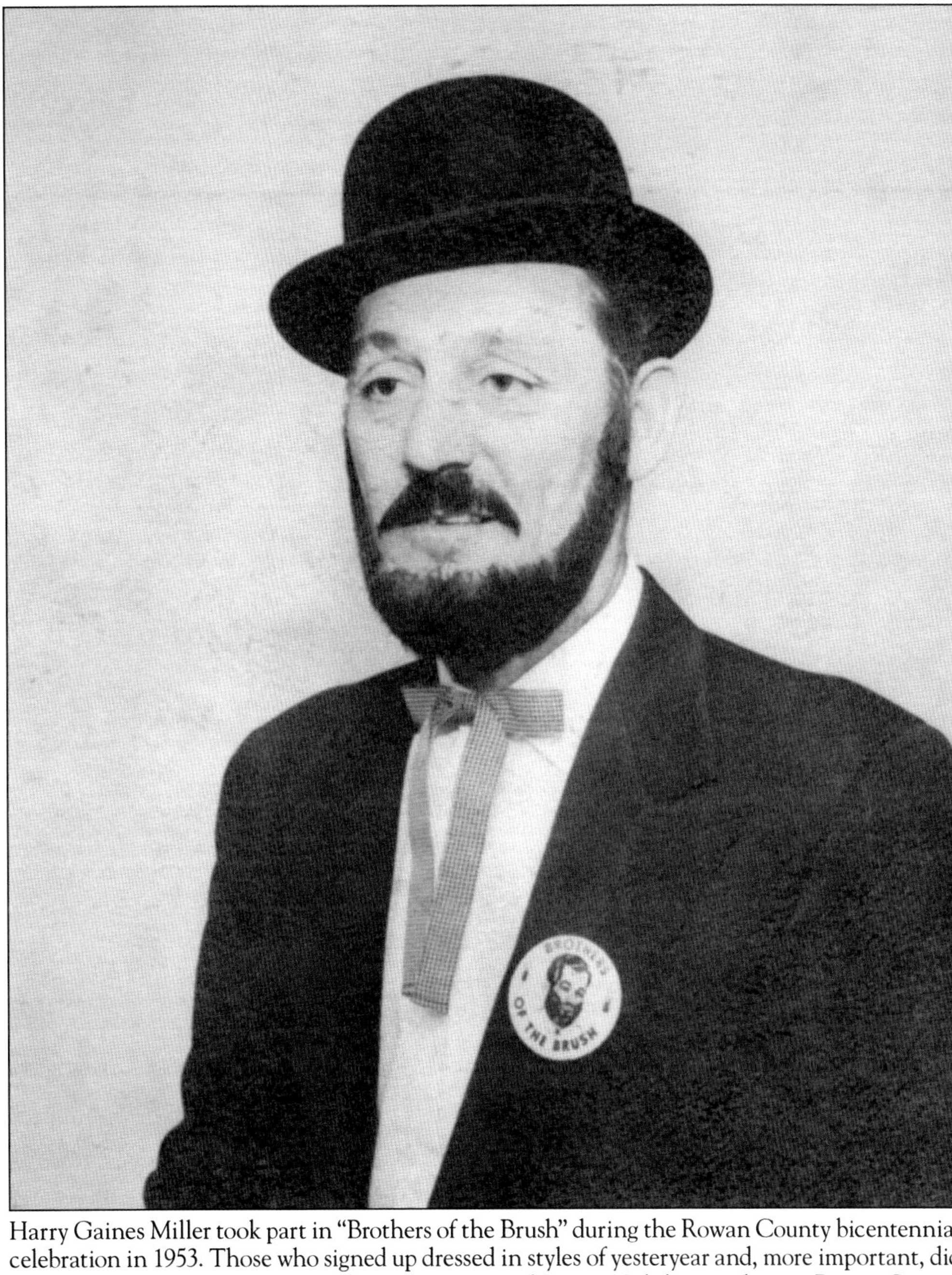

Harry Gaines Miller took part in "Brothers of the Brush" during the Rowan County bicentennial celebration in 1953. Those who signed up dressed in styles of yesteryear and, more important, did not shave their beards throughout the year. Many gentlemen in Salisbury and across Rowan County signed up to participate. (Courtesy Edith M. Clark History Room of the Rowan Public Library.)

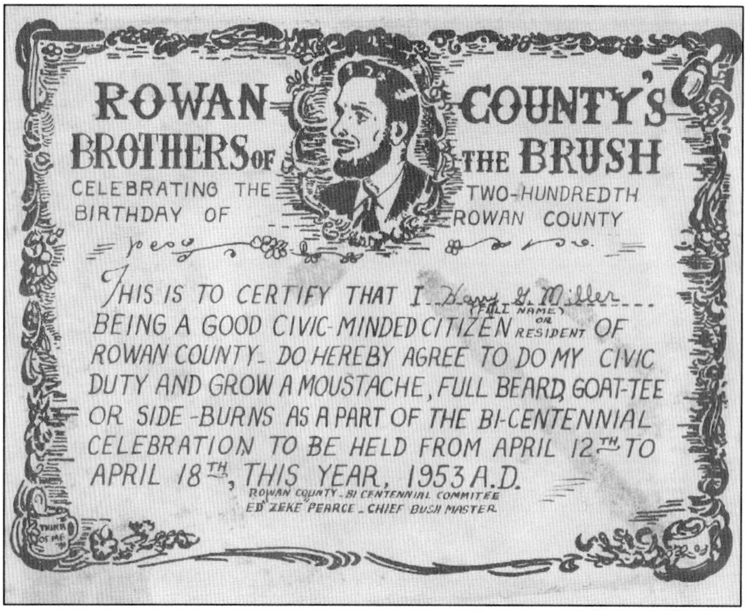

ROWAN COUNTY'S BROTHERS OF THE BRUSH

CELEBRATING THE TWO-HUNDREDTH BIRTHDAY OF ROWAN COUNTY

THIS IS TO CERTIFY THAT I Harry G. Miller (FULL NAME) BEING A GOOD CIVIC-MINDED CITIZEN OR RESIDENT OF ROWAN COUNTY DO HEREBY AGREE TO DO MY CIVIC DUTY AND GROW A MOUSTACHE, FULL BEARD, GOAT-TEE OR SIDE-BURNS AS A PART OF THE BI-CENTENNIAL CELEBRATION TO BE HELD FROM APRIL 12TH TO APRIL 18TH, THIS YEAR, 1953 A.D.

ROWAN COUNTY BI CENTENNIAL COMMITEE
ED ZEKE PEARCE CHIEF BUSH MASTER

The certificate was given to Harry G. Miller for his participation in "Brothers of the Brush." The Ladies of Salisbury and Rowan County participated as well, creating old-style dresses to wear during parades and festivities. (Courtesy Edith M. Clark History Room of the Rowan Public Library.)

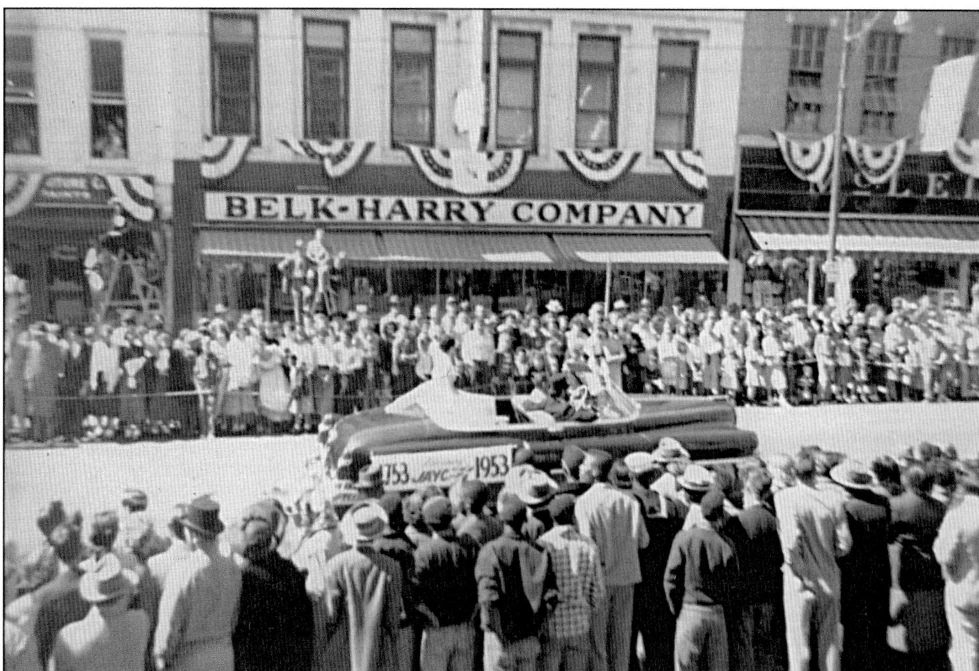

The Belk-Harry store was a great place to observe the bicentennial parade on April 18, 1953. Dignitaries can be seen riding in a 1953 Cadillac, waving to the crowd. President Eisenhower came through Salisbury on his way to Catawba College to speak. (Courtesy Rowan Museum Collection.)

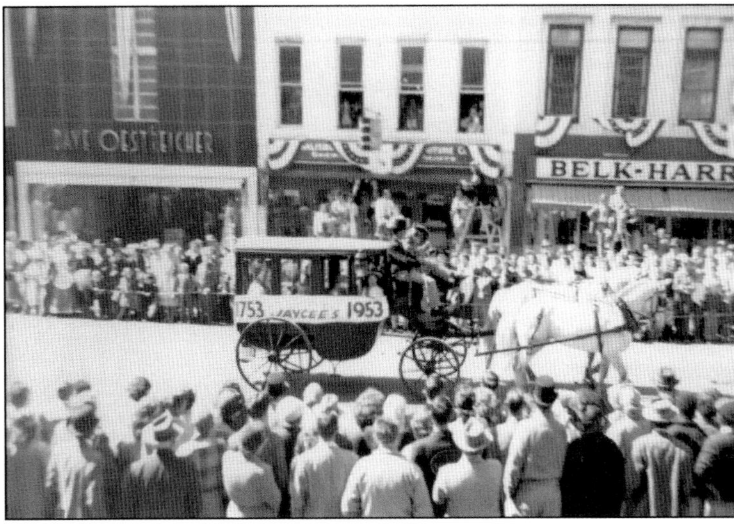

Another parade entry harkens back to the early days with horse-drawn carriages similar to those seen in the early 1900s on Main Street. (Courtesy Rowan Museum Collection.)

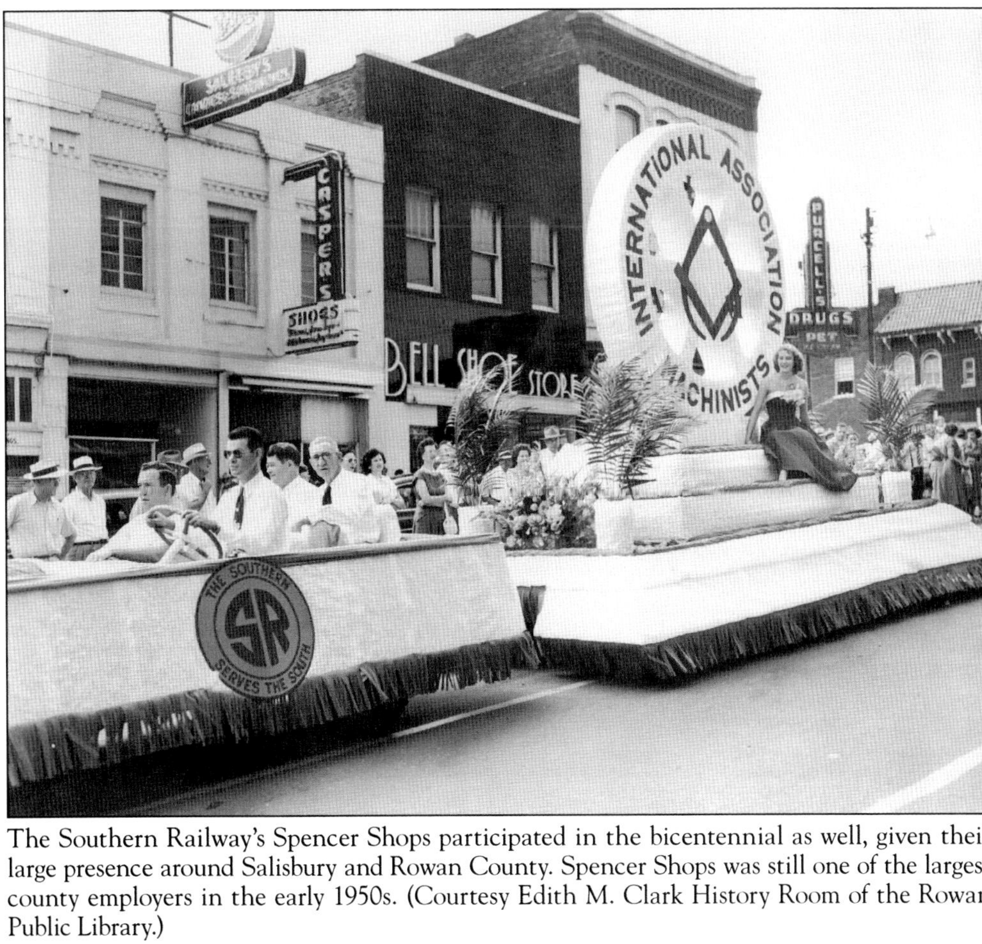

The Southern Railway's Spencer Shops participated in the bicentennial as well, given their large presence around Salisbury and Rowan County. Spencer Shops was still one of the largest county employers in the early 1950s. (Courtesy Edith M. Clark History Room of the Rowan Public Library.)

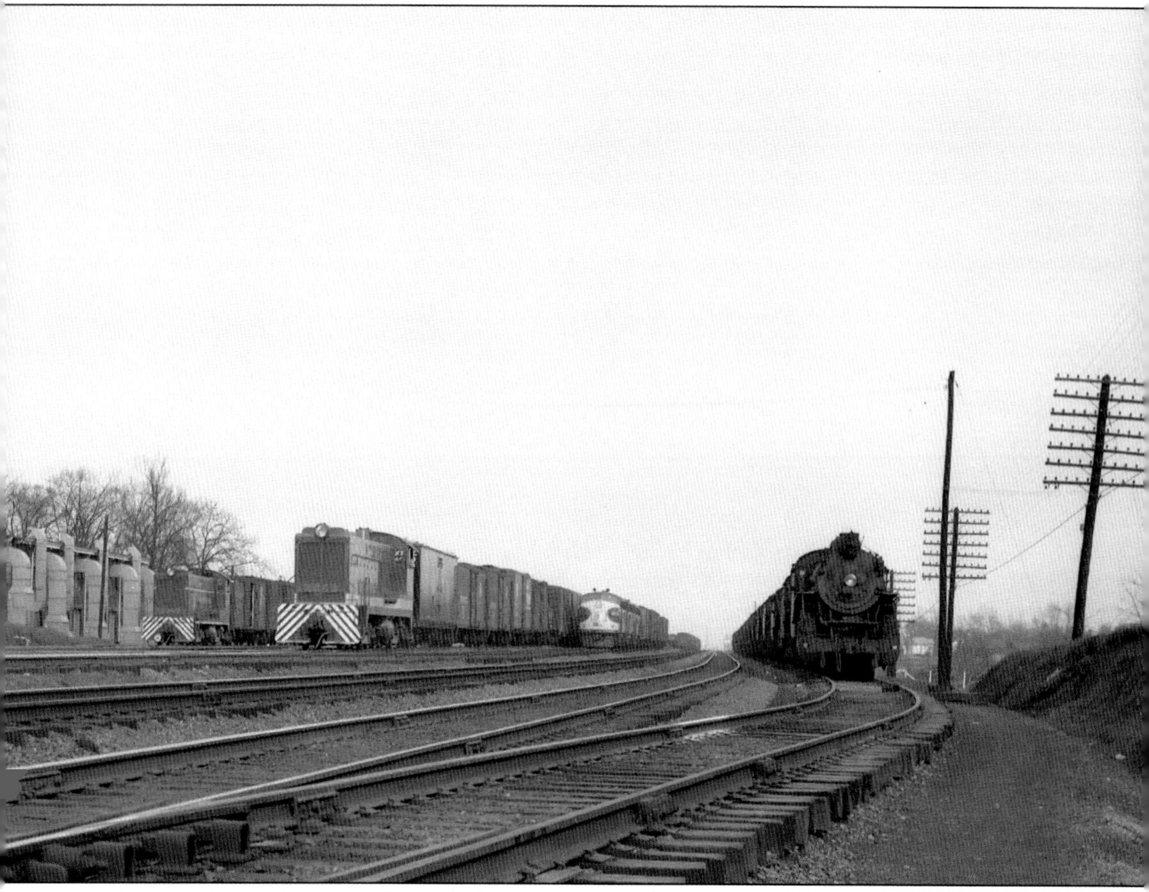

Salisbury bore witness to the end of steam power when Spencer Shops retired all of its steam locomotives by 1953. Here, a long line of steam locomotives waits at Eleventh Street in Salisbury to be transported north to scrap yards, a sad ending to a long and illustrious career. (Courtesy Robert Graham collection.)

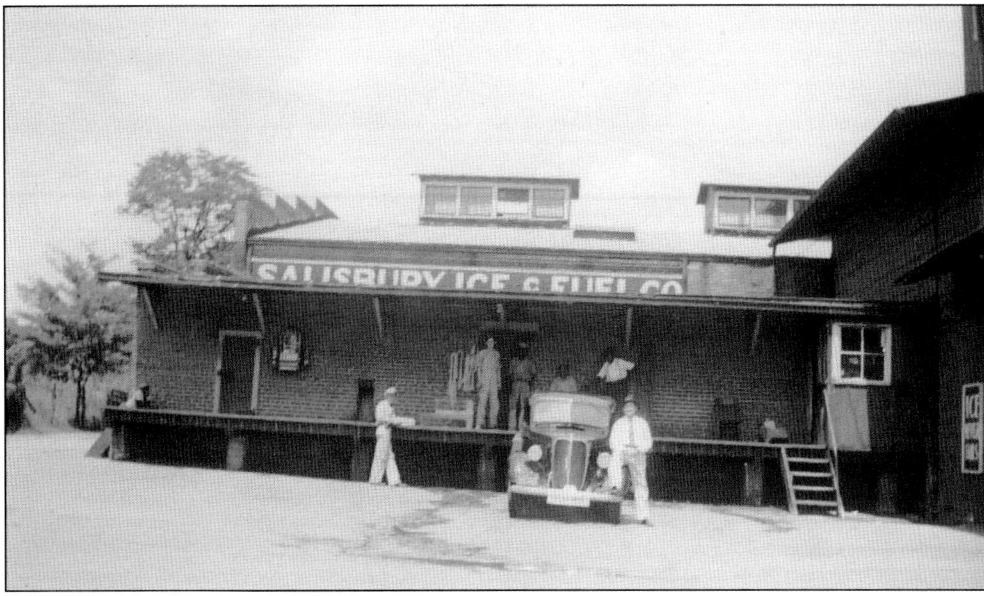

Salisbury Ice & Fuel Company was located off the tracks of the Southern Railway on Monroe Street. It not only serviced local residents, but also loaded ice blocks into refrigerated freight cars, as shown below. The tall section of the building still stands today. (Both, courtesy Edith M. Clark History Room of the Rowan Public Library.)

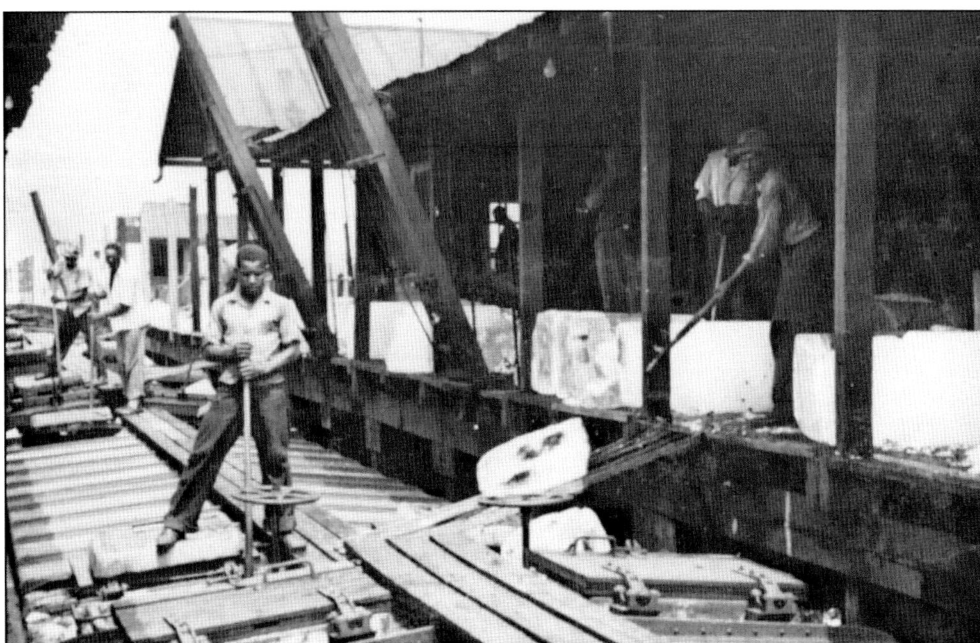

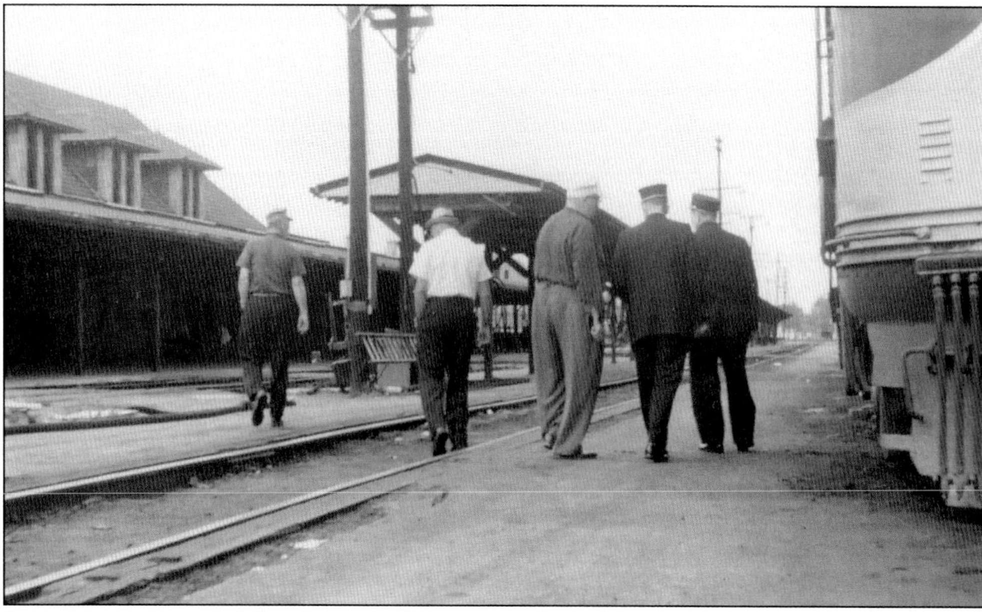

Passenger service to Salisbury remained strong into the early 1960s. The "Crescent," "Piedmont," and "Asheville Special" all made stops at the station. Travelers could ride to New York; Washington, DC; head south to New Orleans; or tour the Biltmore House in Asheville. Southern Railway continued to take pride in its passenger trains well into the 1970s, when only one train was available on its routes, the "Southern Crescent." (Courtesy North Carolina Division of Archives and History.)

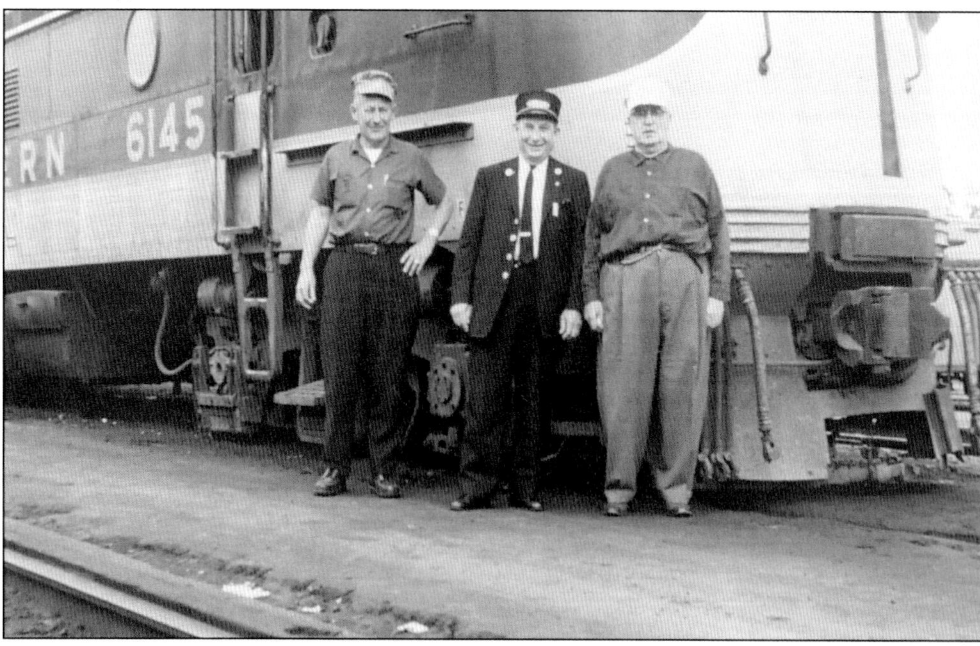

In a time-honored tradition, the passenger train crew pauses for a moment to have their photograph taken beside the locomotive. The railroads still had some mystique in the 1960s, before jet airliners completely dominated vacation travel plans. (Courtesy North Carolina Division of Archives and History.)

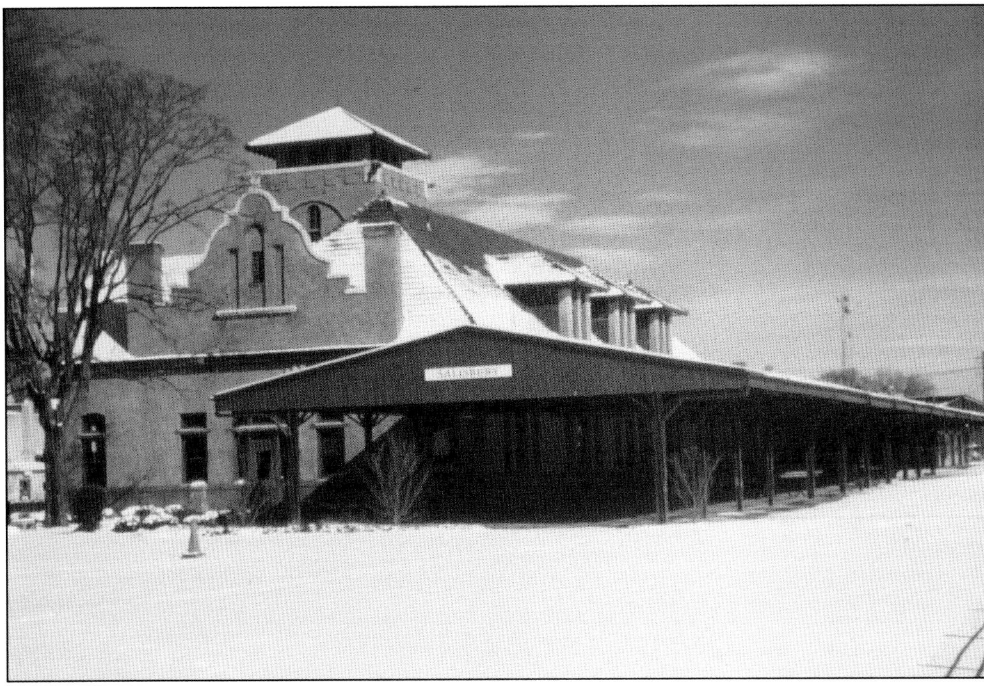

Amtrack eventually constructed a new waiting area in a different section of the old station, which left the old waiting area vacant. Unfortunately, this part of the station fell into disrepair and needed a major renovation. The Historic Salisbury Foundation (HSF) acquired the building in 1984 and began restoration in 1990. The restoration was completed in 1996, and the old waiting room is now used as rental space by the HSF. (Courtesy Larry K. Neal Jr. collection.)

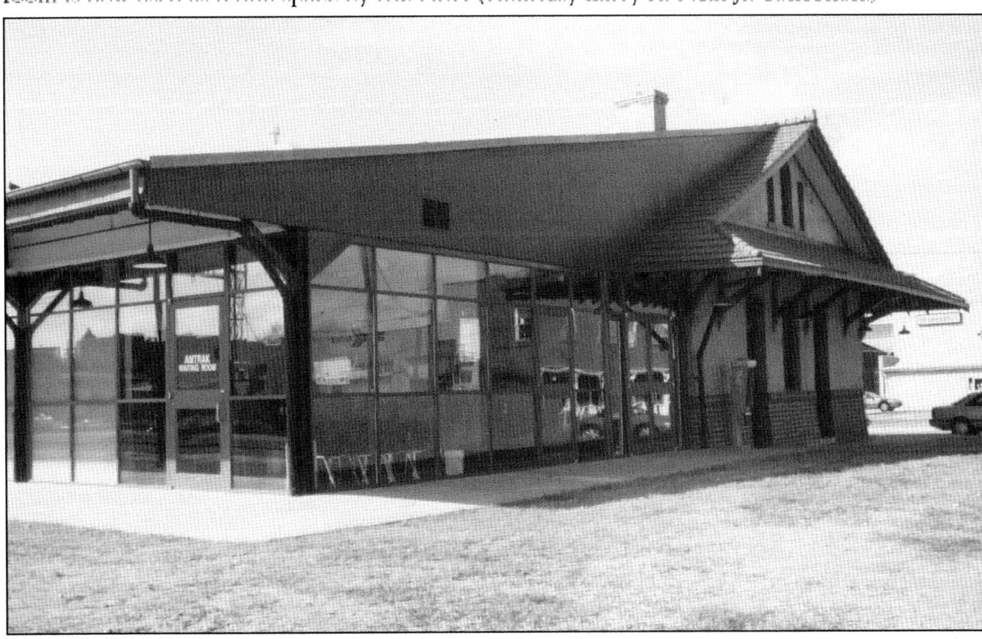

Amtrack still uses the waiting room at the north end of the building. Recently, a new train shed similar to the original was constructed from the main station building across the tracks, allowing passengers a covered walkway to the trains. (Courtesy Larry K. Neal Jr. collection.)

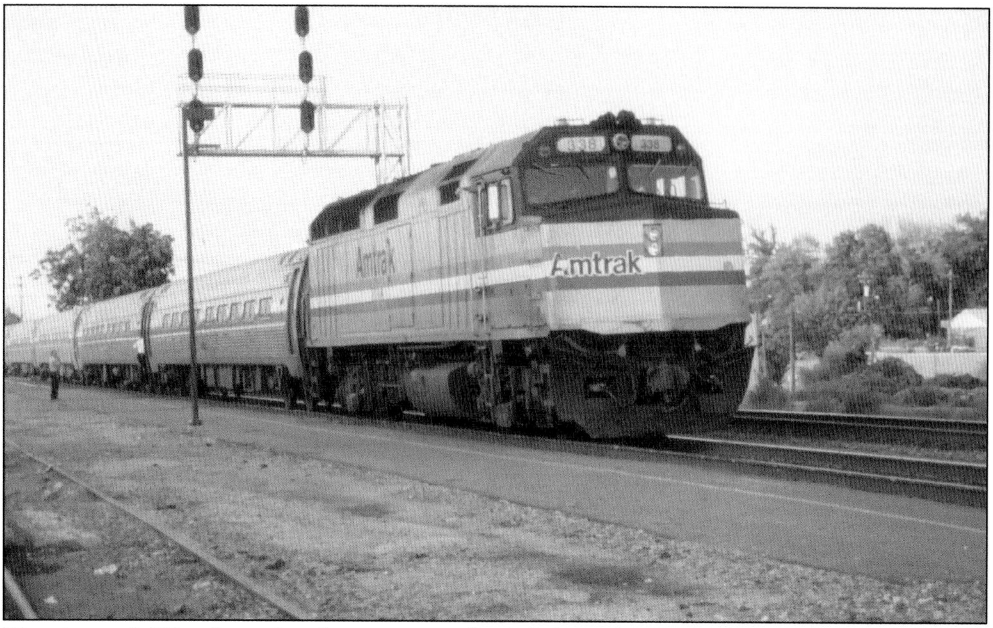

The Amtrack "Carolinian" makes a stop at the Salisbury depot in July 1991. This train route, begun in the 1980s, ran between Charlotte, North Carolina, and New York City and gave travelers more options for train service. Riders can depart north early in the morning and return late in the evening. (Courtesy Larry K. Neal Jr. collection.)

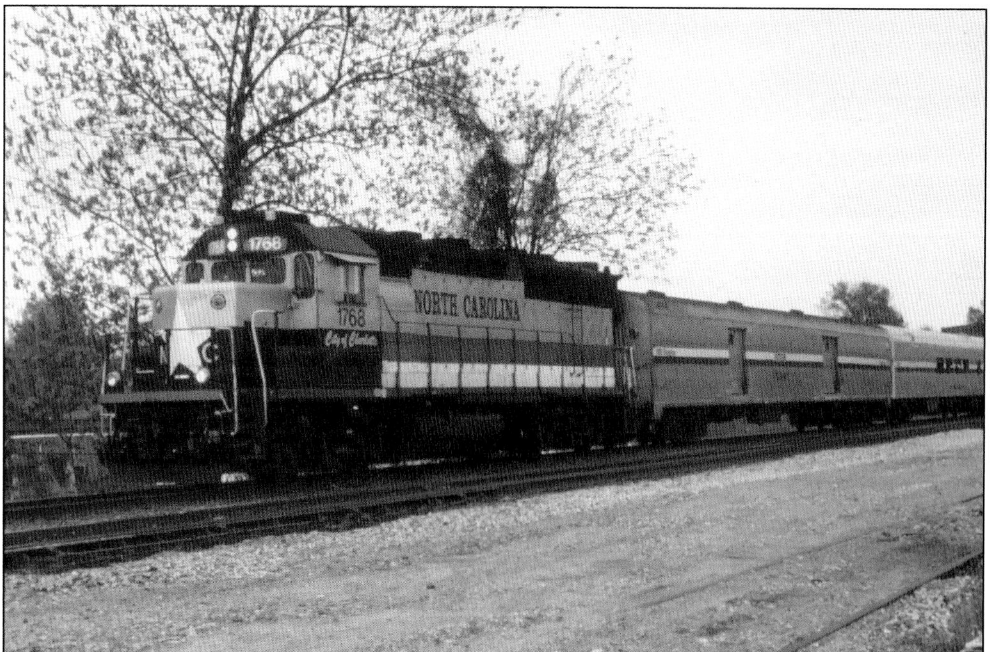

The "Piedmont," operated by the State of North Carolina in conjunction with Amtrack, offers daily service between Charlotte and Raleigh. Two trains are scheduled in opposite directions and offer business travelers or vacationers a viable option to the highway. (Courtesy Larry K. Neal Jr. collection.)

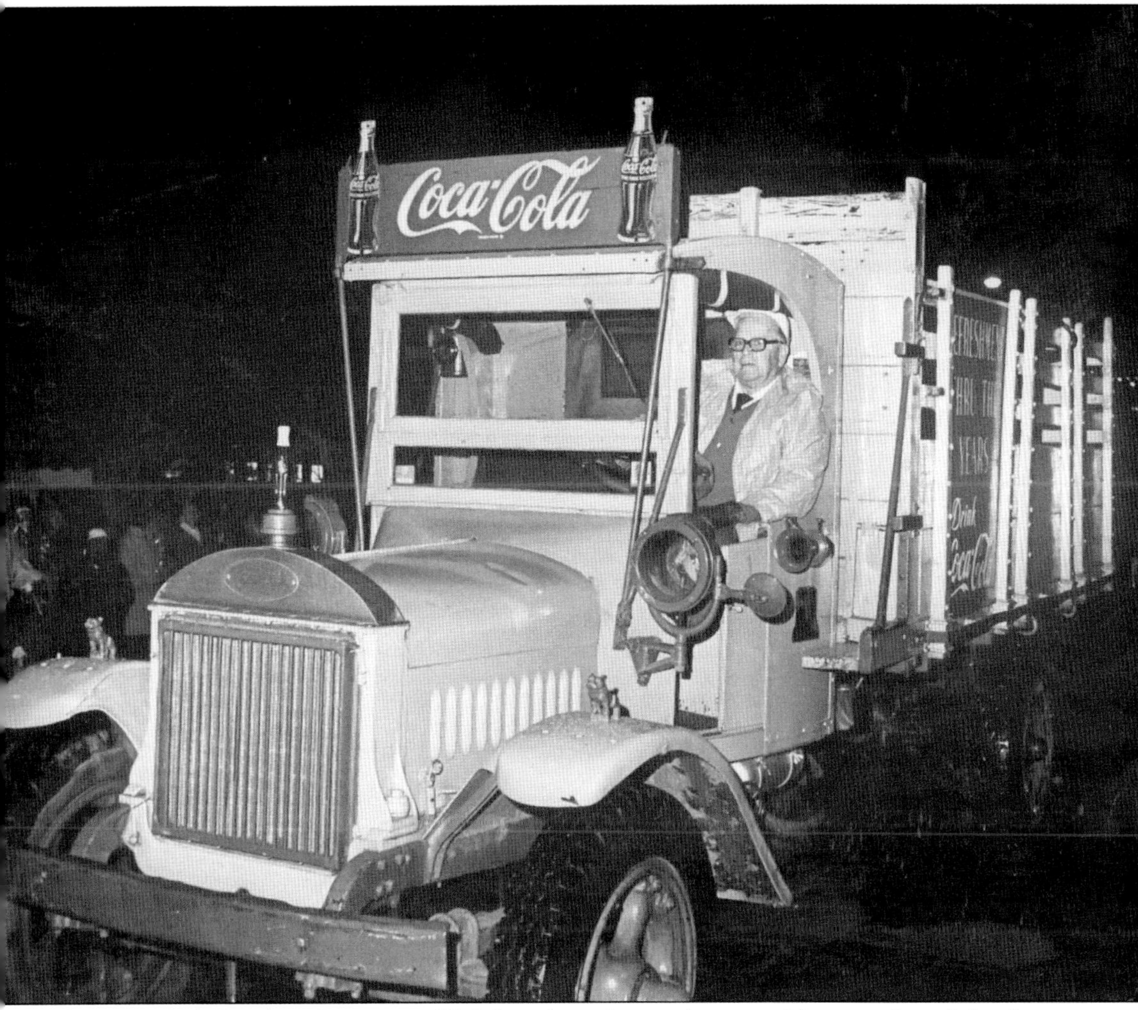

The Coca-Cola Bottling Company of Salisbury brought out this very old, restored truck for the Salisbury Christmas parade in 1973. In later years, the plant moved to South Main Street and was a large distribution point. Unfortunately, it closed several years ago based on a corporate realignment of Coca-Cola in North Carolina. (Courtesy Edith M. Clark History Room of the Rowan Public Library.)

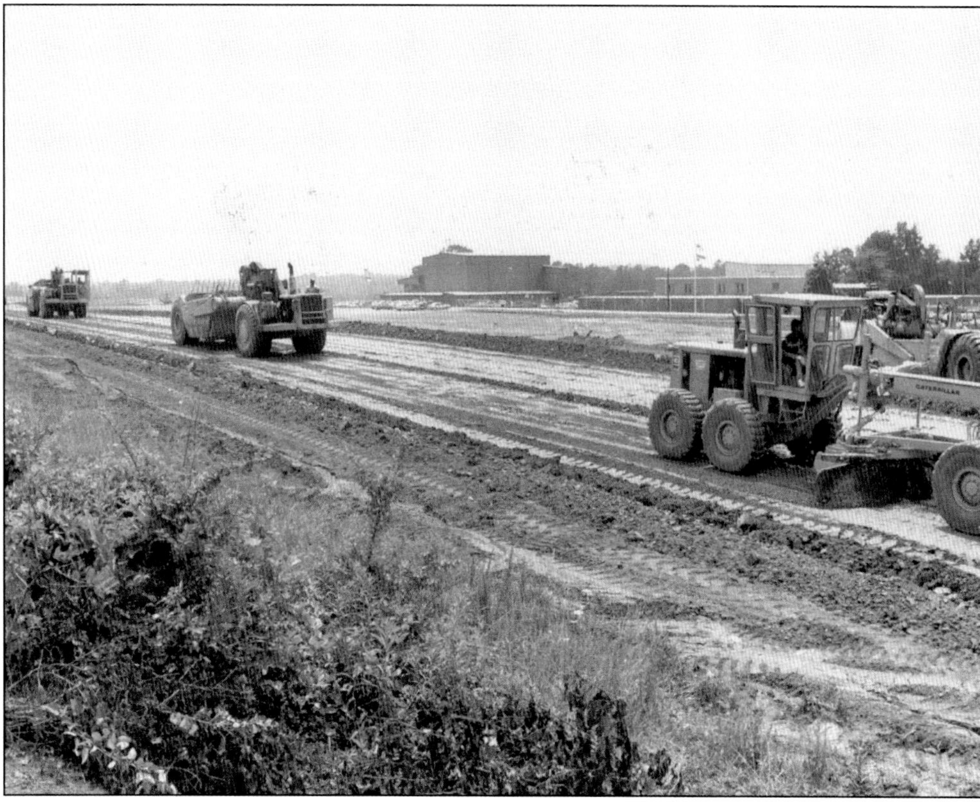

In June 1991, the Rowan County Airport enlarged its runway and made improvements to the hangars and terminal. (Both, courtesy Edith M. Clark History Room of the Rowan Public Library.)

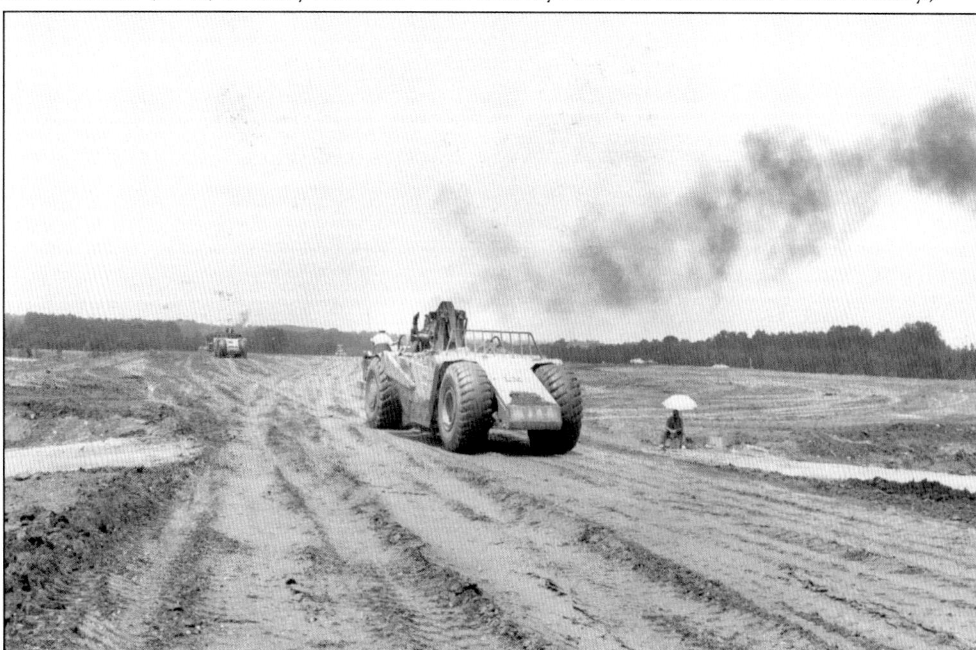

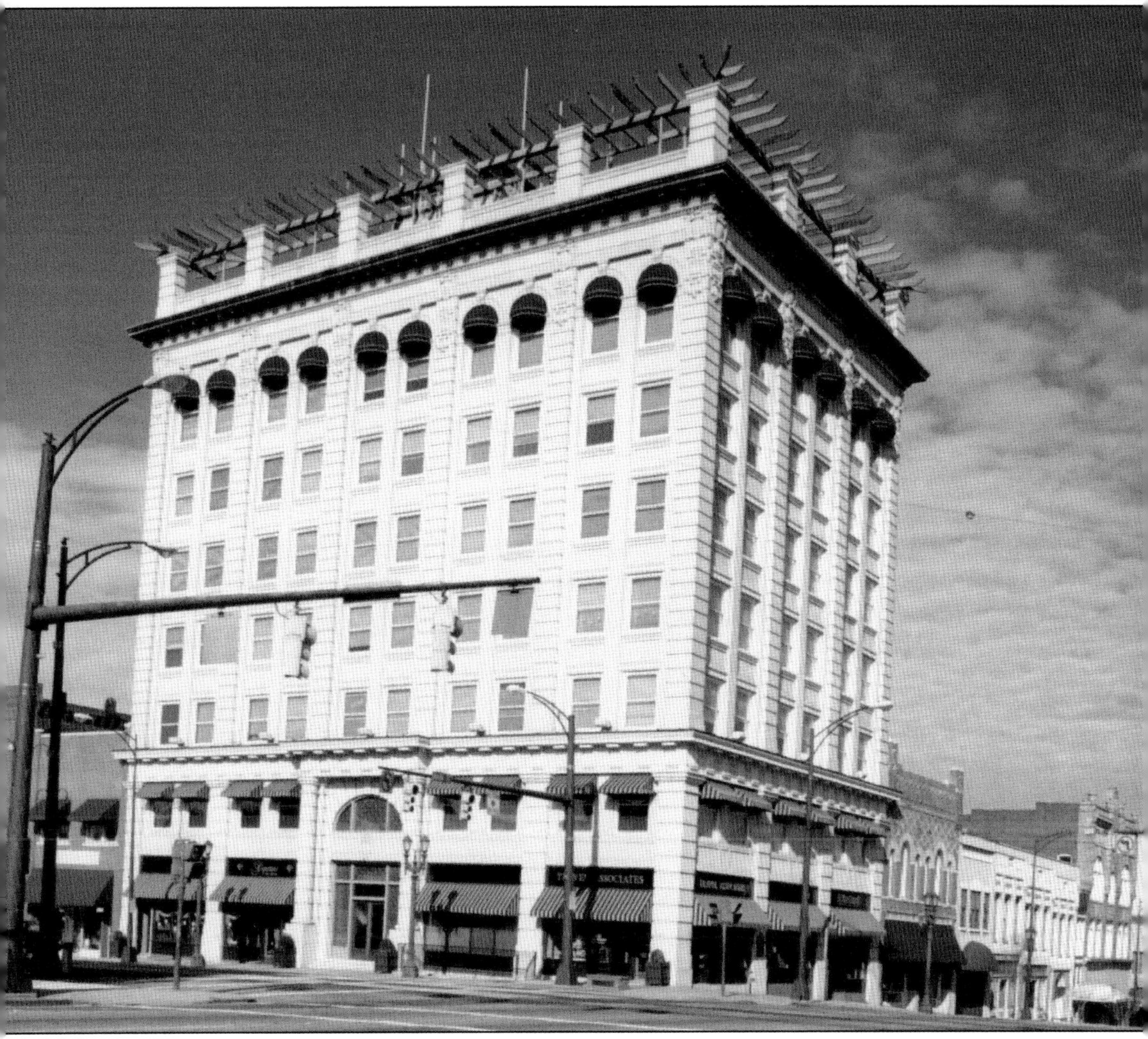

Salisbury's history has been full of interesting twists and turns, but the city continues to prosper and remains a great place to live. Who knows what the next 200 years will bring to Rowan County. (Courtesy Larry K. Neal Jr. collection.)